MW00754417

City Reading

POPULAR CULTURES, EVERYDAY LIVES

CITY READING

~

Written Words and Public Spaces in
Antebellum New York

DAVID M. HENKIN

COLUMBIA UNIVERSITY PRESS

NEW YORK

Frontispiece: Lower Hudson Street, c. 1865. Photograph by Marcus Ormsbee.
© Collection of the New-York Historical Society.

COLUMBIA UNIVERSITY PRESS
Publishers Since 1893

New York   Chichester, West Sussex
Copyright © 1998 Columbia University Press

All rights reserved

Library of Congress Cataloging-in-Publication Data
Henkin, David M.
City reading : written words and public spaces in antebellum New York / David M. Henkin.
p. cm. — (Popular cultures, everyday lives)
Includes bibliographical references and index.
ISBN 0-231-10744-7 (alk. paper). — ISBN 0-231-10745-5 (pbk. : alk. paper)
1. City and town life—New York (State)—New York—History—19th century. 2. New York
(N.Y.)—Social life and customs. 3. Written communication—New York (State)—New York—
History—19th century. 4. Books and reading—New York (State)—New York—History—
19th century. 5. Popular culture—New York (State)—New York—History—19th century. 6.
Public spaces—New York (State)—New York—History—19th century. I. Title. II. Series.
F128.44H46   1998
974.7'103—dc21   98-5215

Casebound editions of Columbia University Press books are printed on permanent and
durable acid-free paper.
Printed in the United States of America
c 10 9 8 7 6 5 4 3 2 1
p 10 9 8 7 6 5 4 3 2 1

To the memories of
Rabbi Yosef Eliyahu Henkin (1881–1973)
Irving Lincoln Hartman (1903–1975)
Dorothy Friedman Hartman (1905–1996)
New Yorkers, readers, grandparents

Contents

Preface

Residents of large Western cities typically take for granted what it feels like to walk around in public, to wend one's way through a landscape full of familiar urban signs and landmarks. We are both embraced and alienated; the city acknowledges and addresses us, but keeps us moving and at an impersonal distance. Fundamentally, both the embrace and the alienation have something to do with dense concentrations of people whose habits both depend on and project indifference to the urban crowd. At the same time, this ambiguous sensibility seems no longer tethered to the particular rhythms of city life. In an age of commercial consumption and mass communication, the same feeling crops up when we drive past the mall, peruse the columns of *USA Today*, scan the titles on an airplane magazine rack, flip channels on the television remote control, or browse the Internet. Despite differences in class, gender, ethnicity, and education, most of us know what it is like to be a consumer and a spectator, to be impersonally and indifferently included in the imagined activities of an abstract group. This sensibility is so pervasive, so constitutive of what we call modernity, that it is tempting to mystify its origins. But our perceptions of connectedness to—or disconnectedness from—the world we live in do not suddenly appear with a technological breakthrough, nor are they determined for us in any simple way by powerful economic interests. Our present predicament rests on countless practices and forms of life that have emerged over time in the daily experiences of countless individuals. This book covers a chapter in that rich and complex history.

To understand the origins of the world of promiscuous circulation, abrupt transition, anonymous negotiation, and spectatorial detachment that has spread out from the capitalist metropolis and conquered buried pockets of human experience in remote corners of the globe, it may be worthwhile to take another look at life in the nineteenth century. Instead of developing a timeless sociological account of urban modernity, this study follows the history of a particular and spectacular city during a crucial and atypical forty-year period. And rather than tracking the transformations and dislocations of that city through the writings, productions, and performances of modernist artists and intellectuals, this project casts a net into the sea of everyday life, collecting debris left behind by everyday people. What I am offering, in the way of a reflection on the vast and deceptively familiar theme of urban experience in modern capitalist societies, is a story about unobtrusive street signs, imposing commercial advertisements, incendiary political broadsides, hackneyed parade banners, cheap daily newspapers, and devalued dollar bills. It is a story about how people living in and visiting New York City during the nineteenth century began to read in public, consuming the disparate, impersonal, and ubiquitous texts of a changing cityscape in a new and recognizably modern fashion. At the thematic core of this tour of urban texts is the proposition that those forms of engagement and disengagement that characterize big-city living emerged fairly early in New York around the experience of written words posted, circulated, fixed, and flashed in public view.

It will surely strike many readers as perverse (or perhaps predictably academic) to trace the origins of a modern urban sensibility to acts of reading. And while the historical relationship between the written word and the city is both long and profound, and their respective roles in modernization are well known, the best defense for attaching so much weight to public reading lies in the evidence itself. In this book, I demonstrate just how ubiquitous urban texts were in antebellum New York and how they became both indispensable guides and apt symbols for a new kind of public life.

This argument may prove more immediately compelling for those who travel in foreign cities. Dislodged from our habitual pathways, we scour walls, lampposts, streetcars, storefronts, bus shelters, customs forms, magazine stands, and strange paper currency for any words or symbols that might quickly facilitate our navigation of an unfamiliar cityscape. Urban texts (many of which validate the stranger simply by presuming his or her existence), mark the possibilities and limits of understanding a new urban environment, of engaging a place where we can function without necessarily having personal contacts, family history, productive responsibilities, or even conversational skills—a place, in other words, where we both do and do not belong. The predicament of the traveler is emblematic, therefore, of life in the nineteenth-century metropolis, where a legible cityscape presumed, reflected, and encouraged the circulation of indefinite numbers of people who were, at least by earlier standards of acquaintance and engagement, complete strangers to one another.

Significantly, such a predicament is emblematic as well of the practice of the historian, whose access to an unfamiliar city is similarly enabled and constrained by the appearance of legible signs, by traces of text available to an impersonal public. And while this affinity should alert us to the risks of fashioning antebellum urbanites in our own image, of assuming that reading was important to them simply because it remains central to our own understanding of their lives, we might keep in mind that as students of nineteenth-century urban culture we are also its heirs. The impulse to redescribe the familiar artifacts of daily life and give them new meaning owes as much to the tradition of sensationalist journalism as it does to the protocols of academic inquiry. While reading the city, cultural historians become wide-eyed travelers, voracious consumers, shameless hucksters, and precarious citizens, much like modern urban dwellers themselves.

Acknowledgments

Many of my largest intellectual creditors bankrolled this project most unwittingly, and are therefore acknowledged (however dispassionately and inadequately) in bibliographical citations throughout the book. There are, however, a number of institutions and individuals whose support merits a different kind of mention.

This book began as a doctoral dissertation, and its timely completion was made possible by fellowship support from the Woodrow Wilson Foundation and from the University of California. Afterward, I was able to devote considerable time to the project thanks to the generosity of a Mellon Fellowship in the Humanities at Stanford University, which I held from 1995 to 1997.

Less material, but no less essential, assistance came from several teachers at UC Berkeley. My interest in signs and posters in antebellum New York was first sparked in a research seminar with Gunther Barth, whose engagement with cultural history and supportive attunement to my work remained with me well beyond the semester I was his student. A seminar and a fruitful independent study with Randy Starn fostered and directed many of my theoretical interests in the history of reading. Robin Einhorn's willingness to sit on my dissertation committee may have been something of an ecumenical gesture toward other ways of studying urban history, but she read my work with great skill and much generosity, asking tough questions in a kind and helpful manner. Though we only met face to face on a few occasions, Sam Otter offered countless useful suggestions—bibliographical, theoretical, and strategic—and helped give analytic focus to my interpretations of American literature and culture.

To acquit Mary Ryan of any responsibility for the errors or eccentricities of this book is more than a nod to academic piety; it is testimony to her great virtue as a teacher. Despite the proximity of my subject to her own interests and areas of substantial expertise, Mary never sought to mold this project. It is a rare adviser who can inspire, support, and challenge her students without trying to reproduce herself in them. I have learned much from her, in no small part from example, and I hope this book reflects some portion of that rich education.

At various stages along the way, several friends and colleagues read some version of the manuscript. In particular, I wish to thank Tom Augst, Leif Brown, Paula Fass, and Waldo Martin for helpful and insightful suggestions. Amy Mae King did the same, but belongs, for many reasons, in her own category. Most of all, I should mention an anonymous reader for Columbia University Press, who gave the work unusually detailed and sustained attention. To the extent that the following chapters present a clearer articulation of the implications of city reading than did the original dissertation, I have her (or him) to thank. I am grateful as well to Ann Miller at Columbia, who solicited the manuscript and guided its revision, and to Leslie Kriesel, who helped make my prose tidier and more felicitous while making the final stages of the revision far more pleasant than I had anticipated. Sarah Jackson provided important editorial and research assistance, and did heroic work in securing permissions for the images that appear here. The index was prepared with extraordinary care, sophistication, and hard work by my friend Q. Julia Švihra. None of these helpful labors would have been necessary, of course, if not for series editor Janice Radway, who attended a panel on the history of reading in the early hours of a Nashville morning and glimpsed in a hasty presentation the possibility of a book. I am especially thankful for the sleep she missed and the opportunity she provided.

Though this book situates itself squarely in the streets of Manhattan, in some respects it is also about another city. I was living in San Francisco before I alighted upon this topic, while I conducted the research (flying to New York frequently, but rarely staying long), and during the manuscript's composition and revision. I continue to live there. My sense of the meanings and the stakes of city living have been thoroughly shaped by this experience. Thus while Laura Comay Bloch, Kenny Dinkin, [Marc] Chief [Goodman], and Kathleen Ritchey did not read or discuss the contents of this paradoxically private project, they have been major partners in the construction of my own city life throughout this endeavor.

In the same vein, though my encounters with them long antedated this work, its publication provides an occasion to acknowledge two great teachers who inspired my intellectual development and perhaps even plotted many of its trajectories. Professor David Brion Davis of Yale University and Rabbi Jay Miller, formerly (and briefly) of the Ramaz School, still command my most sincere gratitude and respect.

To my parents, Alice and Lou Henkin, is due the kind of acknowledgment that eludes the rhetoric of this genre, but I should not use that as an excuse to neglect mentioning their commitments to urban life, to my education, and to my happiness. They are wise readers, fastidious custodians of the treasures of human memory, conscientious citizens of a global community, and wonderful parents. My brothers, Josh and Daniel, are acknowledged and implicated every time I see my own name—even on the cover of a book.

City Reading

1

Introduction

~

Public Reading, Public Space

Walking down Wall Street on April 3, 1865, George Templeton Strong caught sight of the *Commercial Advertiser* bulletin board. As he recorded in his famous diary, the prominent New York lawyer noticed the announcement "Petersburg is taken" and went inside the office for more information. "The man behind the counter was slowly painting in large letters on a large sheet of brown paper another annunciation for the board outside: 'Richmond is'— 'What's that about Richmond?' said I. 'Anything more?' He was too busy for speech, but he went on with a capital C, a capital A, and so on, till I read the word *CAPTURED!!!*"[1] Though the surrender of the Confederate Army was hardly a typical news item, and though the author's dramatic rendering of the event emphasizes the fortuitous nature of his discovery, Strong's experience alerts us to several important features of the role of reading in the nineteenth-century city. Whereas in earlier times writing and print had been used to codify information that was already available in authoritative oral forms, here the relationship is reversed: oral transmission of the news is delayed until the signs are in place. The man behind the counter is "too busy for speech," and only after Strong reads the news is he in a position to go to Trinity Church to suggest ringing the chimes. At the same time, the encounter takes place in the bustling public space of New York, rather than in one of the domestic interiors in which we often set the modern reading experience. And though Strong's diary tends to paint the city as a stage for the interaction of his well-connected acquaintances, there is no mistaking the democratic impersonality of this scene. Strong receives news of the war not by virtue of his privileged social position (his request for private information yields nothing) but in the same manner as countless, nameless other New Yorkers: by crowding around news offices and reading words posted for a large and indeterminate readership.

For the historian, Strong's diary opens a window to a fascinating moment in the development of urban life, when modern modes of urban interaction were emerging against the backdrop of what we often romanticize as the "walking city." Though his story predates recorded sound, motion pictures, telephones, linotype machines, radio transmission, and many other of the hallmark technologies of the modern era, it reflects a change in public communication no less astonishing, and no less significant. Instead of seeing hand-painted letters on brown paper as quaint relics of a bygone era or archaic prototypes of later techniques, we can appreciate the striking modernity of this scene. We might wonder, for example, about the historical process by which an urban public came to rely upon a newspaper bulletin board for authoritative announcements on important issues, and how city residents came to use freestanding signs exhibited in public space to mediate their relationships to their neighbors. We might also wonder about the impact of these signs, whose ubiquitous character we now take for granted, on public life in a heterogeneous and contentious city.

Between the opening of the Erie Canal in 1825 and the end of the Civil War in 1865, as New York grew from a small port city into a multicultural metropolis, a remarkable network of public words appeared in the streets. From shop signs and banners to books and newspapers, written and printed words proliferated across the cityscape, directing the daily movements of New York's burgeoning population, promoting competing visions of the urban community, and dramatizing the circulation of strangers through public space. While these words represented a wide range of private interests, mutually indifferent pursuits, antagonistic ideologies, and discrete messages, their spectacular juxtaposition turned the city's public spaces into a strikingly inclusive arena for impersonal communication. At a time when demographic, economic, and physical changes were disrupting continuities and similarities in the daily experiences of New York's residents and visitors, public words appeared to address everyone, though often with quite varying implications. Throughout the antebellum period, news articles, lithographs, travel literature, personal reminiscences, popular humor, and posted signs themselves all registered an increased awareness of the way disparate urban texts marked the streets as a site of public reading, a palimpsest of shared information upon which claims to personal authority blurred into one another and receded into a larger verbal collage. It is in the context of this emerging public arena of city reading that George Strong's encounter with the *Commercial Advertiser* bulletin board acquires historical meaning. Behind that encounter, we can discern the contours of a modern urban community.

The story of New York's public words that unfolds in the following chapters is deceptively familiar. After all, we have come to expect cityscapes to be legible, much as we expect consumer goods to come with labels, instructions, and promotional copy. But there was once something novel in the spectacle of so many words, and something radical in the notion that buildings and streets ought to be marked. Urban texts have a contingent history that reflects, among other things, changing patterns of residence, work, commerce, education, social control, and visual representation. Many current uses of signs, posters, newspapers, and paper money are in fact fairly recent. Signs regulating traffic, for example, were virtually unknown in antebellum New York, despite the fact that traffic accidents occurred with some frequency. To that extent, traveling around Manhattan's streets required less reading in 1850 than it does today. On the other hand, since national currency did not exist, the passing of dollar bills (notes of credit from banks of varying geographical locations and states of solvency) among strangers in public occasioned considerably more reading. To recover the history of these texts and the daily practices that grew up around them, we first need to divest modern modes of urban communication of their cloak of normalcy.

We also need to rethink the profound relationship between cities and writing, which dates back to their more or less contemporaneous introduction in Mesopotamia five thousand years ago. Both the written word and the city developed in part as means of storing and registering agricultural surplus, and both institutions have retained a symbolic residue of this purpose in their shared association with a world removed from primary production. More concretely, cities and writing share a long-standing connection to money and the spread of commerce, a connection that helps to explain the considerable weight attached to both print culture and urbanization in histories of modernization. In the early modern period, writing and print played an important role in both urbanization (the concentration of larger proportions of people in cities) and city growth (the increase in population of particular large cities), a powerful and complex reminder that the kind of community people create both influences and depends upon their ability to communicate with one another. Speaking from the experience of a particular and often idealized city-state, Aristotle had expressed doubts about an urban community whose magnitude would preclude the possibility of a town meeting. The subsequent history of city growth in the West is replete with examples that test his normative assumptions about meaningful urban life, but his notion of a city struggling with the possibilities of communication remains crucially relevant. The growth of large cities encourages and reflects expanded technologies of communication, and, though it is sometimes overlooked, the city itself is a prime component of that technology. From ancient times, Lewis Mumford reminds us, the city has been a "special receptacle for storing and transmitting messages."[2]

Yet the implications of these oft-acknowledged links have been insufficiently pursued in studies of the nineteenth-century city. In part, such links have slipped through the cracks that separate various academic fields and disciplines as they have constituted themselves in recent decades.[3] But there is more here than merely a division of scholarly labor. In a larger sense, any insistence on the historical interconnectedness of cities and reading runs counter to the way we typically construct their modern incarnations. In the historical imagination, the nineteenth-century city appears as a place of cacophonous commotion, while the nineteenth-century reader sits in silent solitude, engrossed in the pleasures of a novel. These images are not without basis, to be sure, yet they are deeply misleading. To begin with, beneath the bustle and noise of any big city lies a broad foundation of quiet agreements and assumptions. In antebellum New York, for example, both residents and visitors

4

needed all kinds of knowledge in order to function in a world of strangers. From a street name or an omnibus destination to the existence of a vacant apartment or a haberdashery, from the location and nature of a riot to the exchange value of personal property, crucial bits of information undergirded all the activities, gestures, and encounters that comprised city life. Increasingly, this information came in the form of writing or print.

Both cultural historians and urban critics have explored the problem of how city residents orient themselves to and make sense of chaotic and unfamiliar environments, but the broad importance of reading in this process has to a large extent eluded their notice. It is interesting that while "reading the city" has become a familiar and fashionable theme in urban studies, actual reading practices receive limited attention. What urbanists such as Kevin Lynch have characterized as the "legibility" of the cityscape invokes the model of the text to explain the nontextual.[4] Recent historical studies of the nineteenth-century American city employ the same metaphor. An article on civic parades sees in its subject "the vocabulary and the syntax by which social and cultural order was created," while a book on manners devotes a chapter to the "semiotics of everyday life" and refers to cities as "the great signifying structures of the age."[5] Central to what allowed a city like New York to function as a signifying structure, though, was the availability of actual texts.

With the notable exceptions of the penny press and the "Mysteries of the City" genre, however, urban texts and reading practices have not been accorded their proper place in the history of the antebellum American city. When historians do speak of the city in print, it is something of a metaphor—just as the city forms a text that must be read, actual texts (newspapers, sensationalist city guides, urban novels) bear some analogous relationship to the city they describe. This can be a useful point. As we will see, New York's daily papers and New York's crowded thoroughfares had much in common; they were mutually clarifying spectacles of a new urban life. Still, too fine a distinction between what historian Peter Fritzsche calls the "word city" and the "built city" obscures the fact that the two became deeply intertwined in the nineteenth century.[6] Cities were built, in part, of words, words that took material form in public space. Newspapers did not simply resemble the streets of Manhattan; they littered them as well.

That scholars and critics often ignore this obvious fact has much to do with the persistently powerful image of the private reader. The association between reading and privacy assumes several forms and draws on a cluster of myths, some of which romanticize the written word, others of which romanticize a preliterate world of oral communication. Without dwelling here on the peculiar origins and appeal of either the notion that reading is an inherently private activity trapped irrecoverably in the mind of the reader, or the related (if somewhat contradictory) thesis that the history of reading in the modern West has been a process of steadily increasing privatization,[7] it is worth observing how the familiar model implicitly relegates nineteenth-century reading to the periphery of urban life by locating it indoors rather than outdoors and in seclusion rather than in the company of strangers.[8] Reading appears in this model as a means of escaping from or coping with urban interactions (and social and economic life generally), rather than as a constitutive component of those interactions. Thus while historians stress that reading the daily *Sun* or a sketch of life in the Five Points slum could provide a city dweller with symbolic tools with which to organize his or her relationship to the growing metropolis, in this model the act of reading itself becomes removed from the realm of primary urban experience.

Part of the problem with this model of reading is the disproportionate weight it attaches to the novel as the paradigmatic object of literate consumption. In antebellum New York (as in today's cities), books of prose fiction accounted for but a small fraction of the reading matter of everyday life.[9] Writing and print appeared on buildings, sidewalks, sandwich-board advertisements, the pages of personal diaries, classroom walls, Staffordshire pottery, needlepoint samples, election tickets, and two-dollar bills, to name just a few locations and contexts. Obviously, the relationships of these texts to outdoor and interactive life varied considerably. But even conventional texts, such as newspapers and books, often appeared and functioned outside of a domestic or private context, much as they do today (consider how much of our reading takes place on airplanes or in doctors' waiting rooms). Newspapers were hawked in the streets, displayed on racks, perused outdoors, and otherwise introduced into meaningful public view. As anecdotal evidence suggests, books found their way into the urban bustle as well. Every morning, cartman and bibliophile Isaac Lyon sat reading by his stand on Broadway and Houston as he awaited the day's first job.[10] A music critic employed by a daily newspaper was spotted on one occasion "walking in Broadway reading a copy of Punch, extended at arms' length before him, when his toe caught in a pile of lumber lying across the side walk, and he was precipitated from his loft attitude to the ground."[11] These acts of reading may have been silent and individual, but to call them private is to ignore the way they function on the stage of public life. Even when people use books to create a barrier between themselves and the people around them, they do so in public view. Ten-year-old Catherine Elizabeth Havens understood the wider urban audience before which she appeared as a reader, as she admitted in her 1849 diary: "Sometimes we get some of the big girls' books, and carry them in our arms, with the titles on the outside, so the people will see them."[12] Whether they were trying to impress their neighbors, escape their surroundings, or simply keep up with the news at the bulletin board, New Yorkers did a great deal of reading in public. Most often, this was because making one's way in an expanding city of strangers required consulting texts at every turn. During his visit to New York in the 1840s, Charles Dickens observed "two laborers in holiday clothes, of whom one carries in his hand a crumpled scrap of paper from which he tries to spell out a hard name, while the other looks about for it on all the doors and windows."[13] These two complementary acts of city reading, which may have amused the English novelist, provide an especially compelling reminder of what is lost when historians stress the private character of the literate experience rather than its relationship to the spectacle of public life. Far from being confined to private moments and secluded spaces, city reading pervaded a range of daily activities and stretched across a diverse and expanding cityscape.

By broadening our view to include the rich variety of texts and contexts in which the practice of reading took place, we can discern the ties that bind the city and the written word at this particular historical juncture. In focusing on urban texts, we begin to notice how acts of reading and textual interpretation figured in a set of broadly inclusive practices that were embedded in the everyday life of the growing city. Cut loose from personal authority and circulating promiscuously in a world of strangers, the signs, cards, posters, newspapers, and bills described in this study provided new vehicles and new models for communication in an urban environment. Around these urban texts, a new kind of public was born.

To speak of the public as a historical phenomenon is to invoke a category of experience fraught with much ambiguity and confusion. Phrases like "public policy," "public opinion," "public relations," and "public space," to take a few examples, suggest radically divergent relationships to the state, politics, commercial interests, and everyday life. While the word "public" almost always suggests a realm of activity that involves, includes, or implicates a large number of people, it is not always clear what these different publics have in common. Much recent scholarly discussion of the public takes a cue and a frame of reference from German political philosopher Jürgen Habermas's landmark 1962 study *The Structural Transformation of the Public Sphere*, which was translated into English in 1989. Habermas is interested particularly in the concept of public opinion and in the formation during the eighteenth century of a sphere of critical deliberation through which bourgeois citizens could regulate the actions of government. According to Habermas, a courtly publicity in which royalty represented itself before its subjects was replaced by a new public in which the subjects themselves appeared, and in which a broadly inclusive discourse invoked the principle of its own constitutive publicity to subordinate political domination to reason. Under new conditions brought about by the proliferation of printing and the related expansion of capitalism and commerce, Habermas writes, private people came together and claimed a "public sphere regulated from above against the public authorities themselves to engage in a debate over the rules governing relations in the basically privatized but publicly relevant sphere of commodity exchange and social labor."[14] Standing between the absolutist state and the capitalist marketplace, the bourgeois public "sphere" (the German noun *Öffentlichkeit* hovers ambiguously between describing a realm and a concept) is thus both a network of institutions and sites of rational discussion and a critical ideal through which public interests can in principle be identified and enforced.

Though the details of this complex historical and theoretical construct (as well as the controversies it has spawned) lie beyond the scope of our study, it is worth emphasizing how Habermas's inquiry both opens up and restricts discussion of the historical construction of public life. By directing our attention to the social and cultural preconditions for the formation of the bourgeois public sphere, Habermas reminds historians to look at forces and developments outside the domain of political ideology, law, and state action in explaining how large collectivities are constructed, transformed, and experienced. At the same time, by defining the public sphere narrowly, to privilege critical, disinterested deliberation, this model excludes many of the primary sites in which authority is elaborated and contested. To explore what was radically public about city reading in New York, to develop a structural and phenomenological account of the new forms of publicity such reading practices introduced, we need to press at the limits of the central insights of Habermas's work.

First and foremost, Habermas roots the development of the public sphere in commercial life. Second, he treats publicity as a form of subjectivity, not simply as a political institution or concept. Third, he links publicity to reading and print culture. All three interrelated insights are crucial to his argument, but they are by no means straightforward. To begin with, Habermas is profoundly ambivalent about market relations. While the idealized public sphere stands outside the marketplace and is threatened—and ultimately destroyed during the nineteenth century— by the forces of commodification and consumption, it emerges historically from an expanding commercial culture and organizes itself on the model of free trade between equal parties.[15] More specifically, the exchange and consumption of newspapers and books make public information and public opinion possible and meaningful. "The public sphere in the political realm evolved from the public sphere in the world of letters," Habermas explains, since print provided forums, subjects, and models for public discussion. At the same time, reading laid the groundwork for the famous institutions of intellectual sociability—German table societies, French salons, and English coffeehouses—that serve for Habermas as paradigmatic sites of rational-critical discourse. Paradoxically, print plays this foundational role in the formation of a public sphere during an era renowned for the spread of private reading. In an ingenious and telling move, Habermas grounds publicity and public opinion in an audience-oriented subjectivity created within the intimate space of the conjugal family and cultivated in the pages of the popular epistolary novels of the eighteenth century. This subjectivity entailed a sense among participants in the public sphere that they were implicated in public affairs, addressed by their discussion, and engaged in thought that could be communicated to an impersonal and dispersed group of interested others.[16]

The particular significance of a commodified print culture (and a print-based subjectivity) in the emergence of modern publics has been pursued further in Michael Warner's study of the meaning of publication in the political culture of Revolutionary America and in Benedict Anderson's analysis of the role of newspapers and novels in the symbolic construction of the modern nation-state. For Warner and Anderson, as for Habermas, it is not the ideas expressed in a given set of texts that constitute the public, but rather the experience of reading as organized around (and represented in) specific genres under particular historical conditions, which enables individuals to discern connections to one another and assume membership in a collective body or a shared cultural formation.[17]

Strangely absent from all of these publics, though, is any notion of the public as physical space. Despite the powerful spatial overtones of the word "public," Habermas's public sphere (like Warner's republic of letters and Anderson's imagined community) is decidedly abstract and dispersed, not simply in its construction but also in its day-to-day existence. Far from emphasizing the physical congregation and confrontation of people in open spaces, current discussions of the public often turn public space into a metaphor for a set of physically placeless encounters, an aspatial context for political dialogue and debate.[18] The urban public sketched in the following chapters, in contrast, was rooted in the experience of the physical city. The new public created in antebellum New York around shared reading practices was in a fundamental sense the public of the great outdoors, and was firmly situated in public space even as it extended to publication, public relations, and public (i.e. municipal) authority.

The streets of Manhattan—and the surfaces visible from the streets—are an appropriate place to begin reconstructing the modern urban public, not simply because urban streets were, as several historians have emphasized, frequent sites of meetings, parades, rallies, riots, and other recognizable gestures of political ferment and self-expression in nineteenth-century America, but, more simply, because everything that appeared in the open spaces of the city was, by definition, public. To meet a person, witness a scandal, adjust one's dress, or stare at a building façade in the streets of New York was to do so with an awareness that the experience was taking place within the potential view of a heterogeneous and minimally regulated gathering of unidentified (and often unidentifiable) others. To read a street sign, a parade banner, or a sandwich-board advertisement in this urban, spatial public was, as Warner

reading as public spectacle

has argued in the case of print in the eighteenth century, to be aware of the other readers whom the text impersonally addressed, but also, as was not the case in Warner's print republic, to be aware that one's act of reading was itself a public spectacle.[19]

These experiences of public life in the big city diverged in some striking respects from the idealized public sphere described by Habermas and the kinds of abstract collectivities outlined by Warner and Anderson. Situated in physical space rather than in conceptual abstractions, and in the bustle of the streets rather than in domestic retreats or enclosed coffeehouses, the new urban public collapsed the distinction between imagining a community and participating in it. Consequently, it was both less critical and more democratic. Instead of creating a neutral, detached site for rational deliberation, city reading blurred the lines between politics and commerce, interested and disinterested authority, information and exhortation, judgment and promotion. The role of the market in this process is crucial. In Habermas's construction of publicity, commerce and consumption are critically demarcated areas of public deliberation. In a city of shop signs and trade bills, by contrast, commerce and consumption insinuated themselves into the very process of public communication. This is an important point, because part of the resistance among historians of public life to examining signs and newspapers in the nineteenth-century city stems from the ostensibly trivial character of their commercial content. Commercial messages and transactions can have profound effects and far-reaching cultural implications, however, as we will explore throughout this study. Commerce, in the words of historian Jean-Christophe Agnew, "cheapens *and* deepens meaning at the same time, multiplying and complicating cultural exchange in such a way as to render its currency—language—at once reassuringly standardized and disturbingly defamiliarized."[20] Promotional sandwich boards in the streets and patent medicine advertisements in the crowded columns of the penny press did not simply confront readers in public space; they raised central questions about other uses of the written word to mediate social relations. Moreover, the marketplace offered a highly visible model for an inclusive public. Whereas the Enlightenment public sphere excluded or marginalized large groups of people (such as women and workers) in its constitutive self-definition, urban texts posted in public view tended to liquidate differences among people, excluding only those who were illiterate or could read no English (a point to which we will return). To a significant extent, city reading helped to lay the social foundations for what would emerge by the end of the century as a consumer society—a society in which the mere capacity to spend money secured membership, though often on glaringly unequal terms and under increasingly impersonal and potentially alienating conditions.

While extending the logic of an expanding market culture, the public sphere of urban letters also reinforced the formation of a new subjectivity congenial to market relations. If Habermas's public subjects modeled their critical deliberations on the intimate exchanges represented in novels, city reading promoted a strikingly different mode of literate communication. Epistolary novels encouraged readers to imagine their own experiences while reading as similar to the emotionally charged (often written) encounters of the books' characters. Intimate communication led to solitary deliberation: "the empathetic reader repeated within himself the private relationships displayed before him in literature." The nineteenth-century urban public replaced the private reader with the promiscuous reader. By presupposing, inducing, and dramatizing countless rapid and disjointed acts of browsing, the street signs, placards, newspapers, and banknotes of everyday city life cultivated reading subjects whose sense of autonomy lay not in the ability to internalize and resolve exchanges among self-possessed speakers but rather in the ability to peruse, select, discard, and reassemble a range of messages and options. This notion of autonomy, which lies at the foundation of the modern sense of self, fits well, as hardly needs to be stressed, with the exigencies and appeals of mass consumption.[21]

It is tempting, given this link between the market and the urban texts analyzed here, to follow Habermas and many twentieth-century critics of modernization in treating the public life of the nineteenth-century metropolis as a symptom of the disintegration of the Enlightenment public sphere into a privatized, capitalist, mass society. But while signs, cards, newspapers, and banknotes tended to represent private interests and to promote private enterprise, it is misleading to subsume the revolutionary changes they wrought and reflected in the experience of urban life under the rubric of privatization. Addressed impersonally and indifferently to an unprecedentedly broad range of strangers and residents, urban texts actually extended the central features of Enlightenment publicity. As they confronted these texts, city dwellers became public subjects stripped of their particular identities, much like the readers of the

Spectator or the U.S. Constitution.[22] At the same time, city readers were subjects in a far more inclusive and democratic public, in which remarkable numbers of ordinary people consumed and composed written messages in the public spaces of the metropolis. City reading thus marked, shaped, and reinforced the transition from the bourgeois urban public of the early national period, centered around New York's Tontine Coffee House, to a broader-based, more boisterous, and more populous public centered in the streets.

To observe the democratic inclusiveness of the new urban public that developed around writing and print in antebellum New York is not to deny the significant disparities in power, status, ideology, and social experience that persisted and widened during this period. The relationship between this inclusive public and various forms of social and economic inequality was complex and often ambiguous; urban texts could both mask and advertise differences among New Yorkers. For instance, signs appearing in English glossed over the linguistic diversity of the city's heterogeneous population, while signs labeling privately owned buildings and businesses presented a display of individual wealth and economic stratification. Other urban texts, such as broadsides posted on buildings or articles printed in cheap dailies hawked in the streets, actually helped to erode differences by opening up channels for political expression and participation. If the antebellum era marked a major expansion of the franchise, the proliferation of signs, banners, papers, and bills offered political access even to those who could not vote. Women, for example, in traversing the streets, perusing bulletin boards, reading newspapers, and circulating money, gained a foothold in public life denied to them on election day. Public life was highly (and in some cases lethally) contentious, but it mingled actors of different social, economic, and political positions. Still, the network of urban signs increased the distance separating those who could read from a small illiterate minority and intensified the stigmatization of African Americans and the Irish poor, who were frequently identified with illiteracy in the popular imagination.[23] Finally, the expanding urban public could impose new forms of authority and social control. By the end of the period, for example, signs imposing speed limits, restricting access to fields, and otherwise regulating individual behavior had begun to appear in Central Park.

Such varied developments suggest the breadth of impact that urban texts had on everyday life, and remind us of the dangers of oversimplifying that impact. City reading played a crucial, but limited, integrative function in a city that by mid-century was home to half a million people, most of them foreign-born, a city where new and more rigidly defined classes were forming and intense social-political conflict was manifested in frequent violent clashes. An imposing sign marking GENIN, HATTER, a copy of the *Tribune* displayed on a newspaper rack, and a placard marked NO DRAFT held aloft by an Irish-born worker in a bloody riot against federal conscription articulated important (sometimes gaping) social differences—but within a common system of reference and before an inclusive and integrated readership. While acknowledging that city reading functioned in different ways and against the backdrop of other distributions of power in antebellum society, we should not lose sight of the central tendency associated with the proliferation of public reading practices. Though New York's urban texts did not level incomes, instill ethnic harmony, bridge neighborhoods, or promote political consensus, they bracketed these ruptures within a shared experience of public space by rendering much of the city legible to strangers and facilitating forms of access and interaction that did not require personal acquaintance, face-to-face contact, or recognizable individual authority.

While many kinds of texts and many kinds of reading promoted public communication and shaped the experience of public space, this study focuses on four principal categories, each of which captures a different and important component of the new urban public, and each of which underwent substantial growth during the period 1825–1865—a time when, as chapter 2 argues, demographic, economic, and physical changes were destabilizing traditional markers of continuity and order. The first set of texts, described in chapter 3, are public in the most obvious sense: they stood fixed in public view and became part of the visible cityscape. We call them signs, as if to confer upon them a status as the most basic units of communication. But if street signs and store signs were in one sense simple, they served a complex function in antebellum New York, providing information and a network of important verbal cues with which residents and visitors negotiated a changing urban environment. Most fixed signs advertised private commercial interests and registered the claims of private property, but they did so in public view, before a public readership. As these signs proliferated, they established an impersonal public discourse through which new forms of written authority became a part of urban life. Chapter 4 considers a related cluster of texts: that portion of New York's sign discourse that was flimsy, mobile, or ephemeral. Like their more permanent counterparts, texts such as trade cards, handbills, posters, and parade banners were familiar markings on the cityscape, but because they were temporary by design and tended to be cheaper to produce and to exhibit, they evoked the frenzy and heterogeneity of urban life in a more dramatic way and, moreover, allowed a wider range of people to participate in new modes of public self-expression. If store signs and street signs tended to link the city's buildings and spaces to their owners (or to the municipal corporation), posters, cards, and banners tended to subvert those connections, treating the streets as an open screen for the projection of messages, manifestoes, gimmicks, jokes, and acts of sabotage. Fixed, sturdy signs created a kind of monumental epigraphy for the city's commercial life; flimsy, mobile signs functioned more like graffiti. Despite their anarchic, patchwork character, though, this flood of written and printed ephemera created a now-familiar language of publicity linking political action, civic pageantry, and commercial promotion, and reinforced the use of the streets for impersonal address.

If certain texts became public simply by virtue of their placement or appearance outdoors, others entered and refashioned this urban public in subtler ways. Chapter 5 recasts the well-documented history of the antebellum metropolitan press in New York as the creation of a new public space. Circulating in public view, passed from hand to hand, newspapers functioned much like temporary signage in nineteenth-century New York. The particular force of the penny daily, however—its privileged status as an embodiment of the city it chronicled—rested in part on the suggestive homologies between its own print space and the open spaces of the city. Much like the streets in which they appeared, New York's daily newspapers presented a grid of uniform columns juxtaposing a broad range of discrete elements, heavily devoted to advertising, traversed simultaneously by increasing numbers of city residents. As much as any other urban text, the daily newspaper became an indispensable source for information about the city, and thus served as a constant reminder of the increasing dependence of New Yorkers on written words, on utterances that in some sense eluded the control and exceeded the accountability of their authors. Newspapers themselves played on the instability of the print medium and, like many of the other texts discussed in this study, struggled with the problem of creating personal credibility within a system whose power lay precisely in the establishment of impersonal authority. While particular papers were famously and often notoriously identified with their idiosyncratic editors, the public power of the metropolitan press lay in the idea that newspaper space as such belonged to no one in particular, that its columns were available for open purchase, and that its words were being read by an impersonal public.

Antebellum New Yorkers encountered this tension between personal accountability and impersonal circulation most forcefully in the dollar bill, the text that is the subject of chapter 6. Though the use of paper money was not limited to cities, much less New York City, a large and heterogeneous metropolis multiplied and dramatized the problems of assigning value to pieces of paper. In the constantly changing public spaces of New York, the promiscuous intermingling of bills and people from all over the country and abroad increased the likelihood that a banknote would be the only thing to pass between two anonymous individuals. Not surprisingly, New York was the national center not only of banking, but also of counterfeiting and counterfeit detection at a time when the American currency system was peculiarly unwieldy and confusing. A vast and hieroglyphic array of banknotes and an assortment of published documents designed to evaluate their legitimacy thus joined broadsides, shop signs, and newspapers in mediating relations among city dwellers and in bracketing their personal identities so as to facilitate the public anonymity characteristic of modern urban life. Marked, littered, and plastered with all of these words, public space in Manhattan became a site of broad visibility and promiscuous intermingling, of seeing and being seen, of abrupt transition and jarring juxtaposition.

All four of these genres of urban text had their particular histories in antebellum New York, yet their cultural functions overlapped and they developed along parallel trajectories. In each case, New Yorkers confronted written words in unfamiliar places and in unprecedented concentrations. Signs, handbills, dailies, and banknotes tended to be word-heavy even by later standards, let alone in comparison to the oral ceremonies, rumors, architectural landmarks, and personal acquaintance networks for which they increasingly substituted. The texts and reading practices analyzed in this study formed a public discourse that revolutionized communication and self-presentation in the city to an extent that is hard to appreciate from our historical vantage point. The various forms of authority we invest in street signs, billboard advertisements, graffiti, daily newspapers, and paper money have an inscrutable and self-evident quality in cities in which face-to-face communication has long receded as a regulating force in public life. But in the middle of the last century, the sudden explosion of writing and print in public was a significant change. It is worth keeping in mind that while writing and print compete today with a variety of oral and iconographic media (whose function and power both extend and exploit those of the verbal sign) the antebellum era saw a substantial gap open up between the respective capacities of literate and other modes of communication. By the second half of this period, telegraphs transmitted election news and sports results across the country almost instantaneously, newspapers transcribed for large readerships the full texts of speeches that could not even be heard by their immediate audiences, and broadsides posted around town advertised events such as an upcoming rally or exhibition faster than word of mouth. Well before recorded sound, radio, telephones, or television, New York was home to a complex network of institutions and technologies that spread the written word quickly throughout the city and well beyond. A full reckoning of these institutions and technologies would have to include the common school, the postal system, the daguerreotype, the newsboy, and even the city grid, as well as more obvious candidates such as the cylinder press and the telegraph.

The history of public reading in antebellum New York is thus very much a story about an era. While marking a moment in the larger histories of urban growth and mass literacy in the West, this history also involves amply documented (though often separately analyzed) contemporaneous developments, many of them revolutionary, in such areas as education, publishing, property value, immigration, residential mobility, banking, and labor organization. By describing a set of practices that pervade everyday life, the concept of public reading inevitably extends to many different sectors of the historical landscape and allows us to view familiar features of that landscape from a new perspective. At the heart of these practices, though, lay something more specific: a novel and concrete redefinition of a public as those spaces in which mass subjects could be addressed anonymously, impersonally, and without reference to particularities of status.

The specific parameters and premises of this project still require a bit of explanation. First, why single out reading among the variety of practices through which New Yorkers communicated in public and made sense of their changing environment? Why distinguish written words from pictures, flags, buildings, shouts, grimaces, and gunshots? Why privilege texts and ignore the myriad nontextual markers that make up, according to urban scholars, "the image of the city"?[24] Part of the point of expanding the history of reading to include signs, banners, and bills, of course, is that written words do much of the cultural work often associated with other public symbols and communicative media, and that writing and print need to be studied with the same attention to material detail ordinarily reserved for nonlinguistic cultural artifacts. Still, written texts do their cultural work differently from both nonverbal signs and speech acts. The relationship between texts and icons is complicated, and this study might be accused of complicating it further by insisting on the textuality of verbal signs that seem like icons. Words are different from pictures, though, not because language is a stable, univocal, and self-adequate system of representation, but rather because its forms of instability, ambiguity, and inadequacy are so particular. Both because we cannot escape language to evaluate its own claims, and because language carries the illusion of corresponding fully to things in the world, words have a certain privileged claim to transparency in our culture, however deceptive. As historian Randolph Starn has argued with respect to the appearance of texts in Renaissance paintings, words "serve as a uniform class of signification amidst changes in line and color."[25] In the case of a street scene, the uniformity of verbal signs sets up a referential relationship among ostensibly unrelated urban texts that does not exist between signs and nonverbal landmarks. When posted in public space, words in public could also be arranged and rearranged, as New Yorkers frequently and playfully pointed out.

There are also compelling historical grounds for insisting upon the distinction between texts and other images and symbols. As this book suggests, written words were coming into their own as self-sufficient public markers in the nineteenth century. Shop signs and trade cards were becoming more verbose and less emblematic, and newspapers were developing into crowded seas of largely undifferentiated type. Whereas new styles and techniques of visual display would enhance the role and power of nonverbal images in city life *after* the Civil War, the proliferation of the written word on the streets of antebellum New York tended to reinforce the distinction between words and pictures. Therefore, the historical change charted here belongs to what paleographer Armando Petrucci, writing about the bourgeois adoption of classical typography in the nineteenth century, labels "the greatest moment of separation between sign systems of phonetic value (i.e. writing) and sign systems of purely symbolic value (i.e. the figurative arts since ancient times)."[26]

Within the context of antebellum New York, writing and print also occupied a specific cultural position opposed to speech. While scholars and critics such as Jack Goody, Walter Ong, Marshall McLuhan, and others have overessentialized the consequences of literacy and oversimplified the cultural divide between oral and literate societies, it is nonetheless true that an expanded reliance on print can have powerful cultural implications at a particular historical moment. There is a difference between writing and speaking, even if that difference is not everywhere the same and even if it only has meaning in a specific cultural context. Antebellum Americans were particularly attuned to the differences between words spoken and words consigned by an absent author to the impersonal world of print, though they were profoundly ambivalent about what that difference meant. The expanding world of print and writing evoked larger anxieties about such problems as community, confidence, and authority that dominated moral, economic, and political discourse.[27] More specifically, the shift from oral to literate practices figured in critiques of urban society and the decline of traditional, *gemeinschaft*, communal ties. In William Alexander Caruthers's 1834 novel, *The Kentuckian in New-York*, a visitor from the South is surprised by New York elections, in which oratory, drinking, and brawls are replaced by "little bits of paper." As another character of southern origins explains, "New-Yorkers never have what we call 'stump speeches,' and never personally know, or even see their representatives."[28] The proliferation of "little bits of paper" in the expanding city signaled a world far removed from the exchanges of spoken words among the personally acquainted.

For residents of a growing, fast-paced city, written words also lent themselves to two important and contrasting forms of reception. Unlike spoken words, texts could be skimmed quickly by residents and strangers as they passed through the streets. At the same time, they could be held in sustained view as objects of intense deliberation, or detached from their contexts and transferred elsewhere. City reading thus promoted two radically modern forms of promiscuous urban spectatorship: browsing and quoting. While spoken rumors, shouted threats, seductive glances, and brute force remained central to everyday life; while the mass of the moving crowd, the promotional cries of street merchants, the cacophony of hurtling street cars, the flash of new clothing styles, and the stench of human refuse shaped the experiences of circulating in public; city texts provided a mode of detached access distinct from other media and sensory stimuli.

Another reason to distinguish writing and print from other vehicles of urban communication is that they require a specific set of skills that are not always available or well distributed in a specific historical community. The particular importance of written words in antebellum New York had a great deal to do, obviously, with the wide diffusion of what we generally call literacy. Literacy is a tricky concept, though, and its frequent appearance in interpretations of social and cultural history often obscures more than it reveals. Historians are fond of charting and comparing literacy rates in different times and places, and such data often form the foundation of a certain kind of history of reading. But this fondness stems less from the fact that literacy rates represent a solid body of information about the past than from the fact that quantifiable evidence seems somehow more solid than other kinds. In fact, despite the arduous researches of scores of scholars, we know relatively little about the diffusion of reading skills over the centuries. Probate records may measure what portion of a certain population owned books; petitions and depositions can suggest how many individuals in a sample group could sign their names; and census records indicate how many people were able to read or write in the estimation of the heads of household who responded to official surveys; but none of this says very much about a community's reading abilities. In addition to the many lacunae in these surveys, a signature is an incomplete index of literacy. One can learn to write one's own name without being able to comprehend a newspaper, or without even mastering an alphabet. Conversely, an inability to write does not necessarily imply an inability to read, especially in societies where reading and writing are taught separately.[29] The very concept of literacy, understood as a skill people either possess or lack, tends to blur distinctions among radically different kinds of reading communities and practices. The emphasis on a minimal threshold of reading ability as a prerequisite for individual economic and social mobility, as a barometer of cultural assimilation, or as the mark of a certain mentality exaggerates and simplifies the necessary consequences of participation in written exchanges (assuming that learning to read suddenly and automatically opens up a world of enlightenment and opportunity) and tells us very little about how and why people read, how much they read, and how necessary or useful reading was for their everyday lives. It is crucial, of course, to know whether written words were so broadly unfamiliar in a particular community that any use of them constituted a code among elites. But in societies where most people have *some* ability to produce or decipher *some* written messages, the study of literacy rates becomes less central to the task of assessing the meaning of reading.

In thinking about reading practices in antebellum New York, then, we should not get too bogged down in the narrow question of literacy as such. The northern United States in the eighteenth and nineteenth centuries did indeed boast extremely high literacy rates, even by the standards of the highly literate countries in Protestant Europe, and New York was no exception. Despite persistent poverty and extreme cultural heterogeneity, a number of forces helped to maintain high rates of literacy in the city, including the emergence of the common school system; a powerful ideology of educational reform that linked literacy training to republican citizenship, economic well-being, and the maintenance of social order; evangelical commitment to the diffusion of religious knowledge; and the explosion of cheap newspapers, magazines, pamphlets, and books.[30] According to the 1840 census, only 4 percent of the state's population was illiterate. The figure can be misleading, given transience and the vagaries of self-reporting, but the number does suggest a remarkably high proportion of readers. Unfortunately, we have no way of determining from that statistic how many people could make sense of the number 5 on a banknote, a name on a street sign, the contents of a political poster, or the financial column of the *Herald*. We have no precise notion of how broad and, more significantly, how practically excluded from the texts of the city was the class of New Yorkers described by prostitute Helen Jewett when she laments in an 1835 letter to a client that she often wishes that she "had never been educated, but like those I every day meet, I could not read my name in print."[31]

Certainly, there were New Yorkers who could not read all of the texts that appeared in public, either because they lacked reading skills or because they had not yet learned to read English (though it is worth remembering in this context that the overwhelming majority of immigrants to New York before the Civil War came from countries that used the Latin alphabet). Nonetheless, all available evidence supports the hypothesis that most New Yorkers could read most of those texts. In fact, the best evidence for this claim may be the texts themselves. Street signs, parade banners, sandwich-board advertising, banknotes, and even most daily newspapers addressed themselves to a readership that was in principle universal. These texts presumed a widespread ability to read, and provided practical motivations to cultivate and maintain that ability. Michael Schudson has even argued that the proliferation of written words in advertising posters and shop signs offers more compelling evidence of the spread of literacy than signatures on marriage records.[32] And while it is not the point of this study to explain the origins of mass literacy, the story told here does speak to the process by which reading habits were expanded and democratized in the nineteenth century.[33] What is most important to emphasize at the outset is that public writing was not a private code passing among members of an educated minority over the heads of the unknowing masses. The impersonality of these public verbal exchanges rested on the assumption, justified or not, that a stranger of unspecified background could use a sign, newspaper, trade card, or banknote to get around the city.

If the distinction between reading and other ways of perceiving the city makes historical and theoretical sense, the choice to focus on the years 1825 to 1865 may seem a bit more arbitrary. Certainly, the emergence of new sites and networks of public communication took place less suddenly and more unevenly then such a neat time frame might suggest. Nonetheless, 1825 makes a useful starting point for a description of city reading in New York, since the opening of the Erie Canal that October marked the advent of the city's preeminence within the market revolution, and helped initiate the commercial and demographic growth of subsequent decades against which this story is set. This year also saw the introduction of gas lighting in Manhattan, a less momentous event in traditional narratives of our nation's growth, though it marks (but does not itself explain) a significant transformation in the spectacle of urban life and the role of visual signs in the cityscape. At the same time, universal manhood suffrage (which became law in New York State in 1826) codified a more inclusive notion of the polity and provided additional inducements for the cultivation of reading skills and habits. It is more than a coincidence that the proliferation of written words in New York appears to have taken off around this time.[34] End points are harder to fix, both because the population and economy of the city continued to grow at impressive rates well into the next century, and because the proliferation of writing and print has continued (and in certain respects intensified) as well. To extend the study much beyond the end of the war, into the age of color printing, national currency, elevated railroads, tall buildings, telephones, and new waves of immigrants from southern and eastern Europe, would alter or obscure some of the peculiar features of city reading in the antebellum period. To stop the study at 1860 (the standard cutoff for the antebellum era), on the other hand, would be to miss the way the reception of the war in New York dramatized the power of writing and print within the new urban public they helped to construct.

The location of this inquiry within the confines of a single city is in part a pragmatic necessity, but it obviously has significant consequences. As with any local history (and of course all history is in some sense local), the very features of a community or region that make it a compelling point of research tend to limit the sorts of generalizations that can be drawn from the findings. New York was the largest city in the Western Hemisphere by mid-century, the center of commerce in North America, and the port of entry for a historically distinctive collection of immigrants. In areas related to reading, the city's dominance was even more pronounced. With only 2 percent of the nation's population in the 1850s, New York claimed 18 percent of the country's newspaper circulation, handled 22 percent of its mail, and produced over 37 percent of its total publishing revenue.[35] Though the demographic, economic, physical, and cultural transformations taking place in New York were bound up in broader historical changes, it would be absurd to suggest that one could substitute Philadelphia or Charleston or Nauvoo and tell the same story. At the same time, New York did function as a metonym for the big city within a predominantly nonurban American society, especially in the pages of a print discourse about city life that was disproportionately produced in Manhattan. To the extent that this is a story about antebellum America, the focus on an atypical urban environment may actually extend rather than narrow its relevance to the cultural history of the American city.

A systematic comparison of reading practices in New York and those in other cities lies beyond the scope of this project, however, and except where the issue is raised in the sources themselves (as is often the case with travel literature, where visitors frequently comment on the unusual concentration and prominence of signs in New York's public spaces), I do not emphasize the extent to which the relationship between reading and public life that existed in New York was either typical or unique. This study sets out to describe the particular practices of a specific group of people (however large, diverse, and transient), and similar research would have to be conducted to assess the role of reading in the public life of different urban environments in the nineteenth-century West. Still, the experience of New York suggests familiar features of modern city life, and therefore inevitably alludes to larger patterns in urban history and in the well-described shift from *Gemeinschaft* to *Gesellschaft* communities. Peter Fritzsche's recent exploration of print culture in Berlin at the beginning of the twentieth century finds many of the same themes explored in this study. The proliferation in Berlin of "small bits and rich streams of text," argues Fritzsche, offered a compelling and confusing spectacle of transitory urban life and "fashioned the nature of metropolitan experience."[36] Significantly, this phenomenon occurred decades later in Berlin than in New York, where commercial culture, the metropolitan press, and mass literacy took hold much earlier. In the most general terms, the formation of a subjectivity characteristic of modern urban life, what Georg Simmel describes as a kind of blasé sophistication and Dana Brand associates with "the passive yet compulsive consumer of a rapidly and perpetually changing spectacle," appears throughout much of the urbanized West, though undoubtedly with varying political and cultural implications. The case of antebellum New York can help us to explore the implications of print for this story.[37]

This book, then, is both an account of a specific time period in an unusual city and a glimpse at the emergence of urban modernity in the capitalist West. While peering over the shoulders of residents and visitors in antebellum New York to view the signs, posters, newspapers, and banknotes that they would have seen, and while reconstructing the specific conditions of print's reception and consumption by a heterogeneous urban population, we must also keep our eyes open for the larger relationship between print and the city. The power and complexity of the link between written words and urban spaces in the nineteenth century is especially striking from the perspective of an era in which both institutions seem threatened. In recent decades, champions of both the city and the written word have grown uneasy. For if cities and writing have traditionally served as instruments of memory, as forces of preservation and continuity, their explosive growth in the age of market capitalism has tended to produce the opposite effect. More to the point of our story, the relationship between community and communication, between reading and public space, seems particularly fragile at this point in history. The centrifugal thrust of both information proliferation and city development makes it harder to see the spatial contours of an urban public. "The contemporary metropolis," writes architectural historian M. Christine Boyer, "represents a physical site in which images and messages seem to swirl about, devoid of a sustaining context,"[38] a thematic complaint reformulated by countless critics of the digital age who mourn the loss of spatial relationships associated with printed texts.[39]

In some respects, though, the dislocations augured by the decentered metropolis and electronic media represent extensions of the historical changes charted in this study. Ironically, the cities and texts of the nineteenth century, which now appear as the stable objects of premature nostalgia, were themselves sites of jarring juxtaposition and spectacular instability. The paradoxical fact that for a period of time the disparate print messages of a contentious and competitive urban community helped to construct a stage for public communication in the physical spaces of a city—rather than in the abstract or privatized realms we associate with print—should caution us against too narrowly deterministic an approach to the consequences of technology or to the implications of formal changes in both reading and urban life. It makes a difference, of course, how people communicate and how they build communities, whether they are writing or speaking, whether they get information from town criers or electronic mail, whether they live in a stable kin-based community or in a Residence Inn by Marriott. But print and cities do not have technological or sociological destinies; they have contingent social, cultural, and political histories that are being constantly retold and remade. To consider what differences the public use of writing and print made to antebellum New Yorkers (and to ourselves as ambivalent inheritors of the nineteenth-century urban legacy) is to beg another telling of those histories.

2

Brick, Paper, and the Spectacle of Urban Growth

~

The Rise of a New Metropolis

In 1836, the Boston-based *American Magazine of Useful and Entertaining Knowledge* printed an adaptation of a steel engraving depicting Coffee House Slip on Wall Street near the East River. Accompanying the picture, a text written anonymously by the magazine's young editor, Nathaniel Hawthorne, observed the "singular truth, that the mere shadowy image of a building, on the frail material of paper . . . is likely to have a longer term of existence than the piled brick and mortar of the building." For future generations, Hawthorne predicted, mechanically reproduced images would provide the only reliable evidence of the existence of the "proud structure[s]" of his own day.[1] Significantly, Hawthorne's prophetic reliance (expressed three years before the introduction of photography) on the "shadowy image" to preserve the sturdy building evokes the flimsiness of the printed object even as he stresses its relative durability. To some extent, this ambivalent attitude toward the world of paper was symptomatic of a more widespread dilemma about print culture in the antebellum period. Americans' increasing dependence on paper to mediate their relationships to political events, wealth, and cultural authority did not by any means remove their anxieties about that mediation. Hawthorne's comments have a particular meaning, though, in the context of the enormous physical, economic, and demographic transformation of New York during the forty years following the opening of the Erie Canal in 1825.

Massive immigration, high residential mobility, economic expansion and dislocation, and technological advances all shook the foundations of public life in the metropolis by destabilizing the various grounds upon which city residents had come to anchor their assumptions about the identity of New York. In the wake of these changes, writing and print would come to occupy more prominent positions in public space and public discourse, fulfilling many of the cultural roles traditionally played by people, political institutions, shared cultures, and face-to-face communication. But as Hawthorne's text suggests, one of the most dramatic symbols of urban change in antebellum Manhattan was the striking lack of continuity in the city's appearance. Hawthorne leans anxiously on emerging arts and technologies of visual reproduction to provide a stable frame of reference for making sense of this discontinuity, a tactic that proved both popular and lucrative in antebellum New York. Still, the displacement of brick by paper (and by the semiotic systems associated with paper) had, as subsequent chapters will demonstrate, a dramatic verbal component as well. Of course, what made this verbal cityscape so central to everyday life in New York was the fact that the city's population was so transient. Since by mid-century most of the people who walked the streets of Manhattan had arrived from elsewhere, the city was by definition unfamiliar. City reading operated against the backdrop of new presumptions about recognition and acquaintanceship generated by this demographic instability. To reconstruct the appearance and impact of the city's network of urban texts, however, requires underscoring at the outset that written words were flooding the streets at a time when the relationship between the city and its physical forms and structures was becoming increasingly abstract, when the very meaning of public space was being called into question.

Most accounts of the growth of New York in the nineteenth century begin, quite properly, with the enormous increase in the city's population. From only 33,000 residents in 1790, New York grew fivefold over the next thirty-five years and supplanted Philadelphia as the nation's leader. Yet by the standards of the next several decades, New York was still a small port town in 1825. While the overall rate of growth over the next thirty-five years was similar, the sheer numbers were far more impressive and the impact on the nature of the urban community far more spectacular. Fueled by spurts in the late 1830s and the early 1850s, New York's population grew to exceed 800,000 by the start of the Civil War, vastly outstripping its nearest American rivals (as well as twenty out of the thirty-three states in the Union) and surpassing Mexico City as the largest city in the Western Hemisphere.[2] Considering that vast portions of the northern half of the island remained uninhabited and that only a handful of city buildings stood higher than five stories (passenger elevators were not introduced until the end of the 1850s, though their use had been proposed earlier as a means of solving the city's housing crisis),[3] New York's population density was phenomenal even by modern standards. Manhattan's population in 1860, despite these significant limitations, was numerically closer to that of 1990 than that of 1820. Moreover, the city was beginning to support a network of suburbs in surrounding New York and New Jersey counties, communities linked to Manhattan by an expanding system of ferry service. By 1860 there were almost 30,000 people living in Jersey City and more than 70,000 in Newark. Brooklyn, which had annexed Williamsburg in 1855, was home to nearly 280,000 people and ranked fourth among American cities. In all, the New York metropolitan area accommodated some 1.5 million residents by the time of the war.[4]

Besides leading to subhuman living conditions in many of the city's poorer wards, and contributing to a sense that New York was the major metropolis of the New World, this massive demographic increase signaled the emergence of New York as a recognizably modern city, a place in which daily encounters among strangers represented the norm. Lydia Maria Child complained of New York in the 1840s that over the course of "eight weary months, I have met in the crowded streets but two faces I have ever seen before."[5] The meaning of public life within this urban environment would have to be readjusted to accommodate the presence of more people than could conceivably become familiar with one another, even in the most general way.[6]

Compounding and accentuating the disorienting effects of this unprecedented concentration and amalgamation of people, the character of Manhattan's population was changing as well. In contrast to earlier growth, which was supported primarily by natural increase, internal migration (especially from New England), and (to a lesser extent) immigration from England, New York's antebellum explosion came primarily from a new stream of immigrants. In the four decades before the Civil War, 3.6 million foreigners arrived in New York, and enough stayed to transform the city entirely. Whereas net migration accounted for 25 percent of New York's population increase between 1810 and 1820 (with the rest accountable to an excess of births over deaths), the figure rose to over 67 percent the following decade, over 69 percent in the 1830s, and over 80 percent in the 1840s, and stayed over 75 percent in the 1850s. At the same time, the proportion of migrants coming from other parts of the United States was declining, so that by 1855 a majority of New York's residents were foreign-born, more than 85 percent coming from Ireland or from German-speaking countries in Central Europe. That year, the number of New Yorkers born in Ireland exceeded the city's total population thirty years earlier. Even France, a less obvious source of the city's population growth, was the birthplace of more New Yorkers in 1855 than Massachusetts.[7] Each year saw the influx of new people with different histories, bearing different community identities, practicing different religions, and in many cases speaking different languages. Whatever cultural continuities and commonalities had been invoked by New Yorkers to identify the nature of their community had to be revised in light of this dramatic demographic development.[8] From the perspective of the immigrant majority, moreover, cultural continuity with the city's past would acquire different meanings.

Compounding the impact of a highly transient population were an increasing number of visitors to the city, who had no intention of taking up residence in New York but contributed both to the heterogeneous spectacle of urban life and to its audience. "A Strangers List," published in 1835 when the city's population hovered around 270,000, enumerated 59,700 guests (over 22 percent of the total population) at city hotels over a 207-day period, or about 270 per day for average stays of three days.[9] In subsequent years, "Strangers Lists" would become unthinkable, not simply because it would have been impracticable to count all of the hotel guests, short-term boarders, and immigrants bound for inland destinations passing a few nights with their relatives, but because the category itself became harder to define. The entire city was, in a sense, a world of strangers.

While the impact of population explosion and ethnic heterogeneity on city life is sometimes mitigated, stabilized, or at least obscured from general view by the formation of distinct neighborhoods, it is important to remember that New Yorkers (the overwhelming majority of whom did not own their homes) moved rapidly and frequently around the city during the antebellum era. The massive carnival of May 1 or Moving Day, in which countless New Yorkers changed individual addresses for the next year, dramatized persistently high patterns of residential mobility, and though this ritual provided a mechanism for geographical segregation and land use specialization, New York's residential districts remained largely heterogeneous and unstable through the Civil War.[10] Histories of antebellum New York often focus on cities within the city (Five Points, Wall Street, the Bowery) in a misleading way. The great majority of New Yorkers lived in areas that reflected the demographic fluidity of the larger city. The waves of newcomers from Ireland and Germany, for example, were not simply forming ethnic enclaves in previously uninhabited sections of the island, but were negotiating and reshaping the unstable landscape of a city in which spatial differentiation was relatively inchoate.[11] At the same time, an enormous mass-transit system of omnibuses and horse-drawn railroad cars moved passengers (more than 50 million of them a year in 1857) quickly and frequently up and down the island, bridging distances and blurring boundaries between various districts and exposing most residents to the diversity of people and activities in the city.[12] It would be overstating the case to claim, as some historians have, that the forced intermingling of different classes, ethnicities, and subcultures gave New York a "social wholeness."[13] The point is not that the city's new population formed a unified social world, but rather that the many explosive conflicts and jarring discontinuities within this society were highly and broadly visible.

Though the forces behind the growth of New York's population were complex and varied (including, naturally, economic and political developments in Europe), demographic increase was intimately linked with the city's economic expansion. Activity in New York's port had been increasing since the turn of the century (especially after the end of the War of 1812), but the opening of the Erie Canal in 1825 cemented New York's position as the commercial capital of the United States by providing access to markets in the developing West. Over the next few decades, the city enhanced its preeminence as an inlet for foreign trade (especially in textiles, sugar, iron, tin, and alcohol), and by 1860 New

York was handling almost two thirds of the nation's imports. While the total volume of foreign goods entered in New York's port in 1825 had weighed less than 300 tons, by the Civil War the figure approached 2,000 tons (a rate of increase exceeding the population growth over the same period). The increase in export volume was only slightly less considerable.[14] Alongside and beyond the bustle of the port, manufacturing flourished in Manhattan as well. New York led the nation in such fields as piano making, shipbuilding, clothing production, and publishing, and in the twenty years leading up to the war the value added by New York manufacturing increased twice as much as the city's population. By 1860 the city's 4,355 manufacturing firms were employing close to 90,000 workers and had capital valued at about $65 million.[15]

As New York's economy expanded, it also grew more complex and diverse. Unlike in some other cities, the industrial takeoff of the 1830s did not consolidate economic relations around the demands of a single industry. New York at mid-century was, in the words of historian Sean Wilentz, "a metropolitan labyrinth of factories and tiny artisan establishments, central workrooms and outworks' cellars, luxury firms and sweat work strapping shops."[16] By the 1840s, the public markets were in decline, struggling to compete with the myriad private shops that were multiplying in lower Manhattan. But the new urban economy did not simply offer a bazaar of commercial options and opportunities. Much of the wealth that poured into New York as it became the nation's center of trade and finance wound up in the hands of a privileged minority (115 of whom were millionaires in 1860), while an alarming number of city residents suffered in squalor, disease, and penury. According to one contemporary estimate, New York's homeless population had reached 50,000 by the 1840s.[17] Between these two dramatically and increasingly stratified poles lay a wide range of conditions and experiences, but few New Yorkers remained insulated from the destabilizing forces of economic change. An ever-growing middle class was becoming more dependent on the vagaries of a speculative market. Traditional crafts were being reshaped by a revolutionary process of subdivision and subcontracting, and artisanal identities were further threatened by high occupational mobility, the breakdown of the apprentice system, and the city's new demographics (historian Richard Stott estimates that over 80 percent of the city's manual workers were foreign-born by 1855). And for most city dwellers—most painfully for the tens of thousands of unskilled laborers, domestic servants, and journeyman artisans—the rising price of land (which substantially reduced the real value of wages) severely constrained the opportunities offered by the new economy. As the capital of America's market revolution, New York became the site of significant destabilization and dislocation.[18]

Between 1825 and 1865, these well-documented and oft-discussed demographic and economic changes undoubtedly altered the way New York residents conceived of their relationship to the larger urban community. Even for the small minority of New Yorkers who lived in the city continuously during these decades, unprecedented numbers of people from unfamiliar places, moving perpetually to and from private dwellings, boarding houses, tenements, and police stations and performing new tasks in a new urban economy presented a powerful cultural and epistemological challenge. On what perceptible grounds could the city called New York at the time of the opening of the canal be recognized as such forty years later? Rather than providing continuity, the city's core physical plant—its internal geography and topography, general pattern of settlement, and public spaces—became the most telling indices and the most obvious symbols of urban transformation.

Most palpably, urban life was spreading northward to parts of the island that had been hinterland a few years earlier. While as late as 1835 less than 10 percent of the city's population lived above Fourteenth Street, a majority of New Yorkers were living north of that point only twenty-five years later. By 1860, more people inhabited the wards north of Fourteenth Street than had lived in the entire city just two decades before.[19] As New York's avenues pushed inexorably up the island, forging graded paths of macadam through a once-hilly terrain, and as multi-story buildings sprouted up in previously rural areas, the city attained a conspicuous density. While in 1825 parks and squares were spread throughout the inhabited section of the island, the following decades saw the sale of most of the land previously designated as open space. By 1850, the largest park area within the confines of urban settlement covered only twenty-one acres.[20] Developer Samuel B. Ruggles, who made a handsome living constructing elite residential districts within the city, pointed out that since no public squares had been created between 1845 and 1853, the stretch of land between Twenty-sixth and Fifty-seventh Streets was left "without one single breathing space other than adjacent roads and avenues."[21]

But even in areas that had been inhabited for decades, the city's look was constantly changing. New York was a "modern city of ruins," one newspaper declared in the 1840s, where "no sooner is a fine building put up than it is torn down."[22] Arriving during the previous decade, English actress Fanny Kemble had found in New York "an irregular collection of temporary buildings, erected for some casual purpose, full of life, animation, and variety, but not meant to endure for any length of time."[23] In "one short month," wrote Cornelius Mathews in his mid-century panorama of city life, "houses are down that were up—brick piles, inspired with life by the magic glances of the architect, spring up to be houses."[24] Several years after the Civil War, local cartman Isaac Lyon maintained that "of the buildings that have been erected since 1834 there have been burned and torn down, and again rebuilt, more than there are now standing that were built prior to that time."[25] As Lyon's remark suggests, some of this impermanence was more or less accidental, resulting from several devastating fires (most notably in 1835 and 1845) that took a considerable toll on the physical condition of lower Manhattan. But while a few major conflagrations became memorable catastrophes, fires were a regular feature of life in antebellum New York. Upon his arrival in 1846, Swedish immigrant Erik Janson was struck by the fact "there are fires almost all the time in many places and the bells in the city's towers ring the whole night through." Janson echoed a singularly pervasive theme in the recorded observations of tourists, immigrants, novelists, and journalists, all of whom were impressed by the particular importance of fires and fire fighting in city culture. Between 1837 and 1848, 2,500 fires blazed in New York, reinforcing perceptions that homes and stores were ephemeral objects.[26] Asa Greene, in his 1837 description of the city, stressed the "slightness of modern structures in New York" as well, regaling his readers with stories of collapsing buildings. Thirteen years later, former mayor Philip Hone related in his diary the collapse of a boarding house on Broadway (which fell "with a crash so astounding" it was mistaken for an earthquake) as a dramatization of more regular processes of change. "If they do not pull down the houses in the annual renovation of Broadway," he quipped, "they fall of their own accord."[27]

Tragic fires and shoddy buildings (many of which were quite sturdy by earlier standards) made good news stories and offered compelling symbols for a changing cityscape. Most of the demolition and construction, however, was deliberate. To some observers, this perpetual cycle was partly a matter of fashion, or what poet Walt Whitman called the "pull-down-and-build-over-again-spirit."[28] Isaac Lyon noted that all the landmarks of the previous generation had been "swept away to make room for 'something new,' " casting skeptical quotation marks around what Hone had derided as the "annual renovation" of the city's major thoroughfare.[29] But the real engine behind the frenzy, as Hone and other property owners clearly understood, was not simply a thirst for novelty but the growth and movement of the city's population, which created the need for new housing, expanded markets for new businesses, and raised the value of real estate. In the decade 1841–1850 an average of 1,485 new buildings were constructed each year in Manhattan, though even this was inadequate to avert a serious housing crisis.[30] Whether or not New Yorkers longed for changes in the physical appearance of their city, demographic developments guaranteed that such changes would take place. Though a handful of structures—such as City Hall (1811), the Merchants' Exchange (1841), and Stewart's Dry Goods (1846)—made lasting impressions upon city residents, the physical plant as a whole was extremely volatile and could hardly have served as a stable symbol with which the city might be identified.

Well before even a third of Manhattan was inhabited, before buildings had begun to rise and fall in staggering numbers, the groundwork had been laid for divesting the city's physical structures of their privileged status as reliable metonyms for the public or for public space. In 1811, when fewer than 100,000 people lived in the city and urban settlement barely reached Houston Street, a commission appointed by the state legislature to lay out new streets in New York City established a uniform rectilinear grid for organizing all future development on the island. In addition to facilitating the purchase of property and planning for convenient and wide thoroughfares, the mapping of streets prior to their physical construction implicitly subordinated the significance of particular buildings in defining the city. The Commissioners' Plan dealt in space, not in monumental architecture. And like Hawthorne's engraving, the published map represents an inversion of the hierarchical relationship between brick and paper, though here the printed document is relied upon to anticipate (and in some sense make possible) the physical structure, not to preserve it.

Historians and critics have debated the significance of the Commissioners' Plan, some (like Lewis Mumford and John Reps) stressing its bland and brazen artificiality and its value to speculators, and others (like Hendrik Hartog and Elizabeth Blackmar) emphasizing its vision of republican neutrality.[31] But the shared insight of the competing interpretations is clear enough. What made the grid a blueprint for speculation was precisely its neutral treatment of land. Much like Thomas Jefferson's 1785 Land Ordinance, which had mapped the nation's western territories as a series of identical and endlessly repeating rectilinear subdivisions, the 1811 map plotted the streets of Manhattan on the coordinates of what literary scholar Philip Fisher has aptly characterized as a "Cartesian social space" in which the uniqueness of place disappears.[32] Within the grid, land is homogenized, its unique features liquidated into a uniform currency. Points on the map become interchangeable units of space distinct from one another only in terms of size and relative location.

Underlying this homogenization was a notion of land as commodity, an important ideological development in early American history that the Plan both endorsed and reinforced. No longer a privileged form of wealth or a unique determinant of status, land was becoming an object of free exchange. The impact of this development on the economy of the city was considerable, but it also had social implications. Turning places into spaces, critics were quick to point out, tended to obscure differences among people as well. As a French visitor observed in 1864, "a city where the streets are numbers is like . . . a vast hotel open to anyone who comes along, where only money distinguishes one man from another."[33] The grid promulgated a radically integrative vision of urban space in which land values (based largely on accessibility to concentrations of population) could be represented on paper at any given time and social knowledge was flattened and refashioned by market relations.[34]

This further reduction of "real" estate to its representation in print would manifest itself quite dramatically as New York grew in accordance with the commissioners' prescriptive vision. In 1836, the year Philip Hone sold his Broadway home for $60,000 (netting him a profit of $35,000 in fourteen years) to a party intent on converting it to commercial use, the assessed value of real estate in Manhattan rose an astonishing 62.5 percent over the previous year. Though this atypical leap was fueled largely by flurries of speculation, and though some of that increase would be eroded by the depression of the following year, New York's real estate market was on the rise during most of the antebellum era, outstripping both the rise in population and the construction of new buildings.[35] The newspapers were rife with stories of investors making enormous profits almost overnight by purchasing property in underpopulated areas, dividing it into lots, and selling it at auction, much in the manner satirized by James Fenimore Cooper's *Home as Found* (1838), in which land units (even some at the bottom of the sea) skyrocket in value simply by virtue of being mapped, "brought into visible lines, with feet and inches."[36]

Such dramatic and well-publicized changes in the value of land fed popular anxieties about the stability of wealth and status, and figured with particular prominence in the moralistic rhetoric of the Jacksonians and in a republican discourse that made explicit the opposition between real property and its paper representations. James Gordon Bennett, who as editor of the immensely popular New York *Herald* played a powerful and lucrative role in the city's paper revolution, invoked this suspicion in his (mechanically reproduced) analysis of the Panic of 1837 when he urged a return "to tilling the earth instead of selling it—to ploughing the soil instead of lithographing it." Bennett's diagnosis may seem so ironic as to be disingenuous (he goes on to recommend "dwelling in the country instead of starving and agitating in large cities"), but the rhetorical thrust of his juxtapositions would not have been lost on many readers.[37]

To be sure, despite the alarming volatility of the real estate market and widespread uncertainty about the relationship between reality and representation—between ploughshares and lithographs—in the urban economy, property ownership remained a central constitutive feature of public life in antebellum New York. In many respects, the 1820s marked the ascendancy of a notion of public interest in the city's affairs based primarily on the desire to enhance private property—a departure from earlier understandings of the municipal corporation of New York, as a chartered commercial enterprise with its own property rights. Still, this propertied conception of the urban public did not maintain with any rigidity the traditional distinction between land and other commodities that generated tax revenue, and in no way identified the public with the city's buildings.[38]

Hawthorne's observation about the image of Coffee House Slip thus alludes to a multifaceted displacement of brick by paper in which physical buildings depend on plans to give them spatial meaning, on dollars and price quotations to give them value, and on print technology to give them durability. But it would be a mistake to read in this displacement a drift from the real to the symbolic, a disintegration of the built environment of the traditional city into what Lewis Mumford simplistically denounces as the "pseudo-environment of paper."[39] After all, the public significance of buildings is itself a matter of symbolism (consider the metonymic use and value of the skyline in Chicago, or the Capitol in Washington, D.C.), and lithographic prints and published maps are material objects as well as symbolic representations. Moreover, in the experience of most New Yorkers, the world of paper and the world of brick were becoming increasingly hard to separate during the antebellum period, especially in the case of written words.

In city directories, municipal brochures, and bird's-eye views, in woodcuts, lithographs, steel engravings, and photographs (by mid-century, just eleven years after Daguerre's inventions were announced, there were about a hundred daguerreotype studios in New York), new arts and technologies of print representation assumed, as Hawthorne suggests, increased importance in organizing the changing city as an object of visual consciousness. Photography in particular came to represent a genre of public inventory, such that when *Putnam's* published an extensive verbal survey of major architecture in the city in 1853, the article was entitled "New York Daguerreotyped"—despite the utter absence of photographs.[40] But while nonverbal images in lithographs and photographs could give New Yorkers a sense of control over the changing built environment, the written word could be imprinted upon that environment itself. Writing and print were sprouting up everywhere in the destabilized public spaces of the city, covering streets, homes, stores, warehouses, carriages, buses, trees, fences, lampposts, and people. Some of these words appeared on sturdy, monumental signboards and became more or less fixed features of the cityscape, while others were mobilized for more ephemeral or transient signage, such as broadsides, parade banners, and sandwich-board advertising. In both cases, though, as the following two chapters illustrate, the proliferation of the written word in public view represented an important development in the way residents in an increasingly heterogeneous and unwieldy urban community related to one another and to their shared spaces. In an unstable physical environment refashioned by a uniform grid and by market relations, where coffeehouses and coffeehouse cultures were crumbling, a city of strangers turned to urban texts to obtain, share, and project new forms of social knowledge.

3

Commercial Impudence and the Dictatorship of the Perpendicular

~

Signs of the City

Looking back with nostalgia at the New York of his childhood in a book published in 1896, octogenarian Charles Haswell remembered old street names that few of his living contemporaries could identify. After going through a litany of forgotten names, Haswell, an engineer, recalled a narrow alley downtown that had, at the beginning of the century, been known "colloquially, if not legally" as Tin Pot Alley. This colloquial designation did not, however, go unchallenged.

> Some absurd person of more or less authority has endeavored to effect a change by putting on an adjacent street-lamp the name "Exchange Alley," to denote a passage wherein less exchange takes place than in any other throughout the city. We have noted with singular pleasure that . . . the Rev. Dr. Morgan Dix . . . prepared, at his own care and cost, a decorated tablet of graceful design, bearing the old name.

Yet even the civic-minded gesture of Dr. Dix was undone by "a tailor's impudent sign that has been suffered to cover full one-half of this tablet." Still, Haswell had hope that the tailor's "sense of the trade interest with old New-Yorkers may induce him to place this sign a little lower."[1]

Peering over Haswell's shoulder across a considerably larger historical divide, modern urbanites may be amused by the anarchy that seems to surround the naming of streets in this period of New York's history. But the jarring instability of a sign system that present city dwellers and cultural historians alike have come to take for granted should alert us to some of the ways in which the streets and buildings of Manhattan became a battleground for competing expressions of power and authority during the antebellum era. With demographic and economic growth, written and printed words multiplied in number, increased in size and prominence, and came to form a large part of the shared visual experience of New Yorkers of different ethnicities, genders, and classes, as well as an indispensable (though highly disjointed) map with which residents and visitors could negotiate the city. Significantly, the vast majority of these words belonged to the class of trade labels and advertisements represented by Haswell's impudent tailor, rather than the kind of sign associated with the community-oriented initiative of Dr. Dix or even with the intriguingly absent figure of the street inspector (or some other municipal agent), whom we might expect to resolve the dispute with duly constituted authority. Amid the impressive collage of signs that proliferated across the cityscape during this time of intense urban growth, publicly sponsored signs were barely and decreasingly conspicuous. Instead, the most prominent and imposing words in the Manhattan cityscape inscribed claims of private property and reinforced the spectacle of competitive commerce. At the same time, however, these private signs addressed a broad, impersonal public and, ironically, helped to construct a medium through which new kinds of public authority could be expressed. While advertising the juxtaposition of disparate economic interests, commercial signs nonetheless projected some more uniform images—organized around the written word and conveyed largely in English. And while these signs marked many of the city's nonresidential buildings as belonging to private individuals, they simultaneously marked the streets as belonging to an inclusive and undifferentiated public of potential readers.

Though certainly among the most mundane and unspectacular signs in the modern city, street name markers play an integral role in mapping public space and spreading the imprimatur of the public throughout the cityscape. While different street names, in the words of sociologist Priscilla Parkhurst Ferguson, are used to "socialize space and celebrate cultural identity,"[2] the mere presence of the street sign serves a more profound and subtle function—authorizing a perpetually visible designation of public space to strangers and insiders alike. As a broadly literate and highly transient urban community whose economic development had already been linked (as of 1811) to the orderly northward extension of settlement over a preestablished street map, New York had the social and cultural conditions that made such a sign system both useful and necessary. But if what makes street signs so important (and at the same time so inconspicuous) in most Western cities today is their omnipresence and their uncomplicated relation to public authority, what is most striking about the street signs of antebellum New York is that their coverage of the city was so inadequate, incomplete, and even, at times, contested.

Signs inscribed with street names had appeared in New York as early as the previous century, and had been conceived of primarily as a means of giving directions. A letter to the New York *Journal* in 1774, when the city's population was barely 25,000, listed among several laudable city improvements "that of affixing the names of the streets at every corner." The letter went on to complain, however, that these signs were not being posted with any consistency, that the contracted painters had reneged on their commitments, and that only the streets of the politically well-connected had been properly labeled.[3] This gap between public objectives (commercial, to be sure, but understood in terms of shared economic interests) and reality in the erection of street signs resurfaces throughout the early national period in the letters of citizens who felt that these signs were necessary "for the assistance of Strangers &c." and fell under the municipal corporation's responsibility to instruct people how to get around the city.[4] Though the fulfillment of that responsibility would involve a long, uneven, and complicated process of establishing authority in public signs, New York was reaching a point in size, transience, and heterogeneity where what one historian of eighteenth-century Paris has characterized as a "system of addresses and descriptions . . . based on familiarity with the neighborhood"[5] would have to give way to a system of verbal (and numerical) signs legible to strangers.

In the early decades of the nineteenth century, the Common Council frequently ordered either the Street Commissioner or (later) the Superintendent of Repairs to "affix the names to all the Streets that require it."[6] By virtue of some combination of growth and neglect, these orders had to be repeated often, particularly after the massive expansion following the opening of the Erie Canal in 1825. In 1833, for example, the Board of Aldermen adopted a resolution calling on the Superintendent of Repairs "to place sign boards, legibly painted, on the corners, in the usual manner, of all new streets; also on all corners where there are none, and where the present sign boards are defaced."[7] Referring both to "a usual manner" of painting and placing signs on street corners and to "corners where there are none," the resolution leaves us a mixed message about the prevalence of street signs, and finishes with a suggestive reminder of the kind of resistance and interference these signs encountered. The haphazard appearance of such resolutions in the government documents indicates that the general policy of labeling streets was not, as might be expected, incorporated into some regular pattern of appropriation and maintenance. What might have been a simple matter of putting sign boards on all street corners somehow became an irregular and inexplicably recalcitrant process over which the records of city planning and expenditure pass largely in silence.[8]

It is hard to determine with any precision how widely (and how prominently) street signs were spread across Manhattan during the antebellum era. The bulk of the visual sources (lithographs, engravings, etchings) upon which historians depend to describe what the city looked like in the first half of the nineteenth century supply surprisingly little evidence of street signs, and much of that evidence is inconsistent.[9] It is also difficult to know where to look for the street signs in the pictorial documents. Frequent references in the legal sources to affixing signs on street corners steer us toward the buildings that sit at intersections, and in fact most of the identifiable street names in the prints are written on small signs attached to corner structures.[10] But there is no way of ruling out the possibility that street names were posted in less conspicuous locations. The Commissioners' Plan called for the placement of 1,549 marble stones on street corners, and a municipal guide in the 1820s boasted that with these "monumental stones . . . planted at every corner . . . every avenue and cross street is clearly seen."[11] And while it is most doubtful that street signs were impressed into the sidewalks (when merchants used this device for advertising, observers cited the practice as a curious novelty),[12] it is clear that they often appeared on or in street lamps, particularly in the later part of the period. In 1825 the Common Council rejected a petition calling for street names to be painted on the glass of street lamps on the grounds that "the Letters would cover nearly the whole of the Glass, and darken the streets."[13] But when English novelist Anthony Trollope visited the city in 1861, he complained of being unable to determine when to get off the streetcar because the street names were written only on the lampposts.[14] This placement had the advantage of making signs easier to read at night, though they wound up being quite small. An 1865 photograph of Astor Place (fig. 3.1) provides a tiny glimpse of how such a sign looked (see lamp at bottom of image), and several stereographs of lower Manhattan from the '60s appear, under a magnifying glass, to indicate signs in the lamps, though the content of the signs is often illegible.[15] The possibility that street names were posted idiosyncratically and in places we might not suspect limits the way we use pictures to reconstruct this segment of New York's signs.

Even allowing for the problematic nature of this evidence, though, it is significant that only a small fraction of the street views from this period include street signs.[16] Even when artists recorded other small signs with great detail, and even when an indication of a street name would have been useful, street signs are usually omitted. Moreover, street signs appear very rarely in the street photography (mostly daguerreotypes and stereographs) that began to flourish in the 1850s and 1860s. Presumably, the signs that were too small or insignificant to merit the attention of a lithographer would not elude the gaze of the camera. Nonetheless, street signs diminish in visibility in the iconography of nineteenth-century New York. From the sleepy watercolors of the Jeffersonian era to the bustling lithographs of the 1830s and '40s to the photographs of the '50s and '60s, street names form a progressively smaller portion of the words appearing in street views, despite the escalating capacities of the different art forms to register detail. Though many factors may have contributed, the visual record of the period would seem to support the argument that the names of streets were not well marked before the Civil War.[17]

The relative absence of street signs is intriguing in light of the city's growth. As the population increased and diversified, the streets multiplied and extended northward, residents switched neighborhoods with bewildering frequency, and improved internal transportation moved the local population about the city with unprecedented speed, the need for

FIGURE 3.1 Broadway, north of Astor Place, c. 1865. Stereograph
by E. & H. T. Anthony & Co.

• • •

marking the streets became more and more pressing. New York was a
world of strangers in which street signs could facilitate the silent navigation of masses of literate and semi-literate people. Local government
implicitly acknowledged this function of street signs in its frequent deliberations on the naming and renaming of streets. The Board of
Aldermen turned down numerous (though by no means all) requests for
name changes with arguments that unnecessary changes create "confusion and perplexity," especially with "persons not well acquainted with"
a particular neighborhood. A petition to change the name of part of
Monroe Street was rejected in 1838 by a board concerned about the
impropriety of such a change "for the accommodation of the whole
public, and especially strangers." These arguments and the petitions to
which they responded presumed a context of signs by which street names

44

were made known both to residents and merchants seeking to project new identities and to strangers seeking to make their way through the city.[18]

This striking gap between civic policy and urban reality was substantial. Despite an official commitment to the orderly marking of public space, the actual practices of labeling streets often eluded central control. Haswell's story of the battle over the naming of Tin Pot Alley takes place within a political space apparently vacated by municipal authority, or at least beyond its reach. In 1841, the inhabitants of part of Clinton Street also sought to take the naming of their street into their own hands, though this time it was residential elitism and not commercial impudence that clashed with the public interest. Aspiring to the dignity associated with the term "Place," residents changed the street sign and replaced all the numbers on their houses. *Longworth's Directory*, part of the expanding network of institutional inducements to maintain an orderly system of street names and house numbers, defended its initial decision not to recognize "Clinton Place" on the grounds that the new name was not authorized by the law and was not "agreeable to public sentiment." But having been attacked for his "obstinacy," the sales-conscious editor agreed to print the new name (which lasted until 1899) "with the view of ascertaining whether it possesses ennobling power sufficient to elevate the residents above the use of a borrowed Directory."[19] That the power to label streets could be distributed among self-important householders, private directory editors, aggressive merchants, and what Haswell called "absurd person[s] of more or less authority" reflected a sign system stamped only very lightly by the municipal corporation.

A partial but significant exception to the pattern of irregularity and disorder that prevailed within New York's street sign system was the house number. Documents of the period show a widespread dependence on numbers in identifying Manhattan's residences, businesses, and public buildings, even when describing buildings that no longer existed.[20] Like the numbered streets of the Commissioners' Plan, house numbers had the effect of homogenizing land, and of quantifying urban growth while masking and containing change. As houses and stores rose and fell, as the personal or functional identities of the city's edifices were being continually dissolved and refashioned, numbers either remained the same or at least created a common field of reference.[21] Of course, since streets changed names or joined with other streets, and since not all growth proceeded in an upward numerical direction, there was some instability here as well. The *Evening Post* complained in 1839 of the "inconvenience" and "confusion" caused by these changes, which were "often made without notice to the occupier of a dwelling . . . so that he who goes to bed at No. 50 in his street, may wake up the next morning at No. 100."[22] But this complaint testifies also to the relative vigilance of municipal agents in attending to the numbering of houses, as well as to the degree of New Yorkers' reliance on the number system. The proliferation of directories such as *Longworth's* reinforced this dependence, as evidenced by an 1850 report of the Street Committee calling for a renumbering of a portion of Broadway, "as the period is near at hand when a new directory will be published."[23]

House numbers, though, are an anomalous component of a street sign system, not simply because they don't involve words, but because they designate specific buildings rather than streets—private property rather than public space. It is therefore not surprising that numbers took firmer hold than street signs in antebellum Manhattan, where the explosive proliferation of fixed signs consisted initially and most conspicuously of words identifying private establishments. The irregularity of street signs was part of a larger phenomenon: the scant use of signs for the explicit articulation of public authority during the second quarter of the century. Ironically, the very demographic, economic, and physical transformations that would seem from our own experience of big cities to necessitate the establishment of a public advisory sign discourse were subtly overwhelming any possibility of such a discourse emerging. More striking than the maldistribution of street signs is the almost utter absence of any signs that tell people what to do. By the time of the Civil War, as we will see later, signs would begin to wield the kind of authority to advise, admonish, and forbid with which they are now heavily and seamlessly invested. But for most of the period under discussion, I have been unable to locate any street sign that regulated or directed traffic, publicized the law, warned about epidemics, or performed any similar public function.[24] The one intriguing exception, a placard paraded up and down Chatham Street in the 1850s (at the behest of the mayor) with the message STRANGERS BEWARE OF MOCK AUCTIONS is striking for its mobility, its detachment from the streets and buildings that anchored New York's more permanent sign discourse.[25]

Though in fundamental ways the absence of advisory signs can be understood in terms of the inchoate nature of impersonal sign communication in New York prior to the Civil War, this absence marked, in some cases, a retreat from earlier sign uses. Dating back to the eighteenth century, Charles Haswell relates, travelers relied on mile markers along the Bowery, "stout stones, deeply incised with advice . . . of the distance to 'City Hall, New York.' "[26] Documents from the first few decades of the nineteenth century confirm the importance of these milestones in helping residents map their city. The reminiscences of Oliver Morhouse, who arrived in New York in 1803, identify a particular bridge from his youth as " 'Two miles from the Battery,' as a milestone then told us." In letters to his daughter Eliza from 1820 and 1821, philanthropist John Pintard refers to a fair held "at the 4 mile stone" and an aunt living "at the 2 mile stone." As late as 1830, the Common Council used the "Six mile Stone" as a northern limit in its call to have Third Avenue macadamized.[27] But as the population marched up the island, these milestones vanished from the historical record. Haswell reports that only three of the milestones were still standing in 1840, noting with regret that the remaining stones had been plastered over with handbills, a practice he would like to see outlawed, as "surely every care should be taken to preserve in place, unharmed, these memorials of the past."[28] These mile markers were archaeological relics of a time antedating urban intensification, and Haswell characteristically highlights the role of commerce (represented metonymically by the handbills) in burying that past. Clearly, the stones' function had been eliminated despite the fact that the distances remained as accurate in 1840 as they has been fifty years earlier, and Haswell's objection to their effective interment is based solely on some combination of nostalgia and historical interest. Of course, much of what rendered these signs obsolete was the northward spread of the city. As streets were laid and given ordered numerical names, and as homes and businesses covered the island, new urban landmarks could serve as informal distance markers and tended anyhow to transform the significance of the distance to City Hall or the Battery. But it is also true that this traditional use of signs for directions was out of place in an urbanizing New York.

The overwhelming majority of signs in New York, those that hid mile markers, obscured street signs, and otherwise dominated the verbal landscape, were commercial in nature. For the most part they were labels identifying the names and trades of the businesses inside the buildings on whose exteriors they appeared. As labels, these signs resembled house numbers and street signs to the extent that they provided a visible name for identifying and referring to the physical space of the city. In some cases, private signs served as street signs, displaying the full address of the store or business.[29] Unlike house numbers or street names, however, commercial signs also supplied information about what was going on inside a given building, and thus participated in the public self-presentation of private individuals and interests. Moreover, this self-presentation asserted a claim to private property, to the extent that signs (HOLT'S HOTEL, BARNUM'S AMERICAN MUSEUM, JOHN G. LIGHTBODY'S PRINTING INK MANUFACTORY) named landlords as well as commercial ventures. Finally, these signs were advertisements designed to promote the businesses they identified. As such, they were quite simple. They rarely quoted prices, did not make bold pitches, and did not express intricate messages; yet they were extremely powerful. Not restricted to self-selecting newspaper readerships, and not dependent on customers remembering and locating addresses, the commercial value of these signs should not be underestimated. Still, the cumulative effect on urban readers extended beyond the particular purposes and functions of individual store signs to the spectacle of competitive commerce that they collectively presented.

Visitors and residents alike reinforced the image of verbal frenzy depicted in many popular lithographs of Manhattan's street life in the antebellum era (see fig. 3.2). Writing in 1846, antiquarian and chronicler John F. Watson emphasized the unintended visual effects of so many signs:

> New York is distinguished for its display in the way of signs; every device and expense is resorted to, to make them attractive, crowding them upon every story, and even upon the tops and ends of some houses, above. One small house in Beekman street had twelve signs of lawyers; and at 155 Pearl street, the name of Tilldon and Roberts was painted on the stone steps of the door! . . . In truth it struck me as defeating their own purpose, for the glare of them was so uniform as to lose the power of discrimination. It is not unlike the perpetual din of their own carriage-wheels along Broadway, unnoticed by themselves, though astounding to others.[30]

Though Watson may well have been right that the visual cacophony (to adopt his mixed metaphor) proved counterproductive for the interests of

FIGURE 3.2 "Broadway, New York." Broadway at Canal Street, c. 1835.
Drawing by T. Hornor.

■■■

individual businesses, the overall impact on street life was probably considerable. Watson's suggestion that New York distinguished itself from all other cities in this respect was occasionally disputed by other visitors, yet even they saw fit to remark on buildings "covered with signs, posters, and advertisements from top to bottom."[31] Captain Frederick Marryat, the English novelist who visited the city in 1837, thought that New York's tradesmen exceeded the English in advertising zeal "by having large marble tablets, like horizontal tombstones, let into the flag pavements of the *trottoir* in front of their shops" in order to meet the gaze of obstinate pedestrians who stared down to avoid more traditionally placed signs.[32]

Whether or not New York's commercial signs created a qualitatively different cityscape from those of comparably populous cities in Europe, there can be no doubt that the commercial expansion of New York in the four decades after 1825 was reflected dramatically and inescapably in the proliferation of signs, particularly on major business streets such as Broadway and Nassau Street. Over the forty-year span of this study, the number, density, size, and prominence of these signs increased substantially, reaching a point in the relationship between signs and people cap-

49

FIGURE 3.3 Lower Hudson Street, c. 1865. Photograph by Marcus Ormsbee. © Collection of the New-York Historical Society.

• • •

tured so compellingly in Marcus Ormsbee's photograph from the end of the Civil War era, an image to which we will return (fig. 3.3). An exact periodization is hard to pinpoint, though it appears from the visual sources that a major proliferation of signs took place in lower Manhattan during the 1830s and spread northward with the population expansion.[33] Despite changes and variety in size, function, and discursive style, the explosive growth of New York's commercial signage tended toward the development of a monumental architecture of the written word, providing new maps of city space suitable for the silent circulation of strangers, a new semi-official public discourse, and the seeds of new public authority in what has been called (for many good reasons) the private city.

Commercial signs provided a guide to New York. In a city where, every day, strangers would arrive with few, if any, acquaintances and no point of entry into a world of face-to-face contact that might orient them, a sign on a building offered direction indiscriminately. Anyone who could read a little English could be addressed and guided by a placard on a storefront or a name on a place of business. When comic actor Joe Cowell came to New York in 1821, he was hungry and unable to purchase any food with his English coins. Turning down an unpromising street, Cowell found hope in a sign over a "dingy-looking cellar" with the words EXCHANGE OFFICE. FOREIGN GOLD AND SILVER BOUGHT HERE. Ten years later, a young and newly arrived Horace Greeley, who would go on to edit the *Tribune* and run for the presidency, stopped at "168 West Street, where the sign of 'Boarding' . . . fixed my attention." In an 1844 letter, Edgar Allan Poe also highlighted the role of a name posted on a door in helping him find lodging upon arrival in the city. For strangers such as Cowell, Greeley, and Poe, shop signs facilitated an anonymous entry into the city, unsupported and unencumbered by networks of personal acquaintance.[34]

Well after a visitor arrived, commercial signs helped to decode or demystify urban spaces that might otherwise have appeared strange or ominous. English travel writer Isabella Lucy Bird was struck in 1856 by signs for oyster shops, similar to those her compatriot Charles Dickens had described fourteen years earlier as so tempting that their "dainty words . . . make the mouths of idlers water as they read and linger." Bird observed OYSTER SALOON painted outside the basement stories of buildings in busier streets. "If the stranger's curiosity is sufficient to induce him to dive down a flight of steps into a subterranean abode, at the first glance rather suggestive of robbery, one favourite amusement of the people may be seen in perfection."[35]

For more settled New Yorkers, signs formed a network of resources to be consulted in moments of need. In Fanny Fern's novel *Ruth Hall*, an autobiographical depiction of the experience of a woman writer in the city, the protagonist scours the town for signs of prospective employment, wandering "about the business streets, looking into office-entries, reading signs, and trying to gather from their 'know-nothing' hieroglyphics some light to illuminate her darkened pathways."[36] Ruth scans the streets as a reader would pore over the classified section of a newspaper, an important analogy whose implications I will pursue later in this study. The metaphor of know-nothing hieroglyphics, though, pushes in two different directions. The signs are hieroglyphic in their opacity (reflecting her status as a woman seeking employment in a man's world) and know-nothing in their misleading and exclusionary simplicity, yet at the same time they are meaningful symbols that Ruth is not wrong to consult and interpret. Mastering the language of commercial signs, while not very difficult, still served as a badge of urban competence. In the satirical novel *High Life in New York* (1854), narrator-protagonist Jonathan Slick's country naiveté is indicated by misreadings of signs. When he arrives in New York he spots a house with his cousin's name on the door. "It seems that John has gone into a partnership with a Mr. Co," Slick mused, "for that feller's name is on the sign arter his'n large as life."[37] For Scottish writer Thomas Hamilton, who visited in 1831, a noteworthy and inscrutable sign such as HOLLOW WARE, SPIDERS, AND FIRE DOGS "carried with it a certain dim and mystical sublimity," to be stripped only by further familiarity with the trade of the city.[38] Though signs were not always transparent, they were still a privileged point of reference for residents and strangers trying to find their places.

While orienting potential customers in search of goods and services, signs also served as captions for an unstable cityscape. Because they advertised changes of neighborhood, changes of business, and even changes of fashion (the hatter John Genin, who devoted considerable energy and money to advertising, frequently replaced the large signs covering his Broadway establishment to promote new products),[39] commercial signs projected a highly transitory picture of city life. Signs alerted observers to trends in the local economy and in the city's social life. A character in an antebellum novel notices that "signs denoting boarding houses are almost as thick here as lawyers' shingles are in Philadelphia."[40] Signs also marked demographic shifts and thus provided exhibits for New Yorkers with xenophobic nostalgia for some previous period in the city's history. John Watson, while doubting the commercial effectiveness of many of the city's signs, found some interest in what he termed "the nomenclature of the town," from which he concluded that "strangers had got hold of the business and the wealth of the place." By strangers, Watson had in mind the " 'busy tribes' from New England,"[41] but in subsequent years the names on New York's signs increasingly bespoke more distant origins. Looking back from the next century, when business signs distressingly reminded him of "a chapter in Exodus and the words of the prophet who proclaimed that 'all Israel shall be there,' " Charles Harris pined for the signs of the Civil War era, which "breathed of homefolk, old and honored names in American business life."[42]

If commercial signs called attention to New York's rapid and perpetual transformation, they also helped to map the social geography of the city, far more palpably and meaningfully than street signs did. Aleksandr Lakier remarked on what must have been obvious to most Manhattan residents, that "whereas there is not a house on Broadway without an advertisement on it, on Fifth Avenue there are no advertisements at all," an observation he linked with the fact that Fifth Avenue "reminds one most of all the fashionable sections of Europe."[43] Beyond identifying an area with commercial activity, a dense concentration of signs connoted dense concentrations of people, and served to represent social disorder in several depictions of the city's poorer districts.[44] In more specific ways, signs designated streets and neighborhoods throughout the city. The occasional German sign in *Kleindeutschland*, signs for lottery agents along the Bowery, and those for astrologers on Division Street gave information about the area as well as the particular shops.[45]

Signs could also register the flow of seasons. Beginning every February, countless placards would appear on the fronts of buildings announcing dwellings available for rent on May 1, or "Moving Day," as it was commonly called.[46] These signs were in some respects more like broadsides or bills (which I will explore further in the next chapter) than fixed commercial labels, but they shared the critical feature of advertising the buildings on which they were posted and broadcasting a claim to private property. Taken cumulatively, their effect was to publicize and concretize the city's high residential mobility and to confer a certain order upon the process even as the individual signs evoked a competitive and unwieldy housing market. In the editorial page of his *Home Journal*, Nathaniel Parker Willis described the value of this signage even to those New Yorkers who had no need to scramble from tenement to tenement every May: "The eruption on the front doors tells us that Spring is at hand—the placards of 'To Let,' in the city, corresponding with the outbreak of crocuses in the country."[47]

Thus, in a variety of ways, signs designed to identify and promote private commercial interests provided information that helped both residents and visitors negotiate and make sense of New York's complex and changing urban environment. But even when the information communicated by the sign was of minimal substantive significance, signs were also icons and architectural structures that could, in time, become urban landmarks. The use of signs as landmarks had long been associated with inns, which were typically named for the colorful icons (The Blue Boar, Dog's Head in the Porridge Pot, St. George and the Dragon) appearing on their signs.[48] In the antebellum period, though, as signs became increasingly verbal (though icons did not by any means disappear), monumental words provided a sense of place. Certainly large signs, such as the one on P. T. Barnum's American Museum, became sufficiently familiar and prominent within the cityscape to serve the orienting functions of landmarks. Even smaller signs, because their content was both legible and specific enough to be used as a point of reference, could play such a role. A sign for a business that moved often or failed quickly might not last long enough to make an impression. But in some cases signs outlasted the business ventures that had been their intended referents. Figures 3.4 and 3.5 show two photographs of the same Chatham Square building (number 5) separated by five years. Pendleton and Syms appear to have kept S. T. Bailey's signs in place; only the names have changed. In such an instance, the sign masks change instead of advertising it, yet its value as a guidepost in a changing urban environment is at least as great.

Paradoxically, then, private commercial signs fulfilled at least some of the tasks associated with public sign discourse, even as they reinforced the spectacle of a competitive marketplace under which public discourse ostensibly lay buried. This phenomenon seems to reinforce a familiar observation about the city in antebellum America, when private proprietors assumed responsibilities that would later devolve to municipal government. But commercial signs did more than simply provide information; they created a new language of publicity and a new space for public communication. While shop signs (and house numbers) marked buildings as sites of private ownership and enterprise, they marked the streets as sites of public (broad, impersonal, and unrestrained) circulation, consumption, and reading. To follow the ways in which private signs created a public discourse in antebellum New York, it is necessary to explore how disparate signs made an impact in the city streets beyond their individual purposes, and beyond the control and intention of their authors.

Despite their various aims and origins, commercial signs operated in concert. As cultural critic John Berger has observed about modern advertising, "every publicity image confirms and enhances every other."[49] What New York's commercial signs created in common,

FIGURE 3.4 (*left*) Chatham Square, c. 1865. Unattributed photograph.
FIGURE 3.5 (*right*) Chatham Square, c. 1870.
Stereograph by E. & H. T. Anthony & Co.

• • •

though, was more than just a collective summons to consume or a cho-
ruslike testimony to the role of commerce in city life. Signs created a
common language of publicity, a mode of marking buildings and
addressing the public. Most of what gave commercial signs the appearance of unity was precisely that—appearance. The idiosyncratic signatures of merchant signs in the beginning of the century gave way to the
use of print characters, even lettering, and a certain standardization of
style during the antebellum period that is well captured (though perhaps
exaggerated) in the pictorial directories of the 1840s and '50s (see fig.
3.6). Signs set in similar type tended to blend into one another, masking
differences in voice, tone, and perspective under the guise of a single,
official voice.

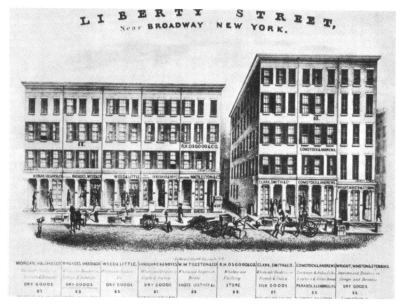

FIGURE 3.6 *Pictorial Directory*, 1836 or 1837. Liberty Street between
Broadway and Nassau Street. Lithograph by J. H. Bufford.

• • •

This trend toward standard, even typography in New York's commercial signs probably served the need for greater visibility to larger
numbers of people moving quickly about town, and may also have
reflected the influence of the newspaper with its columns of regular type.
Interestingly, Armando Petrucci has traced a parallel development in
Italian cities around the same time, when neoclassical monumental
script, arranged in an orderly linear fashion, established itself "as the
most prestigious and universal tool of graphic expression."[50] Whatever
its origins, typographical regularity was a striking feature of New York's
signs. For Argentine educator and statesman Domingo Faustino
Sarmiento, who traveled through the United States (including a stay in
New York) in 1847, the quality of signs in America as a whole provided
"an indisputable example of the progress of the country." Having seen
sloppy signs throughout Spain and South America, Sarmiento was con-
vinced that in the United States "a crooked or fat letter or a mistake in
spelling would be enough to ensure a deserted counter for the shop-
keeper."[51] Orthography, as well as stylistic consistency, presented an

image of uniformity among New York's signs that to some degree coun-teracted the individuality implied by myriad private names. I. N. Phelps Stokes, in his massive iconographic history of Manhattan, goes so far as to impugn the authenticity of a lithograph from the late 1820s on the basis of an error in the spelling of "stationery" on a store sign. Though he is probably wrong (the word is commonly misspelled even in govern-ment documents from around this time, and there are other pictures of the same store with the misspelling), Stokes's position is illuminating insofar as his assumption that a lithographer is more likely than a sign maker to misspell a word reflects a great deal of experience with correct spelling in commercial signs.[52] Words were misspelled, of course, in New York signs (and they still are), but with decreasing frequency—a trend that coincided, interestingly enough, with the dictionary wars of the 1840s and '50s.[53]

If even lettering, correct spelling, and superficial uniformity helped give commercial signs an aura of being official, the fact that English was the dominant language of the city's signs reinforced that aura consider-ably. For newcomers and tourists who read English, there was something reassuringly familiar in the message imparted by this linguistic monop-oly. Visiting from England in 1827, Margaret Hall juxtaposed the "for-eign aspect" of the city with the English signs, and took comfort in "sev-eral covered-waggon sort of things outside of which was written in large letters 'ICE.' " Almost half a century later, British journalist Edward Dicey was struck by the fact that "all the shop-notices . . . are in English, and addressed to English customers," and reported that "there is far less of a foreign look about New York than I expected."[54]

But New Yorkers with different linguistic roots could take no such com-fort. There is scattered testimony of store signs in German in the Bowery (James McCabe estimated that German signs were in the majority there by 1872), though the visual evidence casts some doubt on these claims. On his 1862 visit, Dicey noticed a few signs in shop windows informing potential customers ICI ON PARLE FRANÇAIS or HIER SPRICHT MAN DEUTSCH.[55] Still, these were marginal deviations from a dominant pattern among New York's signs, a pattern that tended to conceal from public view the extent of the Manhattan's changing demographics. In 1860, for exam-ple, there were 119,000 German-born residents in Manhattan, giving New York a population of German speakers matched only by Berlin and Vienna. There were also 8,000 New Yorkers of French birth, as well as immigrants who spoke Italian, Hungarian, Swedish, and numerous other languages. Already by the 1840s, Nathaniel Parker Willis had described the Battery on Sundays as a "Champs-Elysées of foreigners" where only French and German could be heard. Yet presiding over this polyglot oral culture was a written code inscribed almost exclusively in one tongue.[56]

One departure from the English-only pattern was at Castle Garden, which became an immigrant landing depot in 1855. Several drawings of immigrant arrivals in the popular press depict signs in German, though mostly from the post-Civil War period. Figure 3.7, which appeared in the *Illustrated London News* in 1864, shows a German sign used to recruit new bodies into the Union Army. Away from the landing area, however, the city's signs would project a substantially less egalitarian relationship between English and other languages. Significantly, the other exception in New York's commercial sign discourse was the use of Latin mottos, which asserted educational status without legitimizing a rival oral tongue or in any other way undermining the written code. These mottos could cause confusion, though, as in the case of Edward Windust's Park Row saloon, where NUNQUAM NON PARATUS emblazoned over the entrance was rumored to have led vendors to inquire after "Mr. N" or "Mr. P."[57]

Given the brevity and simplicity of most store signs, the predominance of English did not practically exclude many immigrants (the vast majority of whom hailed from countries where the Roman alphabet was used) from participation in everyday commercial life, and may even have enabled newcomers and strangers to find their way around the city without having to ask questions in an unfamiliar language. Still, the imposition of the English language upon the cityscape had a profound significance in the multicultural city. The language and the commercial sign on which it appeared suppressed each other's particularity, reinforcing each other's claims to represent something larger and more inclusive.

While the public significance of signs was enhanced by a trend toward uniform and official language, what made store signs most public was the obvious but neglected point that they were read in public. Scholars have begun to look at the way the spread of print culture worked to construct a "public in print" grounded in the consciousness that a reading experience was being repeated and shared by countless others, a consciousness internalized by the text and inseparable from the reading experience.[58] This insight, which I will pursue in chapter 5, has important implications for the study of newspapers and the popular press in the nineteenth cen-

FIGURE 3.7 "Enlisting Irish and German Emigrants on the Battery." Castle
Garden, 1864. *Illustrated London News.*

• • •

tury, but in many respects public signs present a more powerful example
of how simultaneity and repetition influence written and printed communication. For with texts mounted in the streets, readers incorporate
not only an awareness that what they are reading is to be read by others
in the same way, but also an awareness that other people are reading
alongside them and over their shoulders.

An amusing and probably apocryphal anecdote published during the
Civil War era illustrates how commercial signs were experienced as public texts. A New York sign painter, the story goes, was interrupted in his
task after having painted DEALER IN ALL SORTS OF LADIES and sprained
his ankle, so that until the next day "citizens made themselves busy . . .
in surmises, scurrilous innuendoes, and injurious quizzings; which could
hardly be overcome when the finishing lettering '*and Gentlemen's ready-
made Clothing,*' was at last added."[59] The hubbub surrounding the scandalously misleading sign was rooted in the fact that the scandal was
shared; any New Yorker who walked by could read the shocking message
and could be seen reading it. The words had been published before an
urban readership and could not be retracted.

Jokes about sign mistakes or misreadings, uses of signs for political commentary, and collages of unrelated signs (see fig. 4.1, next chapter) all rely more or less heavily on the notion that once words have been physically and dramatically exposed to public view, they are no longer under the control of their originators. Writing assumes a life of its own in public space and becomes subject to close, literal, and socially unstable reading. Fanny Fern, in an 1853 article appearing in *Musical World and Times*, sets up a critique of the opposite sex in the following manner:

> Walking along the street the other day, my eye fell upon the placard, —
>
> MEN WANTED
>
> Well; they have been "wanted" for some time; but the article is not in the market, although there are plenty of spurious imitations.[60]

In a book of recollections of New York in the antebellum period, Abram C. Dayton relates that oyster houses around town had been in the habit of displaying the sign OYSTERS ON THE CANAL STREET PLAN, until "some malicious fellow was moved to tack on to the familiar phrase the uncomplimentary addendum, 'cheap and nasty.'"[61] Like other forms of graffiti, which both flaunt and flout the claims to private property that more legitimate epigraphs broadcast and stabilize, these reappropriations and mutilations of signs highlighted and drew upon the power of public words.[62]

What made store signs so public was more than their placement in the public space of the city. They achieved increasing prominence within a shared visual world that was expanding not only because the population of Manhattan was getting bigger and more dense, but also because of changes in the technology and iconography of visual representation, especially the introduction of photography in 1839. Signs had a particular place in post-Daguerrean New York. Public words were precisely the sort of details in the urban landscape that photographs were touted as *discovering*. After seeing Daguerre's work in Paris, Samuel Morse reported back in a letter printed in the New York *Observer* in 1839. "In a view up the street," he wrote, "a distant sign would be perceived, and the eye could discern that there were lines of letters upon it, but so minute as not to be read with the naked eye. By the assistance of a powerful lens, every letter was clearly and distinctly legible."[63] Photographs allowed for an accurate representation of the minutiae of city life, of which public signs were paradigmatic examples. Signs also served as captions in urban photographs. When confronting a photograph, a viewer is even more likely to rely on verbal clues than he or she would be in open space.[64] In the case of a street scene, the verbal sign stands out (deceptively) as a uniquely transparent feature of the picture, a singularly straightforward interpretation of and guide to the image in which it appears. More directly, the signs help readers—then and now—to identify the location of the scene.

In these ways, the introduction of photographic technology reinforced the impact of lithography, pictorial directories, and collections of city "views" in encouraging a heightened visual self-consciousness among New York's business owners and sign painters. As photographs became increasingly popular, people began to see themselves through the lens of the camera. A merchant on Broadway had to consider how his or her store would appear in a daguerreotype. The same concern for self-presentation that underwrote the increasing production and consumption of urban photography affected the way the city dressed for its portraits. In Ormsbee's Civil War-era photograph (see again fig. 3.3), the human figures are arrayed and subsumed under the signs for their workplaces. What was for the workers a rare and self-conscious performance is almost lost against the everyday outfits of buildings pasted from head to toe by printers and sign painters who well understood the photogenic qualities of the written word. Signs were no longer addressed exclusively to immediate passersby, but could reach viewers all over New York and well beyond the city limits. Some evidence of the awareness of this expanded readership can be found in store signs that identify their full addresses. In the case of the Hooper and Brother picture-frame factory (fig. 3.8), the building sign reads 333 PEARL STREET, NEW YORK. Presumably, the sign was not intended to apprise pedestrians of what city they were in. Rather, the building is designed as its own advertisement, suitable for transmission and mechanical reproduction.[65]

But if signs were often designed with attention to how they would appear in advertisements, directories, bird's-eye views, or street photographs, their impact on local street traffic was still considerable. In some respects, the self-consciousness encouraged by visual arts and technologies helped to alter the perspective and proportions of New York's street signs in a way that dwarfed the local reader, as the Ormsbee image suggests. While many signs were so small as to require the most immediate proximity of their readers, an increasing number peered down on people from above five-story buildings with letters taller than human beings. The ver-

FIGURE 3.8 Advertisement, Hooper and Brother Looking Glass Warehouse (detail), c. 1849.

■ ■ ■

tical rise of the sign transformed the reading experience associated with it. Except possibly on experimental balloon rides, people had probably never seen words so high, hovering intimidatingly above them in a way that connoted power and may even have evoked the sacred. In the 1840s and 1850s New Yorkers began producing and consuming countless images of their city, images designed to offer a coherent vision of the increasingly unwieldy metropolis. But the impulse to achieve an imaginary perspective from which to grasp the city's intense vertical and horizontal growth, which underlay both the extremely popular bird's-eye views of the period and Ezekiel Porter Belden's remarkably detailed and widely celebrated miniature model of New York (made in 1846), was partially frustrated by the ascent of signs. Instead of reading their city from above, New Yorkers were forced to read it from below.[66]

To be sure, the vertical rise of antebellum New York was not so spectacular by later standards. As the passenger elevator was introduced in 1852, was first installed in 1857, and remained a curiosity for another decade or two, few buildings in Manhattan exceeded five stories before the Civil War. But this cap on building height probably intensified the visual impact of commercial signs. At this stage of building growth, signs could be the highest structures in the cityscape. Later in the century, when skyscrapers began to rise in the city, signs would be lost in the thicket and drop out of the skyline. Even in the fifteen years after the Civil War, elevated railway lines and telephone wires would interfere with the visibility of commercial signs. But during the late antebellum era, signs were quite significant architecturally. In many business streets, signs competed with the buildings they were purportedly labeling and advertising, often overshadowing them. Pictures of the city from this time (see fig. 3.9) reveal the beginnings of an architecture in which symbol—and not simply form—dominates space, an architecture that subverts the traditional relationship between sign and building in the manner described by Robert Venturi and his fellow Yale architectural critics as central to modern Las Vegas and to the modern American experience of public space.[67]

Physically imposing and architecturally prominent, Manhattan's tall and high signs laid claim to a certain degree of authority. Part of this authority derived simply from the relationship between the power of writing and its position in space—a relationship called to mind by Walter Benjamin's description of the historical migration of the written word. "If centuries ago," wrote Benjamin in the 1920s, print "began gradually to lie down, passing from the upright inscription to the manuscript resting on sloping desks before finally taking to bed in the printed book, it now begins just as slowly to rise from the ground," dragged outside by commerce, exposed to the "brutal heteronomies of economic chaos," and arrayed in the "dictatorial perpendicular." Antebellum New York marked an important moment in the cyclical historical transformation that Benjamin astutely, though perhaps belatedly, identified. New York's signs simultaneously ordered an unwieldy public space on the horizontal axis of modern print culture—within the representative systems of flat newspaper typography and the expanding technologies of mechanical reproduction—and reinscribed public writing on the traditional, even primitive, vertical axis of monumental stone epigraphs. While signs

FIGURE 3.9 Hudson Street, c. 1867.
Stereograph by E. & H. T. Anthony & Co.

■ ■ ■

joined a growing army of print documents strewn promiscuously about the city, they drew heavily on the particular authority of altitude, the dictatorship of the perpendicular.[68]

But what gave the perpendicular plane this potential power in antebellum New York was more than the architectural determinism that Benjamin's phrase might be taken to imply. Perpendicular commercial signs, perpetually addressing their readers without having to be picked up or opened, did have a certain advantage in commanding attention. As noted earlier, though, this did not immediately result in the use of signs to express public authority. The striking absence of signs that explicitly directed, encouraged, or prohibited actions (even in stationary advertising) persisted during most of the period, despite the fact that perpendicular signs had been in use for commercial purposes throughout.

Though the size, height, and placement of signs were important, the emergence of sign authority was a more complicated process.

We now live in societies so saturated with signs and so dependent on the kinds of authority they enjoy that it is difficult to think about how such authority might develop. Riding a subway in New York today, we have no problem interpreting the different types of directions or distinguishing the force of various imperatives—UPTOWN PASSENGERS GO DOWNSTAIRS, NO SPITTING, GET MET. IT PAYS, REPORT ALL FARE EVADERS, RE-ELECT LIZ HOLTZMAN—appearing on signs, because we have learned to read them and to recognize their authority (which is not to say that we are in complete control of our responses to them). But this proficiency is the product of considerable sign-reading experience, without which the whole sign system would be unintelligible and ineffective. In antebellum New York, it was the proliferation of commercial signs along the lines identified above—toward superficial uniformity, the appearance of an official code, greater visual self-consciousness, and unprecedented size and height—that helped to construct an impersonal authority associated with the public sign.

To some extent, what was impersonal about this authority was something shared with other forms of published writing in antebellum America. The separation of the written text from the person of the author, which Michael Warner cites as a constitutive feature of both republicanism and print culture in the revolutionary era, was a central source of both the power and the perceived dangers attached to literate communication in the next century.[69] But the authority of signs was also impersonal in the sense that, as I will pursue in the next chapter in connection with parades and processions, signs attached to streets and buildings could give the appearance of speaking on behalf of public spaces themselves without even positing an individual author. The radical publicity of signs, which suited them to appropriations and jokes, also invested them with an authority so distinct from individual identity that they could in some cases speak for, and thereby impersonate, the public.

It is not surprising that the first instances of this new public, authoritarian sign usage appeared in Central Park, which was designed in 1858 and opened for public (though hardly unrestricted) use over the next two years. After all, parks were public property, and the city had traditionally maintained control over what signs were placed in them.[70] Furthermore, Frederick Law Olmsted, who designed Central Park with the belief that the public had to be trained to use it, sought to exercise meticulous supervision over what occurred and appeared within the park's borders. Clearly linking signs with commerce and urban intensification (two of the forces in opposition to which Central Park was created), Olmsted envisioned an environment free of the chaotic intrusions of the written word that cluttered the streets outside. Signs belonging to the shantytowns that had existed in the park area before 1860 were removed, the posting of bills was prohibited, and a special effort was made to control graffiti, though Olmsted reported with great frustration in 1860 that "names and obscene words are frequently found of late cut or marked on the structures of the park and the offenders are seldom detected."[71]

Appropriate to this vision of the park, Olmsted hired gatekeepers to stand at the entrances, give out oral directions, and enforce park regulations with the authority invested in them personally. And in 1859, when the Board of Commissioners passed ordinances prohibiting various "dangerous and improper" activities (such as gambling, obscene language, unlicensed vending, and animals traveling above a certain speed), they publicized the regulations by paying to have them published for ten days in the city's three biggest dailies and three times in every other newspaper, rather than posting the rules on signs inside the park.[72] But once New Yorkers began using the park in large numbers, it became clear that the sort of control Olmsted wanted required the use of signs. In the fall of 1860 a poster appeared enumerating the rules of conduct in Central Park, and in the years that followed signs increased until they formed a comprehensive guide system, directing and regulating the movements of visitors.[73]

Early signs were tentative and even provisional—one placard read FOR THE PRESENT VISITORS ARE PROHIBITED TO TREAD ON THE GRASS[74]—but with the increase in signs came an air of timeless and impersonal authority that renders them recognizably modern. Several years after the end of the Civil War, the park's official sign painter compiled a list of 125 different signs then in use in Central Park, including dozens of directional signs (the kind that do not appear to have been used in the city's streets), complete with arrows, pointing visitors THROUGH THE MARBLE ARCHWAY TO THE MALL, TO COTTAGE FOR GENTLEMEN, to the GATE AT 5TH AVN & 96TH STR., or to DRIVE UP THIS WAY TO THE KNOLL. Other signs publicized laws and regulations, making it known that DRIVING ON CENTRAL PARK AT A GREATER RATE

SPEED THAN 7 MILES PER HOUR IS PROHIBITED, that PEDESTRIANS ARE NOT PERMITTED TO WALK ALONG THE DRIVE, and, in an interesting acknowledgment of the legal status of the sign, that CARRIAGES WAITING, WILL NOT OCCUPY THE OPEN SPACE BETWEEN THE SIGNS. And under every archway appeared the proscription DO NOT MARK OR DEFACE THIS STRUCTURE, affirming the all-important monopoly on the use of written words within the park.[75]

Of course this elaborate system was particular to Central Park in many ways, reflecting both the park's status as an experiment in the organization of urban space and the peculiar obsession of its designer with moving people about and regulating their behavior. Regulatory signs (which were used to prohibit everything from lying down on the benches to picking the flowers to smoking in the summer houses) were emblematic of Olmsted's "elite park" (to adopt the phrase used by historians Elizabeth Blackmar and Roy Rosenzweig to designate Central Park's early period), and to that extent should be understood in the context of a specific historical struggle for control of the city and its public areas.[76] Still, the signs of Central Park, which emerged at the very end of our period, also mark an important chapter in the development of public signs in New York. Encounters with this kind of sign network probably paved the way for more widespread employment of signs to direct and regulate behavior in public. By the same token, the signs of Central Park would have been neither conceivable nor effective without decades of previous sign use in which New Yorkers had grown familiar with words appearing in public.

Ironically, then, the emergence of a public advisory sign discourse depended largely on the proliferation of private commercial signs. The new discourse did not follow automatically from the public recognition that New York was becoming a world of strangers who needed direction (this had been acknowledged for over fifty years), nor was it an extension of the street sign system (which was still sporadic and inadequate). Between the ambitiously exhaustive mapping of the city by the Commissioner's Plan in 1811 and the rise of a sign system through which public authority could be impressed upon the city's public spaces lay a process of historical development in which the medium of urban sign communication was constructed in large part by private businesses. This paradox is important because it complicates the story often told about the nineteenth century, that the commercialization of culture in the West led to "the fall of public man," or, in the formulation of Jürgen Habermas, the disintegration of the bourgeois public sphere.[77] While it is true that in New York, the demographic and economic changes of the middle of the century wreaked havoc with the foundations of the urban public as it had previously been conceptualized, a new public was being constructed on its ruins, in which modes of communication that had been developed in the world of commerce would have significant implications for the way human beings communicated in other realms as well. The very signs that epitomized, reinforced, and advertised the erosion of the traditional urban public laid the groundwork for the development of a new public that impinged more forcefully upon the lives of city residents. This new public may not have appealed to someone like Charles Haswell (whose nostalgic dichotomous opposition between public interest and private good finds echoes throughout the political discourse of antebellum America),[78] nor does it please sociologists and historians who celebrate a particular notion of public life and a particular standard of meaningful political performance and dialogue. Still, a city crammed with verbal signs and highly dependent upon them was, in important and novel respects, a very public city.

4

Word on the Streets

~

Bills, Boards, and Banners

A lithographic advertisement from 1862 depicts a wall plastered completely with overlapping bills promoting everything from esteemed ministers to Tammany politicians to popular actresses (see fig. 4.1). Read "downwards," as the original caption to "The Bill-Poster's Dream" instructs, the notices form such amusing messages as $100 BOUNTY WANTED A JEWESS FOR ONE NIGHT ONLY, THE AMERICAN BIBLE SOCIETY WILL MEET AT THE GAIETIES CONCERT SALOON, GREAT SPARRING EXHIBITION BY THE SIAMESE TWINS AT BARNUM'S MUSEUM, and RESTORATIVE FOR THE HAIR USE SPAULDING'S PREPARED GLUE. The humor in this drawing lies, of course, in the characteristically urban juxtaposition of unlikely combinations of people and events, in which physical proximity forces the promiscuous intermingling of a community's disparate elements. More specifically, the cartoon calls attention to several central features of New York's commercial sign discourse as it emerged in the antebellum period. First, "The Bill-Poster's Dream" seems to make the point that as signs became too numerous, their individual purposes were to a certain extent undermined as the notices buried one another in an avalanche of competing messages. At the same time, the signs blended smoothly into a shared language of publicity in which everything from politics to entertainment to religion became homogenized—it is because of their superficial graphic and discursive resemblances as well as their spatial contiguity that these overlapping words lend themselves to humorous misreadings. In addition, the effectiveness of the collage depends on what was the crucially *public* element in the emerging urban sign system: once a sign was placed in the public domain it was radically severed from its author's control and intentions and acquired a life of its own. Finally, the framing of the plastered wall by a small sign reading POST NO BILLS! in the upper left corner and the sleeping bill poster (whose fantasy of an exhaustively papered wall seems like more than just a dream of day's work completed) in the lower left dramatizes the clash between a barely conspicuous and patently ineffective public authority and a burgeoning commercial culture intent on leaving no vertical space unmarked.

Still, these bills diverged in significant ways from the fixed signs that came to dominate much of the Manhattan cityscape during the second third of the nineteenth century. Light and flimsy, handbills and posters were mobile and had a radically different relation to urban space. Whereas fixed signs mapped and labeled the surfaces on which they appeared and claimed the authority associated with those surfaces (speaking, in some sense, for buildings, streets, and parks), the signs featured in "The Bill-Poster's Dream" have no such connection with the wall they cover. Rather, the bills are subversive of the orderly relationship between private property and public writing asserted in the city's monumental commercial signage; these posted notices draw parasitically upon the visibility of the building in direct defiance of the only sign authorized to speak for it. Moreover, the posted notices are by nature temporary and refer in most cases to current events, so that they reverse the spatially specific and temporally more abstract pattern of the fixed signs discussed in the previous chapter, projecting an image of constant change in urban life.

Posted bills were not the only mobile or temporary signs in New York at this time. A vast array of ephemeral texts could be seen in the public spaces of the city, including cards passed from hand to hand, advertisements suspended over the shoulders of human beings, and banners draped across buildings during moments of civic celebration. These

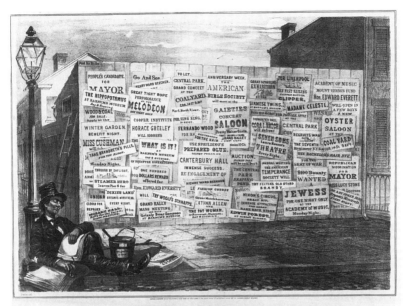

FIGURE 4.1 "The Bill Poster's Dream," 1862. Lithograph by B. Derby.

∎ ∎ ∎

signs did not all share the particular relationship to time and space that
distinguishes the notices in the 1862 lithograph. Nonetheless, they
formed an important and growing body of public texts whose significance needs to be considered separately from that of fixed signs. The
posters, broadsides, sandwich boards, and banners that contributed to
both the hubbub and the pageantry of daily life were in many ways less
like monuments and more like speech acts. Calling them speech acts,
however, obscures several crucial developments in the expanding world
of mobile texts: their potentially subversive anonymity, their reliance on
the impersonal authority of public space, their dramatic detachment
from the control of their authors, and their role in the process by which
writing was replacing speech as the dominant mode of public interaction. The proliferation of nonpermanent public signs thus reinforced
some of the impact of the fixed commercial sign system—facilitating the
anonymous circulation of strangers and constructing public interactions
in New York's bustling streets around shared reading experiences—but

extended that sign system democratically to embrace a broader range of people, everyday circumstances, and political purposes. As "The Bill-Poster's Dream" and similar documents suggest, the relative ease with which these ephemera could be produced and transported underscored the jarring contiguities and transitions of an urban culture rife with new possibilities for individual self-presentation and mass action.

Perhaps the most mobile and ephemeral texts appearing in the public spaces of the growing city were cards and bills passed from person to person in the streets. Wandering amid the din and bustle of a crowded New York in the 1850s, Russian visitor Aleksandr Lakier was struck by the steady flow of "notices and announcements [that] are thrust in your hands."[1] As in the case of store signs, most of these notices and announcements were commercial advertisements, trade cards or handbills promoting everything from patent medicines to daguerreotype studios. Trade cards (which could run as small as 2 by 3 inches but were often more than twice that size) had been used by merchants and craftsmen in urban North America for more than a century, but with the spread of lithography in the 1820s, these cards became a more viable form of large-scale advertising. While in the first two decades of the century trade cards generally contained only neoclassical emblems and the names and trades of individual proprietors, the trend thereafter was toward the kind of verbose and detailed advertising messages exemplified in the 1851 dollar-bill style card of Baker, Godwin, & Co. Steam Printers (fig. 4.2). Trade bills designed to resemble paper money (an increasingly common strategy among New York tradesmen in the late antebellum period) were obviously intended to catch the eye and induce the reader to take a closer look. At the same time, the resemblance is broadly suggestive of the way trade cards circulated as public texts. Like currency (and newspapers), these "circulars" traveled from person to person in the form of numerous identical copies, each implicitly referring to its wider public distribution.[2]

Beyond its role as cheap public advertising, the passing of paper from hand to hand also constituted a particular act of urban self-presentation. A written notice could transform a chance and silent encounter in the streets into a meaningful communicative act. Unlike signs attached to buildings or lampposts, handbills and circulars bore the stamp of a physical confrontation between two people, though the fact that the same text was being distributed to countless others in plain view compromised the

FIGURE 4.2 Baker and Godwin Steam Printers, trade card (front and back), 1851. © Collection of The New-York Historical Society.

• • •

personal quality of that stamp. An 1850s newspaper article describes a German festival in which an energetic woman, having impressed and exhausted her dance partner, presents him with a card "similar to the following: M. Klopfel / LAGERBIER AND OYSTER SALOON / No. _____ Delancey Street / New York."[3] The card appears to cheapen an erotic moment at the festival, and to hint at further links between sex and commerce in the growing city. The indifferent distribution of paper advertisements to strangers in the streets evoked the promiscuity of urban life, and it is fitting that prostitutes advertised their services on cards passed out in the streets by peddler boys.[4] Nonetheless, many trade notices (which in this period still advertised businesses owned by individuals rather than corporations) bore significant substantive and rhetorical resemblances to more personal forms of correspondence, such as the social card, at the same time as they extended the public discourse of commercial signs. The distributed trade card was thus personal and impersonal at the same time, requiring and registering a moment of one-on-one contact while constructing its readership as a group of largely undifferentiated consumers.

Cards were so thoroughly identified with this ambiguous form of personal self-presentation that "card" named a kind of text rather than a mode of communication or a piece of paper with specific material properties. Newspapers from the antebellum era are full of "cards," promoting all kinds of services, products, and causes. The boxer Yankee Sullivan's challenge to Tom Hyer, for example, issued several months before their incredibly well-publicized 1849 bout, identified itself as "a card," even though it appeared in the pages of the *Herald*, simply because it was Sullivan's official public self-presentation.[5] Significantly, published cards tended to merge personal, social, political, and commercial gestures of self-presentation. After the death of the illustrious restaurateur John Delmonico in 1842, his family published "a card" to express their "heartfelt thanks to his friends, benevolent societies, and Northern Liberty Fire Engine Company, who accompanied his remains to his last home," and, incidentally, to announce the restaurant's reopening, for which "no pains of the bereft family will be spared to give general satisfaction."[6]

New Yorkers turned to the newspaper to greet potential voters, clients, customers, and friends; however, they also displayed and circulated signs in the streets as a way of communicating with and appearing before an urban public. Back in the 1820s, gout-stricken actor John Henry had a sign on his carriage depicting a pair of crutches and the words THIS OR THESE as a way of justifying his possession of a private vehicle. This mobile card, unlike the modern-day bumper sticker that it anticipates, seems to assume a familiarity with Henry (or with his public persona) on the part of his readers. Random city residents (whom Henry probably would not recognize) would see the sign and be asked not to judge the actor (whom they probably *would* recognize) too harshly for his use and display of this particular symbol of wealth.[7]

But this presumption of signs operating within a context of personal recognition was becoming increasingly exceptional in antebellum Manhattan, and in fact many signs, notes, and cards relied on anonymity rather than familiarity for their effect. Cartman Isaac Lyon recalled an 1848 encounter with a young beggar girl on Broadway who wore "a thick piece of white pasteboard, about 12x16 inches in size," hanging around her neck by a string. The sign read TO A GENEROUS PUBLIC— PLEASE HELP A POOR BLIND GIRL, and Lyon noted that the girl "bore every appearance of being in reality what she professed to be." A few days later, however, Lyon spotted her dressed elegantly in the streets, and when their eyes met, the girl dashed off.[8] Other paper ruses relied similarly on the anonymity of the public encounter, though some proved less successful. On a summer day in 1850, a boy walked into the millinery establishment in which Henry Southworth was employed as a clerk and handed him a piece of paper. Southworth read the note, which "proved to be a circular 'to the benevolent' setting that *the bearer* was the mother of three children, whose father was dead, that they had left some place in Italy, and were not entirely destitute," [emphasis in original] and asked the boy where his mother was. The boy didn't seem to understand the question, so the clerk followed him to the door, seeking to produce the body promised in the text. Finding no one there, Southworth concluded that the boy "was sent out by some person, as I am informed that there are persons in this City who make it their business to supply these beggars with circulars, and who live upon the proceeds of their begging." The value of these circulars in the scheme Southworth describes lies in their power to supply an identity for an unknown and unnamed beggar. The scheme fails in this case largely because of internal contradictions in the presentation, beginning with the incongruity between the claim that "the bearer" was the mother and the plain fact that it was a young boy. In his diary, moreover, Southworth remarks that what really amused him was "that [although] the bearer should be the mother, the circular was signed by a Mr. Smith."[9] But if the irregularities in the encounter dominate Southworth's narrative, they are set against an illuminating backdrop in which texts (often multiple identical copies of the same text) are passed among anonymous strangers as they present themselves to one another in the city.

While Southworth's encounter took place in the semiprivate space of a store, circulars typically traveled in public. In most cases, a handbill established an ambiguous contact that highlighted the tension between the personal quality of face-to-face (hand-to-hand) communication and the impersonal quality of publishing (multiple copies addressed indiscriminately to numerous anonymous individuals). Right before John Colt's scheduled execution for the murder of Samuel Adams in 1842, for example, the authorities distributed notes around town recruiting witnesses with the message that YOU ARE RESPECTFULLY INVITED TO WITNESS THE EXECUTION OF JOHN C. COLT.[10] (Colt foiled the plans by committing suicide.) This summons to an execution exploited the rhetoric of the personal invitation even as its apparently indiscriminate distribution marked it as a public document.

Handbills and circulars may have presupposed some physical contact between individuals in the streets, and in some of the examples discussed above the portable sign referred to or spoke for the person who passed it out. Clearly, though, in most cases people were simply vehicles for the distribution of signs expressing the authority and promoting the interests of others; individuals tended to function as messengers or simply as advertising space. With the explosion of commerce and the growth of the population, any visible surface might become a forum for transmitting messages and getting attention. "There seems to be no end to the new advertising projects which are daily springing up in all directions," observed a commercial reference book published during the Civil War. Noting with surprise that umbrellas were still left blank, "their ample and conspicuous surface bearing no announcement of any new pill, new adhesive gum, bankrupt's sale, or What is it?," the author half-seriously predicted that this oversight would soon be corrected, allowing the umbrella to realize its destiny as "a tremendous vehicle for information."[11]

Enlisted in the cause of commercial promotion, the written word began to appear on wagons, personal accessories, clothing, and, most dramatically, sandwich boards (see fig. 4.3)—what one visitor described as "huge boards pasted with gigantic posters . . . carried on their shoulders by men and women hired for this purpose."[12] Marked umbrellas and moving billboards may not seem too strange from the perspective of late twentieth-century America, when T-shirts, lapels, hats, and jackets are appropriate and commonplace sites for displaying messages of all kinds. But advertising worn on one's person did not project individual fashion statements or political postures. In extreme contrast to Hester Prynne's scarlet letter, which was to be read as revealing her character (or her character type), sandwich boards effectively buried their bearers' identities under the weight of someone else's words.

Sandwich boards offered a uniquely suggestive representation of how people could be used for advertising, a vivid reminder of the essentially impersonal character of sign communication. But most temporary signs eliminated all appearance of the human middleman, addressing readers from the largely anonymous spaces of building fronts and walls. Though the term "handbill" suggests a particular mode of circulation, bills were usually posters or "show cards" (larger versions of trade cards intended for display rather than distribution) and were generally attached to surfaces that bore no particular relation (proprietary or otherwise) to the authors or distributors of the posted text.[13] In this respect, bills were even further severed from personal authority than fixed signboards; if a store sign appeared to speak for a building, a handbill appeared to speak for itself. This kind of anonymous, free-floating text represented an impor-

FIGURE 4.3 "View of Broadway, New York, from Exchange Alley to Morris
Street," 1855. Lithograph by F. Heppenheimer.

∎ ∎ ∎

tant and potentially subversive medium of urban communication.
Posting a bill that would be read by substantial numbers of city residents
did not require owning or renting property, gaining expensive access to
printing devices, or even assuming much responsibility for its words. At
a time when New York's population was becoming larger and denser and
printing was becoming cheaper and more efficient, handbills dispersed
the power of mass communication quite broadly.

Efforts to regulate bill posting were not terribly effective. Proprietors
and authorities had to resort to the famous and ironically self-defying
POST NO BILLS signs to advertise restrictions, or else a penalty might be
contested. In 1829, for example, Cornelius Hulsart (identified by the
Police Committee report as a poor man) successfully petitioned the

Common Council to be relieved from paying a fine for bill posting, claiming that he had been unaware that his activities were illegal. Eight weeks later, the Council remitted a similar fine of Dr. William Nelson on the grounds that "the Petitioner is a stranger, and pleads ignorance of the Law."[14] In all likelihood, most violators of posting prohibitions were never prosecuted in the first place. Anonymous posters, such as the more inflammatory political handbills discussed later in this chapter, made even the best-publicized restrictions hard to enforce. But whether or not posters identified their producers or distributors, it was hard to assert authority over spaces whose publicity value lay precisely in the suspension of authority.

One particularly fascinating illustration of the possibilities of the free-floating handbill is the case of Martha Clements, who was prosecuted, together with her parents and a friend named Julia Ann Goslin (all four of whom lived together), for indecency in 1830. According to neighbor Rhoda Horton, keeper of a boarding house on Greenwich Street, the teenaged Clements was in the habit of "cutting out large capital letters from play and hand or posting bills, and arranging the said letters together in grammatical order so as to read vulgar and indecent words . . . [and] pasting them on the fences, & places in the yard." Significantly, although Horton cited other offenses and leveled other charges against the character of her "nasty and filthy" neighbor, only the obscene collage art made it into the District Attorney's indictment. Because the rearranged letters were placed "within sight and view of divers other citizens through the said yard," the defendants were charged with corrupting the morals of neighbors and passersby, acting "in contempt of the people of [New York] and their laws, to the evil example of all others in like case offending, and against the peace of the people of the state of New York and their dignity."[15] Though we must resist the temptation to make too much of the D.A.'s tantalizing reference to all those "others in like case offending," the Clements case does register a moment of struggle over the boundaries between public and private, boundaries that the handbill seemed to unsettle. Of course the ostensible essence of the indecent act was simply the public use of language, an offense for which any kind of posted sign could have qualified. Yet the image of cutting and pasting evoked in Horton's testimony seems crucial to the indecency of Clements's action and the symbolic transgression it achieves. Not only was she displaying dirty words in public, not only was she cloaking her identity in the anonymity of a posted sign, but by enlisting other people's publicly circulated words toward her mischievous ends, Clements calls attention to the emerging power of the city's public texts, severed from their original authors and expressive contexts, broken down and refashioned before a promiscuous urban readership.[16]

Though a particular poster might shock to the point of prosecution, most temporary signs blended inoffensively and seamlessly into the vast spectacle of writing and print that had become part of everyday life in the city by the 1840s and '50s. As "The Bill-Poster's Dream" (the 1862 lithograph discussed earlier) suggests, the man who had the job of covering public walls with printed notices provided a compelling figure for the confusions and collisions of New York life. Frazar Kirkland's compendium of business lore celebrates the bill sticker as a "definite, genuine distinct character—one who keeps alive other trades—and who may also be said to live in the public eye as literally as any other man of his day."[17] In the mid-century urban exposés of popular journalist George G. Foster, the bill poster appears as an intrepid connoisseur of the city, much like the author himself. "With his hieroglyphic paper bed-blankets over one arm and his paste-bucket hanging upon the other," the bill poster makes the rounds late at night when only a handful of drunks are left in the street, and "with nice discrimination" spots the fresh posters of his rivals and "neatly plasters them over with his own."[18] Elsewhere, Foster describes the spectacle of a wall papered with ads in a manner much like that of the 1862 cartoon:

> Go to the tumbling dead-walls of the Park Theater . . . and see what is written there. You will perhaps, after scanning its calicoed surface, reply: "Steamer Ali—Sugar-Coat—and Pantaloons for—the Great Anaconda —Whig Nominations—Panorama of Principles—Democrats Rally to the—American Museum"—and so on, reading interminably from the handbills lying like scales (or like political editors) one upon another.[19]

Though such contrived illustrations may be exaggerated, posters and show bills were in fact plastered all over the city (see fig. 4.4), "stuck upon every wall," as one foreign observer noted during the Civil War, "with an utterly English disregard of artistic proprieties," and banners hung from awnings, announcing special sales and merchandise arrivals. "One sees nothing but waving banners, monstrous sign-boards, flamboyant finery," complained Ernest Duvergier de Hauranne in 1864 after a stroll down

Broadway. "There isn't enough room for the advertisements," the Frenchman noted, "and they overflow into the street, on the edge of the sidewalks, between the gutter and the feet of the passers-by." Travel writer Isabella Lucy Bird, who visited from England in the 1850s, wrote of "large squares of calico, with names in scarlet or black upon them, hang[ing] across the streets, to denote the whereabouts of some popular candidate or 'puffing' storekeeper."[20] The streets were the site of countless verbal publicity campaigns whose strategies remained essentially the same, as Bird's comment suggests, whether their purposes were political or commercial. The effect of these campaigns could, of course, be trivializing. Duvergier de Hauranne expressed outrage at the juxtaposition and homogenization of such varied concerns.

> Then I came upon this emphatic advertisement: 'Books at Tremendous low prices;' then a majestic array of signs all alike: 'We need ten thousand volunteers,' with details of the bounties offered and the drinks promised, or else a big flag upon which the picture of a fantastic bottle is displayed in brilliant colors. Everything is done in this way, even serious things, even the purchase of human blood!

Seen together, this collage of paper and ink served, much like the city's store signs and street signs, as a familiar space for staging and receiving public messages. Because posters and bills were visibly transitory, though, they called even more attention to the rapidity of urban change. "That which is really written there is but a single word," Foster observed of the sign collage outside the theater, "MUTABILITY."[21]

The expansion of this style of street advertising in New York was both epitomized and furthered by the activities of Phineas Taylor Barnum, a man whose profound connections with the printed word are aptly commemorated by his eponymous typeface, characterized by bold lettering and eye-catching graphics. Barnum's entire masterful career—as lottery agent, libelous newspaper editor, bookseller, advertising copywriter, curator of the curious and the freakish, concert impresario, circus director, bank president, and autobiographer—traces the trajectory and highlights the dominant themes of the history of print in nineteenth-century America. While various scholars have offered convincing readings of Barnum as the classic Yankee performer, the classic con artist, and the classic self-made man, he is also important as, quite literally, an urban man of letters.[22] Some of the possibilities opened up by taking seriously

FIGURE 4.4 Showbills, 1866. Stereograph by E. & H. T. Anthony & Co.

• • •

Barnum's role in the formation of modern print culture have been explored by literary critic Jennifer Wicke in her provocative study of the relationship between advertising and the novel. Wicke, who credits Barnum with pioneering a mode of "spectacular discourse," describes how he authorized "a textual infinite regress, where every item of publicity worked to create new items," and constructed a new mass public by teaching his readers how to consume new genres of print.[23] Barnum's more immediate impact on the history of reading in New York City was equally significant.

Beyond the general and oft-remarked fact that Barnum recognized and exploited the power of the press and of print advertising to stimulate mass interest in previously unknown people (such as Swedish opera singer Jenny Lind, whose fantastically successful concerts he presented in New York in 1850) or largely unremarkable events and exhibitions (such as his 1842 discovery of a dwarf in Connecticut whom he dubbed General Tom Thumb), Barnum understood two important features of the written word. First, he appreciated the material qualities of a sign, and was often as attentive to the physical appearance of an advertisement as he was to its semantic content. Second, he thrived on the sparsity of the written sign, its ability to make a brief and enigmatic statement without having to elaborate or answer questions. His legendary use of a large canvas bearing the words TO THE EGRESS as a device to reduce crowds at his American Museum on Broadway typified Barnum's strategic use of writing to mislead readers into believing something he didn't actually say; significantly, in Barnum's retelling of the story it seems that his patrons (especially Irish ones) fall for the ruse in part because they *mispronounce* the word "egress," supplementing the sparse written word with a misleading vocalization (suggestive of a wild animal) for which Barnum need not assume legal responsibility.[24] Of course Barnum was not beyond making patently false claims in his printed ads (he once cautioned the Water Commission not "to interpret my show bills too literally").[25] In general, though, Barnum's strategic deployment of writing and print reveled in an intensely literal and close reading. He preferred to rope in customers with advertising messages that remained within the bounds of technical accuracy while refusing to satisfy any further the curiosity they aroused. "The cold type," one of Barnum's friendly critics explained in another context, concealed "the twinkling of the author's eye."[26]

Even before he took over the American Museum in 1841, P. T. Barnum had established himself as one of New York's pioneering practitioners of mobile sign advertising. Six years earlier, when he had exhibited Joice Heth, the woman he alleged to have served as George Washington's nurse, he had distributed "innumerable small bills" and posters "setting forth the peculiar attractions" of the old woman, and had installed a color transparency with the words "Joice Heth 161 Years Old" painted on it. According to Barnum, this was one of the earliest uses of transparencies for advertising in New York.[27]

Throughout his career as New York's preeminent showman, Barnum prided himself on his generous outlays for posters, circulars, and bills, and he frequently hired people to carry signs in the streets. Of course he also took great pains to decorate the façade of his museum—which he compared tellingly to a "pictorial magazine"[28]—but he insisted on changing its appearance regularly, using the building sign space as an opportunity to stage verbal and visual events rather than durable monuments. For in a profound way, temporary signs were more appropriate than permanent ones to the nature of Barnum's business and to the particular style of promotion that he came to represent. Barnum championed the singular artifact or event, and his advertising campaigns continually emphasized changing lineups, unprecedented attractions, and novel exhibitions that his customers would have to consume anew each time like the numerous, slightly variant editions of his best-selling autobiography. Like other forms of periodical literature, disposable signs suited this entertainment culture, and a symbiotic relationship developed between Barnum's promotional literature and his program, wherein changes became mutually reinforcing. In his autobiography, Barnum noted that in the 1840s he printed "but one set of posters (large bills) per week, so that whatever was announced for Monday, was repeated every day and evening during that week" (see fig. 4.5).[29]

If Barnum's promotional uses of the written word were, as he saw it, more "audacious" and "glaring" than those of his neighbors,[30] they were by no means out of place in an urban culture in which public signs and posters, scattered throughout the streets, addressed their readers with brief slogans and enticing hooks. Political posters and broadsides were of course part of this public culture, and placards posted before an election, such as an 1861 sign on the corner of Broadway and Duane Street reading FOR SHERIFF, WILLIAM M. TWEED[31] or a striking Jacksonian summons for voters to GO THE WHOLE HOG (in what a visitor dubbed "sesquipedalian characters"),[32] clearly had more in common with Barnum's commercial posters than with the idealized political broadside literature associated with the development of the public sphere in the eighteenth century. But the continuities between politics and commerce within the city's sign discourse do not mean that public appearances of the written word had become trivial window dressing in the city's political landscape.

Throughout the antebellum era, in campaign advertisements and political broadsides distributed in the streets and posted on trees and buildings, New Yorkers of different ideological commitments and agendas took full advantage of the handbill medium, especially in the staging of protests and riots. Temporary signs extended opportunities for public address to a broad range of people, made the views and tactics of those people visible in public space, and facilitated and orchestrated mass

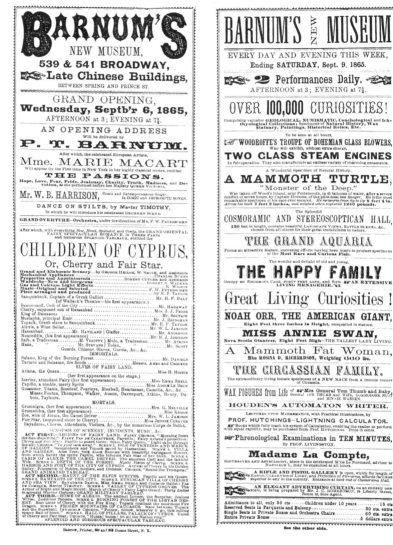

FIGURE 4.5 Showbill for Barnum's Museum, 1865.

. . .

84

action in a city whose size limited the effectiveness of traditional modes of face-to-face political organization. For these reasons, ephemeral signage figured prominently in virtually every major political demonstration of the period.

As food prices rose during the Panic of 1837, for example, Moses Jacques and seven others posted a notice of a meeting "to inquire into the cause of the present unexampled distress, and to devise a suitable remedy." Sketching the history of the "Flour Riot" in his popular 1873 study of New York's riots, Joel Tyler Headley stressed the impact of this sign: "Everywhere knots of men were seen gathered before these placards—some spelling out slowly, and with great difficulty, the words for themselves—others reading the call to those unable to read it." Headley's dramatic account of the poster's reception must be understood in the context of the overwhelming condescension he felt toward the rioters, whom he saw as providing in this case the best "illustration of the insensate character of the mob."[33] Still, the point remains that street posters served as a clarion call for concerted political activity and a centerpiece of political discussion, even among New Yorkers with limited reading skills and experience.

A quarter of a century later, during the ferment of the Civil War, posters were still instrumental in mobilizing crowds and coordinating mass political action. Posters placed around town on the morning of July 4, 1862 and signed "By many Union Men" denounced slavery opponents Horace Greeley and Henry Ward Beecher and called for a meeting later that day in City Hall Park. Antislavery forces tore down the signs within an hour, though, according to one contemporary report, and the meeting was poorly attended.[34] The following year, during the bloody antidraft violence of 1863, a handbill representing a RESOLUTION OF A LARGE MEETING OF THE MERCHANTS AND BANKERS OF NEW YORK urged shop owners to close their businesses and to "meet with their Employees on South side of Wall St., for immediate organization."[35] Shortly thereafter, Archbishop John Hughes used a 2-by-3-foot poster to communicate his partial support for the antidraft forces, convene an audience for a personal address, and defy municipal authority.

ARCHBISHOP HUGHES TO THE MEN OF NEW-YORK, WHO ARE NOW CALLED IN MANY OF THE PAPERS RIOTERS—

Men, I am not able, owing to my rheumatism in my limbs, to visit you, but that is not a reason why you should not pay me a visit in your whole strength. Come then, to-morrow, Friday, at 2 o'clock to my residence, north-west corner of Madison avenue at Thirty-sixth street, I shall have a speech prepared for you. . . . I take upon myself the responsibility of assuring you that in paying me this visit, or in retiring from it, you shall not be disturbed by any exhibition of municipal or military presence. You who are Catholics, or as many of you as are, have a right to visit your Bishop without molestation.[36]

The next day, a crowd of three to four thousand gathered outside the Archbishop's residence and listened as Hughes praised the assembled while advising them to seek constitutional and legislative redress for their grievances rather than resorting to violence.

Perhaps the most impressive evidence of the role of street posters in the organization of political protest comes earlier, from the famous Astor Place Riots of 1849, in which a rivalry between two stage actors became the focal point for cultural and economic anxieties among New York's artisans and journeymen and led to a massacre. The clash between the English actor William Macready at the Astor Place Opera House and the American Edwin Forrest at the Broadway Theatre was dramatized quite visibly by the appearance on May 7 of two posters announcing two different performances of *Macbeth* that evening. The juxtaposition of the competing plays was represented in the familiar mode of commercial advertising—the tone and style of the posters were identical (only the names of the cast members differed)—but the seriousness of the conflict was clear enough. That night Macready was greeted with boos and rotten eggs by the Bowery B'hoys, and was forced to leave the theater. Three days later, on the occasion of Macready's infamously well-guarded repeat performance, bills pasted to walls all over town asked SHALL AMERICANS OR ENGLISH RULE IN THIS CITY? and alleged some threats made by English sailors against "all Americans who shall dare to express their opinion this night at the English Aristocratic Opera House!!" The poster, which seems to have been distributed by Ned Buntline (E.Z.C. Judson) and by Isaiah Rynders's Tammany gang, the Empire Club, received considerable attention in the papers after that evening's unrest culminated in the killing of twenty-two people. When Ned Buntline was tried for his participation in the riots, presiding Judge Daly recognized the significance of the defendant's "words, signs, and gestures."[37]

The day after the violence, several other signs sprouted up, attempting to organize a response to the previous night's massacre. TO THE

PARK! one poster urged New Yorkers "opposed to the destruction of human life," while a more inflammatory bill summoned American patriots, "whose fathers once compelled the base-born miscreants to succumb," to fight the aristocratic English oppressors and defend "the liberty of opinion—so dear to every true American heart."[38] Another notice, signed by the coroner William Walters, invited "persons who witnessed the wounding or death of individuals during the riot at the Opera House Theatre" to meet the next day at his office, and Mayor Caleb Woodhull's proclamation "deploring the loss of life" while reminding "all the citizens that the peace of the City must be maintained" was posted that afternoon.[39] As much as the newspaper, which required a greater time lag and operated on different principles of personal accountability, posted signs served as primary conductors of mass communication during the 1849 tragedy.

Events such as the Astor Place Riots remind us how important bills and posters were in the network of urban communication that made large-scale political action (among other things) possible in antebellum New York. The role of signs in the dissemination of news and information frequently escapes the notice of historians who are (quite properly) impressed by the spread of the newspaper in the nineteenth century. It is easy to overlook the facts that, first of all, since newspapers were hawked in the streets, they could function as public signs, and, moreover, newspaper companies often posted signs to supplement and promote their paper sales. When Jenny Lind landed in New York on a Sunday morning in 1850, the thousands who greeted her ship had learned the approximate time of her arrival from bills posted by various newspaper offices.[40] Especially after the introduction of the telegraph, newspaper offices became sites of public reading where New Yorkers frequently gathered to learn the latest bits of important information as they were posted for general view. News of the Confederate surrender at Richmond, George Templeton Strong's diary reminds us, was first publicized in New York by the bulletin board of the *Commercial Advertiser*.[41] On some occasions, the premature public appearance of a news announcement could cause embarrassment and loss. When false election returns were broadcast on the bulletin board of the *Courier and Enquirer* in 1841, several readers (according to a rival newspaper) were misled by the authority of the posting into placing losing wagers on the outcome.[42] In an urban community where expectations of receiving news quickly were being elevated by the proliferation of commercial telegraphy (during the Hyer-Sullivan fight of 1849, fans crowded newspaper offices for immediate results), signs were often preferable to news editions as a mode of public announcement.

The power of temporary signs derived from more than their capacity to transmit information, however. Signs were well suited for political mobilization because they circulated anonymously. While most commercial handbills and posters subsumed distributors and readers to their roles as nameless wage-earners and consumers, this very anonymity opened up possibilities of public communication. New Yorkers could appear and interact in public unanchored and uncompromised by the burdens and responsibilities of mutual personal recognition. In the realm of politics, this situation had profound implications. Much like the broadside literature of the Revolutionary period, antebellum posters could claim the public interest (or in some cases class or regional interest) not only by addressing an abstract readership, but also by bracketing the personal identities of their composers.[43] Standing freely in public space or floating swiftly from hand to hand, bills often claimed an impersonal authority irreducible to the private interests or ambivalences of an individual. In addition, anonymously authored and distributed signs could attribute their words to other parties and could intervene in political debates without any personal liability.

The special power of anonymous signs showed frequently. On October 2, 1833, the day abolitionists had planned to convene at Clinton Hall, the following poster appeared throughout the city:

NOTICE

To all persons from the South.

All persons interested in the subject of the meeting called by

J. Leavitt, W. Goodell,

W. Green, J. Rankin

Lewis Tappan,

At Clinton Hall, this evening, at 7 o'clock, are requested to attend at the same hour and place.

MANY SOUTHERNERS.

NEW YORK OCTOBER 2D, 1833.

N.B. All citizens who may feel disposed to manifest the true feeling of the State on this subject, are requested to attend.

Using the anonymity of the sign to pose as southerners, and calling explicit negative attention to the personal identities of their abolitionist opponents, the organizers of this demonstration (which was temporarily foiled by a change in venue on the part of the antislavery forces) were able to muster a substantial crowd on the day of the event.[44] The anonymity of the handbill was also exploited by supporters of the striking journeymen tailors convicted in 1836 of forming an illegal combination. THE RICH AGAINST THE POOR! began the well-distributed handbill. "On Monday, the Liberty of the Workingmen will be interred! . . . Go! Go! Go! every Freeman, every Workingman and hear the hollow and the melancholy sound of the earth on the Coffin of Equality!" The Board of Aldermen authorized the mayor to offer a reward to anyone who would identify the parties responsible for this poster, which Philip Hone called "most diabolical and inflammatory."[45]

Political handbills could conceal the identities of their authors and distributors to good effect. More subversively, they could also impersonate the authority of others. IRISHMEN, TO YOUR POSTS OR YOU WILL LOSE AMERICA, announced an 1839 election handbill purporting to endorse Alexander Stewart and Edward Flanagan, two "true Irishmen" running for alderman and assistant alderman. "By perseverance," the bill proclaimed, "you may become its rulers; by negligence, you will become its slaves."[46] Whether or not the scandalously ambitious text was circulated by nativist opponents of Stewart and Flanagan, the potential for mischief under such circumstances was clear enough. Not all handbills and posters went unsigned, of course, and many (such as the announcement of Archbishop Hughes) relied explicitly on personal authority for their legitimacy. Moreover, had bogus campaign advertisements appeared with notorious frequency, they would have destabilized the ephemeral sign system too much to achieve any impact. More plausibly, the light undercurrent of indeterminate origins in every handbill (detached from a physical person and untraceable through recognized publishing networks) was sufficient to color the experience of city reading without precipitating a paralyzing crisis of confidence in publicly posted words. The public posting shifted attention away from the obscured private identity of an individual author and toward the abstract and anonymous readership—toward the scandal of a text shared by a promiscuous public in the streets.

The political culture of antebellum New York depended on both the logistical utility and the radical publicity of posted signs to recruit participants and create an audience. In addition to announcing meetings and paving the way for demonstrations, however, signs were communication devices within the context of crowd activity. Though riots often appear in the historical imagination as events dominated by the spoken (or shouted) word, writing and print occupy a central position in the history of street protest in antebellum New York. When the anti-abolitionists arrived at Clinton Hall in 1833, it was a notice nailed to the door that informed them of the cancellation of the event. Seeing the sign, Joel Headley reports, many of the assembled returned home.[47] Sixteen years later, during the pandemonium of Macready's first disrupted performance of *Macbeth*, the manager of the Opera House chalked a large sign telling the enraged hecklers that MACREADY HAS LEFT THE THEATRE.[48] Before the next performance, a sign was posted on the front of the theater advising the public that all seats had been filled (much to the displeasure of over two hundred people who stood outside waving their tickets menacingly and demanding admission), and the play itself was interrupted by a man walking across the stage bearing a sign that read THE FRIENDS OF ORDER WILL REMAIN SILENT.[49] Written words seemed to hold out a promise of order in a chaotic situation, a possibility of directing the movements of large numbers of people without putting oneself on the line, much as Barnum had duped his visitors with the sign pointing to the egress.

More often, signs were employed during demonstrations not simply to speak over the noise of a crowd, but rather more ceremonially, to represent and celebrate the cause for which the crowd had gathered. Election rallies of the post-Jacksonian era generally featured signs and banners inscribed with brief slogans. In a hostile review of the Democrats' torchlight procession shortly before the presidential election of 1844, Philip Hone remarked that "their banners avowed no political principles." But while DESTRUCTION TO CLAY!, NO $50,000,000 BANK!, and DOWN WITH THE COONS may not have impressed the ex-mayor as political theory, they certainly expressed the heartfelt political sentiments of significant segments of the Democratic constituency and were largely typical of political posters during the middle third of the century.[50] Campaign bills and placards also reinforced the now-familiar power of the pithy slogan as a distinctive and privileged element of political discourse, introducing phrases ("go the whole hog") and postures ("fifty-four forty or

fight") into popular political parlance. Even when signs expressed less
negative or more complex messages, such as placards at an 1862
Democratic meeting at Cooper Institute reading THE CONSTITUTION
AS IT IS, THE UNION AS IT WAS, STAND FIRM, and SHALL ABOLITION
PUT DOWN THE UNION OR SHALL THE UNION PUT DOWN ABOLI-
TION,[51] they framed public understanding of the party positions. In the
context of the rally, though, the projected slogan served to construct a
collective political identity and mark a moment of collective resolution
rather than to transmit information or formulate a new argument. Hone
implicitly acknowledges this point in his diary when he describes a Whig
rally held the day before the Democratic festivity he so smugly derided:

> The great demonstration of the Whigs, which has been in preparation for
> some time, came off to-day. It beggars all description. Nothing so great,
> so magnificent, so enthusiastic, was ever before witnessed in New York.
> The several wards marched in rotation, with all the mechanical crafts on
> stages superbly ornamented and employed in different occupations, with
> banners and flags, and every device which ingenuity and zeal could sug-
> gest. I cannot attempt a description. It will be sufficient for this record of
> the event, to say that the procession was more than five miles in length,
> and composed of the most respectable men of every profession, trade,
> and occupation in the city.[52]

When writing as a sympathizer and participant, Hone recognized that
banners were elements in a visual display, icons of class and occupational
identity, and evidence of "ingenuity and zeal"; the content of their
inscriptions—the "principles" they avowed—did not seem worth mentioning.

Even when political posters functioned ceremonially, though, they
were meaningful speech acts whose ceremonial function depended on a
certain minimal degree of literacy and on emerging conventions of sign
communication. While these verbal banners belonged to the theater of
the street and worked as components of a visual presentation, they were
privileged components with a particular responsibility to articulate and
communicate an interpretation of the whole. At the same time, they
worked as icons, achieving a special prominence within the public spectacle that no spoken words could match. During the draft riots of 1863,
for example, the *Tribune* reported that leaders of a crowd gathered to
burn the telegraph offices at the Bull's Head Hotel carried banners "on

which were written 'Independent,' 'No draft,' &c., and it was unsafe to express a single word of dissent from the proceeding."[53] Clearly, a sign opposing the draft was ceremonial, hardly necessary to inform participants or bystanders of the cause of the demonstration, yet the power of the inscribed words to project an intimidating political message was, as the reporter sensed, considerable. According to a report published in the *Tribune* (whose hostility to the riots was powerful and whose offices were targets of antidraft violence), another kind of poster appeared during the draft riots. A notice reading $100 REWARD FOR A NEGRO was reported to be posted near the docks, threatening further death and destruction to the area's victimized African American population and encouraging rioters with fantasies of the southern slave system they were being conscripted to fight.[54] To be sure, the meaning and impact of posters and banners displayed in political demonstrations depended, as the diverse examples listed here suggest, on whose messages they were transmitting. Still, sign display had become a dominant medium of political speech in public space, through which a wide range of forces within the urban community could combine the ceremonial appeal associated with the public icon, the impersonal authority associated with the monumental epigraph, and the semantic clarity and rhetorical flexibility associated with broadsides, newspapers, and similar uses of print.

Banners and signs also figured prominently in the city's more blatantly ceremonial public displays—the parades and civic processions that filled the streets of Manhattan in the antebellum period. Though particular processions, like a burlesque militia muster held in 1833 (see fig. 4.6) or the march of draft rioters in 1863, used public space to represent the interests of a particular group and to contest or parody norms of public behavior, the parade genre as a whole was a decidedly conventional mode of public display. The rhetoric of these events was sufficiently inclusive (though they tended to be carefully orchestrated and controlled affairs) to prompt historian Mary Ryan to claim that the nineteenth-century civic procession was "the most general and broadly public picture that American cities presented of themselves."[55] Some New York parades were annual events, like the regular commemorations of the fourth of July, Washington's birthday, or Evacuation Day. But the best attended and most interesting public displays were those occasioned by events or achievements of purported public significance. Most such parades fell into one of three categories: welcome processions for foreign visitors (Marquis de Lafayette in 1824, Lajos Kossuth in 1851, the Prince of Wales in 1860), funeral obsequies for fallen statesmen (William Henry Harrison in 1841, Zachary Taylor in 1850, Daniel Webster in 1852, Abraham Lincoln in 1865), and, perhaps the most festive and popular, celebrations honoring momentous political or technological developments (the completion of the Erie Canal in 1825, the opening of the Croton Aqueduct in 1842, the introduction of the Atlantic Cable Telegraph in 1858, the end of the Civil War in 1865).

As with riots and rallies, the powerful role of signs and banners in parades and processions seriously complicates the way scholars interpret those events. Susan Davis introduces her major study of the parade in nineteenth-century Philadelphia by contrasting public enactments with texts and complaining that historians "have often ignored the nonliterate, nonelectronic communication through which movements and events are accomplished, interpreted, and remembered."[56] It is odd, though, to regard the antebellum parade as a form of nonliterate communication. Davis's book is crammed with fascinating details of the myriad verbal banners displayed in those parades, banners both historians and onlookers tend to privilege as keys to identifying the objectives and unraveling the meaning of the public enactments she analyzes. In New York, as in Davis's Philadelphia, banners were essential features of the parade, prominent icons that communicated in a manner simultaneously direct and spectacular. Throughout the antebellum period, verbal signs were used both to identify the various contingents represented in the processions and to offer commentary on or support for the person, cause, or event being celebrated. At any given parade, hundreds of different banners would be held aloft by marchers or hung (sometimes in the form of illuminated transparencies) in prominent locations, each one articulating, more or less explicitly, a relationship between a segment of the urban community and the larger unity that the spirit of the procession emphasized.

Despite this continuity, though, there were striking changes in the way parade banners functioned throughout the period. In the earlier processions, such as the Erie Canal celebration, banners functioned largely as emblems of the corporate identities of traditional social and occupational groupings. Societies of tradesmen such as cordwainers, butchers, or typographers carried banners displaying familiar craft iconography and inscribed with mottos asserting pride in the public value of their

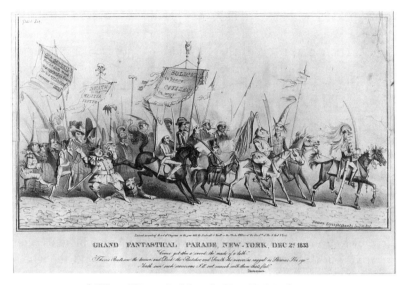

FIGURE 4.6 "Grand Fantastical Parade, New York," 1833. Engraving by "Hassan Straightshanks."

• • •

respective trades. BY THE POWER OF FIRE ALONE, the Potters' Society banner proclaimed, THE FRAGILE CLAY IS TURNED TO STONE, while the Ropemakers' Benevolent Association bragged OUR HEMP IS GOOD, OUR CORDAGE NEAT / WE WILL SUPPLY THE AMERICAN FLEET.[57] This style of banner drew on guild traditions originating in Europe and thus was not too different from parade banners used in earlier craft processions, such as the one held in 1788 to support ratification of the Constitution. Though, as Sean Wilentz has argued, the beginnings of the dissolution of corporate craft identity and the formation of a certain class-consciousness could be detected by 1825 in the way the craft contingents organized themselves, the banners projected the older imagery and often repeated the same slogans.[58] The Erie Canal parade banners were gestures of corporate self-presentation whose relationship to the whole procession lay in the notion that a society's collective, indivisible public interest could be represented by its constituent groups.

In later parades, craft self-presentation gave way to a different kind of promotion. Individual companies and proprietors were beginning to replace corporate social and occupational groups as the relevant constitutive units of a productive society, and this new conception of the urban community was reflected in signs that explicitly advertised the wares and services of specific businesses rather than simply proclaiming the honor or touting the social utility of a craft or trade. In the Atlantic Cable parade of 1858, for example, a banner read: THE BIRTH YEAR OF THE TWO GREAT WONDERS OF THE AGE—THE ATLANTIC TELEGRAPH, AND THE NON EXPLOSIVE GAS GENERATING COOKING RANGES. That same year a brewery truck proclaimed: NO COCCULIS OR CANNABIS CONTROLS OUR POWERS / BUT BOUNDLESS FIELDS OF BARLEY MALT ARE OURS.[59] Two days before the 1858 parade the *Herald* had bemoaned a recent tendency toward commercialism in the city's "illuminations" (the torchlight parades held at night) and expressed the hope "that this great occasion will not be degraded by storekeepers and pill venders as a means to advertise,"[60] but it was clearly a lost cause. Some attempts to use signs for commercial purposes barely managed a perfunctory nod in the direction of the celebrated event. Over one house in the Bowery a poster invited passersby, in good Barnumesque tradition, to observe the contrast between

THE FAT WOMAN FROM MISSOURI,

650 POUNDS,

AND THE SMALLEST MAN IN THE WORLD,

<u>38 POUNDS</u>

THE CABLE IS LAID[61]

By 1865 and the celebration of the end of the Civil War, the use of parade banners for commercial promotion had become well entrenched and highly developed (see the "float" of the petroleum industry in fig. 4.7). *Harper's Weekly* went so far as to assert that businesses' "chief object in participating in the festival, was the opportunity to advertise their wares."[62] In precocious anticipation of later developments in American advertising (this was the year when the first ad agency in the country opened) one liquor banner managed to absorb, deflate, and colonize both the rhetoric of the procession and the city's recent history of bloody ethnic, racial, and class conflict in one grand stroke: MCAULIFFE'S IRISH WHISKEY / CEAD MILLE FAILTHE / DON'T AVOID THE 'DRAUGHT' / BY ORDER OF / PROVOST MARSHALL MCAULIFFE.[63]

It is tempting to explain the shift from the corporate craft banner to sign advertising as reflecting the disruption of artisanal culture brought about by the expansion of the market economy and the division of skilled work into smaller, more strictly regimented tasks. However, the onset of metropolitan industrialization significantly preceded the demise of craft banners, which remained important features of the civic parade at least through the 1842 Croton Aqueduct celebration. This transformation in the parade banner must also be understood as a development in the nature of public communication in antebellum New York—a change from iconic emblem to verbose message that was taking place around the same time, as we have seen, in such disparate sign genres as the trade card and the storefront signboard. Words on banners continued to have iconic value and to coexist alongside nonverbal figures, but the distinctive significance attached to written words, which could be preserved and broadcast effectively either in pictorial representations or in print summaries, became increasingly apparent.

Even more dramatic was the gradual migration of the parade sign from the street to the building. Whereas in earlier parades, banners rode past the assembled crowd, hoisted by the leaders of the various contingents and societies, in the later celebrations the buildings themselves became the visual focus of the procession. In 1842, the newspapers still emphasized the familiar lineup of artisan contingents marching behind temperance organizations, fire companies, and municipal leaders, though the festive decoration of Broadway buildings had already become an important symbol of civic unity and festivity.[64] By the 1850s, however, the priorities were reversed. In the procession honoring Kossuth's visit in 1851, banners decorating the exteriors of buildings were far more numerous and more prominent than signs carried in the street. The *Commercial Advertiser* devoted considerable attention to the banners on houses along Broadway, inscribed with such mottos as UNITED STATES TO THE RUSSIAN BEAR: MIND YOUR OWN BUSINESS.[65] In the Atlantic Cable celebration, building signs were even more conspicuous, and the *Herald* quoted all the banners hanging along the parade route before even describing the mobile displays that formed the actual procession. An implicit distinction was drawn between a civic celebration of "over half a million jubilant people" (a standard and almost certainly exaggerated crowd estimate) and a more modest "turnout of the military, the professions and the trades," which formed only a component of the larger spectacle. Significantly, the report privileged the "inscriptions and decorations on the buildings" rather than the marching procession as expressions of "what the people think of the cable."[66]

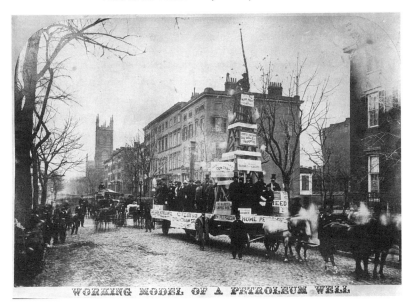

FIGURE 4.7 "Working Model of a Petroleum Well," March 12, 1865.
Fifth Avenue, near Thirteenth Street. © Collection of The New-York
Historical Society.

■ ■ ■

Poems, mottos, quotations, and political pronouncements, emphasizing
different aspects and implications of the telegraph, spoke from the building façades as private residences, commercial establishments, and public
institutions presented themselves to the moving crowd.

This upward migration of the parade banner reflects and highlights
several important features of the growth of the city before the war,
including the rising power of Manhattan's real estate proprietors to
dominate street life and control definitions of the public. Owning buildings did not simply confer the right to determine land use and charge
ground rent; it also allowed for the projection of monumental epigraphs
before a broad readership. While commercial signs cultivated and
exploited these spaces on an everyday basis, parades offered a special
opportunity for timely public communication.

Stationary parade banners were part of a larger ritual through which
public sentiment was made visible in the public spaces of Manhattan.
When obsequies were observed for President Lincoln in 1865, four days
after his assassination was reported in the city, New Yorkers did their best

to project signs of mourning into public view. As the *Times* emphasized the following day:

> From every window in every street its mark may be seen. . . . From the spires of our churches, from the domes of our halls, from every flag-staff, from every pane of glass, on the lappel of the millionaire, about the arm of the laborer . . . everywhere where life or home may be, are the insignia of grief, the physical and outward exponents of the sadness which rings in every breast.[67]

But among the "insignia of grief," verbal expressions on buildings assumed an especially prominent role and received particular attention in the press. On the day of the funeral procession, the city's storefronts eulogized the fallen leader. THERE WAS IN THE MAN SOMETHING THAT COULD CREATE, SUBVERT OR REFORM AN UNDERSTANDING, a piano store proclaimed, A SPIRIT OR AN ELOQUENCE TO SUMMON MANKIND TO SOCIETY. A fruit store on Broadway contributed some tragic irony: BUT IF THIS COUNTRY CANNOT BE SAVED WITHOUT GIVING UP THAT PRINCIPLE, I WAS ABOUT TO SAY, I WOULD RATHER BE ASSASSINATED UPON THIS SPOT THAN TO SURRENDER IT. *Abraham Lincoln, Independence Hall Feb. 22, 1861.*[68]

These signs went well beyond traditional parade banners both in rhetorical diversity and in the kind of narrative voices they projected, reflecting a heightened awareness of the expanded audiences for parade banners created by newspapers and photography. A magisterial banner draped across City Hall reading THE NATION MOURNS (see fig. 4.8) calls dramatic attention to the way this kind of self-consciousness manifested itself in signs that seem to invoke an abstract reader, an appropriate analogue to the impersonal authority of the signs themselves. "No man can walk our streets without feeling the power of the public mind," the *Times* asserted after the assassination.[69] Parade signs claimed to make the "public mind" legible, as well as palpable, from the vantage point of the streets.

In large part, the powerful role of building banners can be understood in the context of the rise of the commercial sign system discussed in the previous chapter. Having grown accustomed to reading storefronts, New Yorkers had no problem conceiving of building façades as appropriate media for public communication or making sense of verbal messages suspended above their heads. Parades were adjusting to and participat-

FIGURE 4.8 Lincoln's funeral cortege at City Hall, 1865. Stereograph by
Jeremiah Gurney. © Collection of The New-York Historical Society.

• • •

ing in the construction of a public space marked, quite literally, by sign
communication. New York was becoming a city plastered with written
words. That these words, whether on fixed signs or, more radically, on
flimsy and disposable bills and cards, were increasingly removed in one
respect or another from the personal identities of their authors was a
telling feature of life in a city whose size and pace had, in forty years,
altered beyond recognition. But this distance from personal authority
was not in all respects a troubling phenomenon. Within the new public

space, visible words were acquiring a new reliability and a new capacity to identify and define fragments of a changing urban environment. Moreover, these visible words made it easier to circulate in public and to participate in emerging forms of popular culture and mass politics. The overlapping signs of the bill poster evoke a world of entertainment, activism, education, and personal refashioning characteristic of modern urban life. Hanging out of small windows or attached to large façades, parade signs reinforced the need to scan the streets for verbal clues to public life, even as they reinforced the power of private property.

Seen from another perspective, however, the transformation of the parade banner points in a different direction. The numerous signs posted along procession routes found their resting places in the pages of an expanded metropolitan press that in many respects had helped to produce them. On the day before the 1858 illumination, the *Herald* confidently announced: "During the day the hotels and public buildings will have their flags hoisted, and the principal streets, at fitting intervals, will be decorated with appropriate devices." Because newspapers provided a highly visible space for the serial display of parade banners, they themselves became a procession site and could dictate the terms of the celebration. "It is to be hoped," the report continued, invoking authority superior to municipal government and private commercial interests, "that both the authorities and private citizens will see the propriety of having inscriptions put up that will be worth reading and quoting." Then, as if giving editorial instruction to its own staff, the *Herald* advised readers that the parade would provide "a fine occasion for the display of terse, epigrammatic sentences, such as will live in the memory long after the occasion that called them out is forgotten."[70]

But what is most significant about the newspaper's emergence as an alternative procession site in New York during the late antebellum period is not the fact that signs in the streets were being replaced by signs in the daily press, but that the two discourses were developing in tandem and were shaping each other. Though the daily press, as I will explore in the following chapter, enjoyed a different relationship to public space than that of signs, bills, and banners, its impact on public life raised many of the same issues about the authority of the written word in an expanding city.

5

Print in Public, Public in Print

~

The Rise of the Daily Paper

"In my last entry I found Cincinnati similar to a chessboard. True! But today I should prefer to compare it to a giant newspaper page." German journalist and travel writer Moritz Busch had a penchant for fanciful similes as he described America's sixth-largest city in 1851. Beneath the extemporaneity of Busch's metaphoric eclecticism, however, lay an important insight about the relationship between streets and sheets in antebellum America.

> To the yard-long columns of the [American] journals correspond the mile-long streets of the city. The former are up to three-quarters advertisements; the latter are six-eighths commercial firms. The former are crowded with woodcuts illustrating the announcements; the latter exaggeratingly exhibit the originals of the illustrations in a superabundant confusion of enormous rifles advertising the gun shop, great golden mortars advertising the physician and the apothecary. . . . Giant plows, likewise put up as high as the building permits, greet the farmer as a customer at three thousand paces.

Understandably, what impressed Busch most was the sheer spectacle of a sign system that exceeded human proportions: "Mammoth bottles, from which a company of soldiers could get drunk, shimmer green, red, and blue from the windows of boutiques."[1] More generally, though, his analogy between the newspaper and the city points to their shared function as means of advertising through graphic representations laid out in rectilinear patterns for all to see. And if Cincinnati provided Busch, as it had Frances Trollope two decades earlier, with a powerful symbol of American commerce on the frontier—a society in which the pursuit of money and trade seemed liminal, unchecked by the gradual development of European culture—the affinity between public space and published papers as particular sites of commercial representation was at least as evident in New York, where the implications of urban growth, economic expansion, mass literacy, and advanced print technology were manifest most dramatically and elaborately.

What made the newspaper such an illuminating metaphor for public space in New York was not simply geometry or commerce, but rather the particular combination of those two elements described earlier in connection with the 1811 Commissioners' Plan. While the value of land was being transformed as commercial and residential development climbed up the island of Manhattan according to the grid, while the city's real estate was being constructed as a series of interchangeable and transferable commodity-units distinguished only by size and relative location, New York's penny papers were reorganizing the printed space of the metropolitan press in an intriguingly analogous manner.

In his provocative study of newspaper culture in nineteenth-century France, literary critic Richard Terdiman describes the way the daily press created an "anti-organicist" discourse in which disparate news items and advertising notices were juxtaposed in the neutral space of the paper. According to Terdiman, this juxtaposition performed two ideologically significant operations. First, the apparent neutrality with which discrete newspaper contents were laid out in relation to one another implicitly trivialized, through a "systematic emptying of any logic of connection," all conflicts those contents might generate. Moreover, the transformation of the Parisian newspaper from a journal of opinion to a self-promoting consumer good whose space was available for purchase converted all news into commodities, even as it obscured and mystified the relationship between news and commerce.[2] Though the layout of a publication like *La Presse* or *Le Petit Journal* differed in some important details from those of its New York contemporaries, newspapers like the *Sun*, the *Herald*, and the *Tribune* presented similar juxtapositions of news and advertising and similar overlaps between politics and commerce. And while there may well have been more to the impact of this layout than the containment of political conflicts and the mystification of economic realities, Terdiman's analysis of the neutral grid of the cheap daily provides a suggestive starting point for an examination of New York's burgeoning newspaper culture in the antebellum era.

By reflecting on the homology between the physical layouts of newsprint and streets in New York, we can develop the spatial component of a familiar and well-documented story about the press in the United States. For unlike street signs and handbills, the rise of cheap daily newspapers beginning in the 1830s figures prominently in recent historiography and forms the centerpiece of much scholarly discussion of public life and the public sphere during the nineteenth century. However, many of these historical treatments tend to frame the story in national terms (even when the papers analyzed were, overwhelmingly, published in Manhattan) and to describe the kind of public created in print as an abstract entity. The newspaper, we are often told, replaced spatial communities with imagined ones, unsettling geographical boundaries and nullifying physical distances. This chapter sets out to describe the emergence and proliferation of New York's daily press in a way that takes seriously the local character of that history and connects the print public to the broader experience of public space in the city. For while the penny press did recast notions of community and the public, the communities and publics projected in their columns were decidedly urban. Cities, after all, were not simply the contingent sites of news production; they were the primary and novel subject of the new dailies. And while there was a grain of truth in the claim put forth by an ambitious New York-based journal in 1848 that "the *Herald*, the *Ledger*, the *Police Gazette*, and other papers, are as local in New Orleans, or Cincinnati, or Boston, as in the cities of their publication,"[3] those newspapers nonetheless bore the stamp of the metropolis in which they were published and had particular connections to its public spaces. Much of the transformative impact of the new urban dailies lay not simply in the construction of broad, imagined links across the country but also in the emerging circuits of communication and navigation within the growing city.

Daily papers reinforced emerging modes of anonymous, market-oriented, urban sociability in New York in two fundamental ways. First, they became a regular feature of the verbal cityscape, rendering new forms of social knowledge visible in the public spaces of the city to a broad and impersonal readership. Second, newspapers constituted their own public space, an arena of print exchange where strangers appeared, circulated, browsed, and presented themselves before the urban crowd. The metropolitan press thus provided both a corpus of material and a compellingly analogous vehicle for the type of city reading that was proliferating in New York during the nineteenth century. Moreover, these two functions overlapped substantially. Newspapers were not simply simulacra of primary urban experience or abstract representations of the real spatial contours of the city. Hawked, posted, traded, and read in public view, they had a palpable material presence in the streets, and the symbolic relationship between rectilinear city blocks and rectilinear print columns was reciprocally clarifying.

To flesh out this spatial history of the newspaper in antebellum New York, it is necessary not only to shift the focus from national trends to local developments, but also to reconstruct the conditions under which newspapers were consumed at this particular place and time. Though direct evidence of how different New Yorkers read their papers is spotty and largely anecdotal, the real obstacle to recapturing the experience of newspaper reading is not that it remains irretrievably trapped within the private interiors of human consciousness, but rather that since the nineteenth century the daily press has become inextricably linked with the events and worlds it describes and the time frames it organizes and narrates. So while scholars have begun to speak critically of the deceptive and bewitching transparency with which modern newspapers claim to represent "the world," "the news," or "the times," it is equally important to trace the significance of that claim for particular reading contexts and communities. By exploring the circulation and reception of the metropolitan press in the city where it achieved fullest flower, we can appreciate the way newspapers participated in a larger process through which the written word facilitated the anonymous circulation of strangers and acquired privileged public authority in daily life.

The history of New York's cheap newspapers in the antebellum era is, in its basic outline, quite familiar. Beginning in 1833, a new kind of daily paper began appearing in the streets, offices, and hotels of

Manhattan. In stark contrast to the staid six-penny commercial journals and political party organs that had dominated the city's press in the first three decades of the century, dailies on the model of Benjamin Day's *Sun* (founded in 1833), Asa Greene's *Transcript* (founded in 1834), and James Gordon Bennett's *Herald* (founded in 1835) charged only one or (more often) two cents a copy and addressed themselves to a wider class of readers. Whereas the older journals had supported themselves through subscriptions and (to a lesser extent, in the case of New York) government printing contracts, the new papers were consumer commodities sold directly by street hawkers, and they generated unprecedented revenues from advertising. In addition to their revolutionary emphasis on local news and sensational crime stories, these New York penny papers produced and exemplified a radical nationwide transformation in the role of newspapers in daily life, sustained in part by important advances in the technologies of printing and distribution. From 1830 to 1840, the number of dailies in the United States rose from 65 to 138, and the average circulation nearly doubled as well, achieving a daily total of approximately 300,000. Weekly journals, often catering to specialized readerships, flourished in a similarly spectacular fashion (if slightly later), though many of their readers were from outside the city. One census of the newspapers published in New York between 1820 and 1850 found more than 300 different journals serving a wide variety of constituencies, ideologies, language groups, and subcultures— and this was before the great decade of growth in weekly publications during the 1850s, which saw the rise of such popular New York-based magazines as the *Ledger*, *Harper's*, the *Home Journal*, and *Frank Leslie's Illustrated Weekly*. (A single 1860 issue of *Frank Leslie's* sold 340,000 copies.) But in many ways the most significant development was in the institution of the daily paper. With the rise of the daily, vast numbers of New Yorkers adopted new and regular reading habits that would thoroughly transform their relationship to the urban community. Whereas New York's combined daily circulation in 1830 measured 1 for every 16 residents, twenty years later the ratio would exceed 1 for every 4.5 (one for every 2.2 on Sundays). During the same period, newspapers (responding to the example of the *Herald*) began competing with one another to report news as quickly as possible, employing carrier pigeons, horses, boats, and rival rail lines to obtain the freshest possible information and eventually forming the Associated Press in 1848 to harness the technological advantages of the telegraph. In the process, the city's press refashioned the relationship between the time the paper was read and the time the paper described and institutionalized the day as a significant unit of news in the experience of most New Yorkers. A new and recognizably modern era of mass-circulation daily journalism had arrived.[4] There are, of course, some important differences among historians about the details of this story, especially the significance of technological innovations and the relationship between the new dailies and Jacksonian politics. However, most historians concur in attributing watershed significance to the rise of the penny press in the development of new habits of reading, new notions of everyday life, new bonds among anonymous (and implicitly urban) individuals, and what Dan Schiller, evoking Habermas, calls "a presumptive claim to the exercise of reason in the public sphere."[5]

As with most attempts to isolate moments of profound historical change, histories of the penny press in New York tend a little toward oversimplification. It is easy to exaggerate, for example, the dichotomy between the cheap papers and the "respectable" six-penny journals, though this obscures important continuities. While the cheaper papers were notorious for sensational crime reporting, many of them served traditional functions as clearinghouses of commercial news and information. James Gordon Bennett's money articles, for example, a regular feature in the *Herald*, were as central to the ideology and as characteristic of the tone of his paper as his pontifications on the trials of accused murderers. Moreover, shipping news, consisting of both regular announcements of departing and arriving vessels and sensational headlines surrounding particular transatlantic voyages, remained a prominent feature in the cheap dailies, especially in the first fifteen years—an enduring reminder of the origins of the newspaper in merchant newsletters.[6] And while penny papers are often described as departures from the more explicitly political partisan press, this generalization accounts for some journals (like the *Sun*) while ignoring others (like the *Tribune*). For their part, six-penny journals such as the *Commercial Advertiser*, the *Evening Post*, and the *Courier and Enquirer* maintained a stance of superiority toward their cheaper rivals (a posture articulated most explicitly in the "Moral War" waged against the *Herald* in 1840, which called for a boycott of the paper and its advertisers), but they nonetheless mirrored the penny papers in many respects, covering similar stories, constructing similar portraits of the day's news, and competing for readership in the same general (and highly expanded) market.

Exaggerated emphasis on the revolution of 1833 also obscures the gradual process by which newspapers came to assume new importance in the daily lives of New Yorkers. Whether the transformation of print technology was the cause or the effect of the nineteenth-century proliferation of newspapers (and it was almost certainly a little of both), the most important technological innovations were introduced at very different points in the early history of the mass-circulation press. While some inventions, such as David Napier's cylinder press, which replaced the flat presses that had dominated the printing craft for centuries, or Fourdrinier's paper-making machine, prior to which paper had been made by hand, appeared before or around the emergence of the first penny daily, others were introduced much later in the period. Robert Hoe's revolutionary ten-cylinder press, which used revolving type and could print 20,000 sheets per hour (ten times the output of the original cylinder press) was not adopted until the mid-1840s. The telegraph, which revolutionized the process of gathering news, was not in use until 1844; the process for making paper out of tree pulp was not introduced in the United States until the Civil War era; and typesetting did not become automated until the 1880s, when Ottmar Mergenthaler introduced his linotype machine.[7] As these developments only begin to suggest, the decades *after* 1833 brought enormous changes in the production and distribution of the new metropolitan press, with important consequences for its reception and cultural impact. The four-page, three-column premiere issue of the *Sun*, more than half of whose scant twenty-five advertisements were ship announcements, looked in many ways less like the *Herald* of the 1860s, with eight pages of six columns each (five pages of which were news) than like the traditional commercial journals it is supposed to have supplanted.

Still, the emergence of both a new genre of newspaper and new patterns of newspaper reading remains undeniable. When the *Sun* announced to its readers on September 2, 1833 that "the object of this paper is to lay before the public, at a price within the means of every one, ALL THE NEWS OF THE DAY, and at the same time afford an advantageous medium for advertising," noting optimistically that "the sheet will be enlarged as soon as the increase of advertisements requires it," the paper was articulating the premises of a textual commodity that would transform the society and culture in which it emerged. To explore what exactly this transformation meant in the lives of New Yorkers and appreciate the way these texts fit into larger patterns in the changing experience of writing and print in New York, this chapter considers in greater local detail several characteristics of the New York papers during their proliferation: their material history, the type of urban space they presented, and the kind of public they constructed.

First and foremost, newspapers were material objects, and much of what made the penny papers seem so radical to contemporaries was their physical character. More conspicuous than any differences in editorial tone or reportorial style was the fact that the new dailies were substantially smaller than their traditional counterparts. The first issue of the *Sun* was 8½ inches wide by 11 inches high, and even though the paper would expand steadily (reaching 12 by 19 inches in 1836), it remained relatively tiny. In 1828, the standard newspaper page measured 24 inches wide and 35 inches high, about three times the spread of the original *Sun*. While other penny dailies, such as the *Transcript*, as well as the shorter-lived *Age*, the *Man*, the *Mechanic*, and the *Penny Daily Gazette* published sheets as small as the *Sun*, the six-cent papers continued to enlarge over the next two decades, with the *Journal of Commerce* reaching an intimidating 35 by 58, or over 2,000 square inches.[8] Size differences became a frequent subject of observation among editors and readers. While the *Courier and Enquirer*, according to one testimony, "would almost serve a small man for a blanket,"[9] the cheaper journals were pocket papers. Looking back from 1855, Isaac Pray, Bennett's friendly biographer, recalled that twenty years earlier "one could scarcely pass his neighbor without seeing him thrusting one or more of the penny papers into his pocket,"[10] and in the first *Herald*, Bennett bragged that with the publication of his journal there "is not a person in this city, male or female, that may not be able to say—'well I have got a paper of my own which will tell me all about what's doing in the world—I'm busy now—but I'll put it in my pocket and read it at my leisure.' "[11]

Penny papers were fond of invoking the metaphorical implications of this size difference to their advantage. In 1836, the first number of the *New Era* (which later became a party organ for the Democrats) cited "the heavy, lumbering, and soporific properties of the sheets which have arrogated to themselves the title of 'respectable sixpennies,' " while another pocket-sized daily, the *Age*, associated size with accuracy, comparing itself in 1838 "to a camera obscura, which gives you the objects that pass before it in the smallest possible compass, and yet in full perfection." The same editorial also went on to suggest that a journal "of such a convenient size" allowed for more conspicuous advertisements, which might be lost "in the ocean of larger papers."[12] For his part, Bennett proffered his diminutive *Herald* (which began in 1835 at 10½ by 15 inches) as a light antidote to the larger journals:

> The broad relief which the lively HERALD will afford to the dull business air of the large morning papers, will naturally induce every patron of the former to take in a copy of the latter, so as to diversify and exhilarate the breakfast table. A glass of champagne makes a dinner pleasant—a pie is good after a piece of roast . . . so will the HERALD minister to its larger, heavier, and more expansive contemporaries, over a cup of coffee or a dish of chocolate.[13]

Calling the sixpenny journals more expansive, not just more expensive, Bennett sought to attach attractive significance to what was one of the most obvious distinctions between the two classes of newspaper.

The small size of the new cheap dailies evoked other qualities as well. As something that could be incorporated so obviously into one's possessions, the pocketable paper advertised its status as a consumer good. Pray, recalling his neighbors thrusting papers into their pockets, linked the rise of the penny daily to the introduction and proliferation of cheap Locofoco matches, noting that "in fact, the progress of matches and newspapers has been somewhat analogous." Both objects became sources of pride to their new owners, who had previously "borrowed coals of fire and newspapers of their richer neighbors."[14] At the same time, the pocket suggested certain possibilities of concealment, something Philip Hone (who like many of his class was scandalized by the new press) emphasized in his 1837 observation that "every man who blames his neighbor for setting so bad an example occasionally puts one in his pocket to carry home to his family for their and his own edification."[15]

This suitability of the pocket press for private—and, as Hone's comment reminds us, domestic—consumption conforms neatly to the general picture historians have presented of the privatization of reading practices in the modern era. To describe the consumption of cheap dailies as private, though, would be a radical misrepresentation of the way newspapers were read in antebellum New York. For although a small paper could be secreted for later perusal, the very gesture of tucking it away constituted a public act. Pray's description of passing a neighbor in the street and seeing him put a penny paper in his pocket describes, most significantly, a public encounter, even as it suggests a postponed scene of private reading. Moreover, for many sectors of the urban population, reading the penny press took place primarily in public view. A report in the Philadelphia *Public Ledger* from 1836 portrays New York as a city covered with cheap journals.

> These papers are to be found in every street, lane, and alley; in every hotel, tavern, counting-house, shop, etc. Almost every porter and drayman, while not engaged in his occupation, may be seen with a paper in his hands.[16]

A similar picture emerges about fifteen years later in a humorous article entitled "Newspaper-dom" written by novelist Fanny Fern, who made a good living contributing to the New York press. In trying to imagine how humanity survived so many centuries without the benefits of the newspaper, Fern wonders "What did cab-drivers do, while waiting for a tardy patron? What did draymen do, when there was 'a great calm' at the dry-goods store of Go Ahead & Co.?"[17] Another observer recalled that around 1850 the *Sun* was popular among "cartmen dozing at street-corners in waiting for a job," while Isabella Lucy Bird, during her visit from England in the 1850s, noticed "groups of extraordinary-looking human beings" constantly lounging near the entrances of the major hotels, "smoking, whittling, and reading newspapers."[18] Nor was the act of newspaper reading an exclusive relationship between a consumer commodity and its owner. In hotels and other places of public gathering, a single copy of one of the cheap dailies would pass through the hands of numerous readers, who, Pray observes, "will no more neglect looking at it . . . than they would to eat their own breakfast and leave that of their neighbors undisturbed."[19] Though it is impossible to reconstruct all the conditions under which New Yorkers read the newspaper, it is clear that while the size of the new dailies may have facilitated certain habits of private reading, these papers remained visible public objects.

Perhaps the most powerful symbol and vehicle of the publicity of the penny press was the newsboy, who hawked the papers in the city streets, shouting names of journals and advertising special editions. A popular figure in the urban sensationalist writings of the second third of the century, the boy who hawked the daily papers belonged, in the words of one guide to the mysteries of the city, to "the race of merry juvenile rogues . . . who are always first at a fire or a fight, and are 'some pumpkins' at a horse-race—who holler on regattas and know the points and speed of every yacht and row-boat in the river . . . —who are as brave as they are mischievous."[20] In a sense, the newsboy stood at the crossroads of two otherwise distinct commercial cultures, merging the traditional orality of the street crier (the hot corn girls, the ragmen, the chimney sweeps) with new print technologies and revolutionary demands for up-to-the-minute news and information. As both the only major group of street criers to survive to the postbellum era and the high-profile engine for spreading the power of print, the newsboys were a double-edged symbol of urban change.[21] Sometimes the values of these two commercial cultures clashed, as they did during the Hyer-Sullivan boxing match of 1849, whose telegraphed results were described in great detail and flashy typography in the New York press. According to one of the more elitist weekly journals, "the newsboys as a class were in favor of Mr. Sullivan, and even permitted their enthusiasm for that personage to interfere with their pecuniary interests—for while vending the 'extrees,' which related the issue of the fight, they boldly proclaimed their disbelief in the contents."[22] But though certain ironies in the role of the newsboys amused critics, these figures were central to the experience of the daily paper in antebellum New York, and the tie between the penny press and the city's masculine, working-class street culture was strong.

Newsboys supplied an important oral dimension to the dissemination of news in the city, and it is tempting to think of them as late-model town criers. Shouts of "extra" often functioned as clarion calls, giving city residents first notice of a major news item.[23] But as descriptions of reactions to these shouts suggest, they fulfilled this function in a complex manner. Ex-cartman Isaac Lyon recalled the way he learned of an 1830s disaster that befell a ship in whose passage he had a particular interest. Noting that "Extras then were not quite so common" as they would become three decades later, Lyon was "startled from my reverie by the sound of a newsboy's voice away down Broadway shouting and screaming: 'Extra *Herald!*'" When the "little dirty, ragged newsboy" approached, catching his breath, he was screaming: "Here's the extra *Herald*, containing a full account of the loss of the steamship 'Home,' with all on board!" Immediately, the boy was surrounded by "an eager and excited crowd of half frantic persons, each one pulling and hauling the other, and all impatient to secure an 'extra' at almost any price."[24] Though the boy's voice introduces and summarizes the news, the powerful institution of the newspaper frames the event. The authority of the ragged newsboy derives from that of the news-gathering apparatus he represents (and whose token he carries), and the story culminates in the (public) purchase and consumption of newspapers. At both ends, experiences of the printed word give meaning to the shout of the newsboy.

For events of compelling general interest, the cry of a running newsboy might set off a public alarm, but the reading of the news gave that alarm meaning. On the night after the opening shots of the Civil War were fired at Fort Sumter in 1861, Walt Whitman was walking down Broadway on his way home from the opera when he "heard in the distance the loud cries of the newsboys, who came presently tearing and yelling up the street . . . even more furiously than usual." At least in Whitman's narration, the substance of the cries remains unknown until the papers are presented:

> I bought an extra and cross'd to the Metropolitan hotel where the great lamps were still brightly blazing, and, with a crowd of others, who gather'd impromptu, read the news, which was evidently authentic. For the benefit of some who had no papers, one of us read the telegram aloud, while all listen'd silently and attentively. No remark was made by any of the crowd, which had increas'd to thirty or forty, but all stood a minute or two, I remember, before they dispers'd. I can almost see them there now, under the lamps at midnight again.

Whitman recalls a remarkable scene of public reading, but what is perhaps most striking is the silent and attentive response to the newspaper, which is "evidently authentic" on the basis of its own authority.[25] New Yorkers were especially attuned to the tension between the vendors' cries and the purportedly authenticating print documents they sold. Stationed in Washington with the Union Army in 1861, Georgeanna Muirson Woolsey complained to her cousin Margaret Hodge of the difficulty in obtaining news. "One longs now and then for a real living and lying 'Extra' boy," she confessed, "with his mouth full of fearful statements, all disproved by his paper which you imprudently buy."[26] News vendors brought the paper into prominent public view and helped make reading it a public activity; they also projected their famous and powerful cries within the cultural context of the spread of the written word and against the backdrop of increased reliance on print's authority.

When not in the conspicuous clutches of ambulatory hawkers, newspapers would also appear in the stands of news dealers along major downtown thoroughfares, arrayed as an advertising display for passersby. Some of the more sensational journals might be positioned in such a way as to reveal just enough of their contents to entice potential customers. In addition to the public spectacle of the display itself, the newsstand offered a key to the social taxonomy of the city, presenting a stage on which silent and anonymous individuals might make themselves legible to the urban connoisseur. Junius Browne observes (or perhaps imagines) such a scene in his 1860s guide to *The Great Metropolis*:

> As the human tide descends, the heaps of papers rapidly diminish. There is no conversation between buyer and seller. The money is laid down, the journal taken up, and the change given, without a word. You might tell from the appearance of the purchaser what paper he wanted. . . . That affected person, with a slightly finical air, wishes the *Home Journal* of course. That crimson, sensual face is searching for the *Day's Doings* and its cheap sensations. This low brow and hard, cruel eye are in quest of the *Clipper*.[27]

Much like the specialized tiers of the nineteenth-century theater, the newsstand arrayed social difference in public view and transformed personal habits into public spectacle. In such newsstands (see fig. 5.1, where the hawked newspapers appear as part of the collage of public print), on newspaper bulletin boards, and in the hands of newsboys or neighbors, the public appearance of newspapers became a significant and legible component of the cityscape.

At the same time that newspapers were leaving their mark on Manhattan's expanding and changing public spaces, they were, of course, creating a public space of their own. Newspapers constructed a regular system of columns and pages, and New Yorkers would grow accustomed to the particular organization of information that this layout established and reinforced. To understand what it meant for unprecedented proportions of the city's population to become regular readers of the metropolitan press, it is necessary to consider the nature of these print spaces.

Though the layout of New York's dailies varied and changed, several

FIGURE 5.1 "Newsboy Selling *New York Herald*," 1857. Painting by James
Henry Cafferty.

• • •

important patterns prevailed during this period. The dominant unit for
organizing and dividing space within the newspaper was the page. Even
as they expanded in height and width, virtually all daily newspapers were
four pages long in the antebellum era, whether they were pocket or blanket sized. The *Herald* experimented with "double sheets" (eight-page editions), which Bennett issued every Tuesday after 1849, but this was more
the exception. Within the standard four-page format, most papers used
the first page for select advertising, serialized fiction, reprints of lengthy
speeches, and miscellaneous features. Some dailies, especially after
1850, put major headlines on the front page, usually in the left-hand column, though several journals avoided even this valuable promotional use
of the front page. In the six-cent *Courier and Enquirer*, for example, the firing on Fort Sumter never made page one. For all dailies, the second page

remained the primary site for editorials and important news. The rest of the advertisements filled the final two pages. No distinct sections existed in the daily papers and few headings segregated categories of news items, though dailies, including the *Tribune* and the *Courier and Enquirer*, employed small headings to designate specific advertising categories such as "Dry Goods," "Tobacco & Segars," and "Mining Companies."

Whatever loose principles of spatial segregation were provided by the dominant four-page format were loosened even further by the explosive and unwieldy character of advertising in the daily press after 1833. One of the most significant changes brought about by the introduction of the cheap papers was an inversion of the relationship between circulation and advertising revenue. Whereas earlier journals had claimed to sell their advertisers to their readers, the new press claimed to sell readers to advertisers. "We lose money on our circulation by itself considered," Horace Greeley announced in an 1841 *Tribune* editorial, "but with 20,000 subscribers we can command such Advertising and such prices for it as will render our enterprise a remunerating one." Five years earlier, the *Transcript* had informed its readers that it made "little or nothing" on the circulation of the paper, and depended largely on advertising income.[28] Because of the new power of advertisements as both symptoms and engines of newspaper growth, they could not be restricted to regular places within the layout of the metropolitan press. As papers succeeded in attracting more advertising patronage, its bulk grew quite conspicuous. Several years into its run, the *Sun* was devoting seventeen of twenty-four columns to ads. When the ostensibly more traditional *Courier and Enquirer* expanded its pages from nine to ten columns in 1845, an editorial explained that "the great extent and character of our circulation, had forced upon our columns an advertising business, which has, of late, nearly excluded from them the current intelligence of the day."[29]

These habitual encroachments upon the space occupied by "the intelligence of the day" may have helped to prevent the establishment of rigid boundaries between different kinds of printed information, but the lines separating news from advertising were blurry for other reasons as well. Critics of the modern newspaper, both then and now, frequently call attention to the way news stories and reviews are purchased, to confluences between financial needs and editorial policies or what Richard Terdiman has described in the case of the Parisian press as the "disguised colonization of 'objective' informational discourse by the commercial."[30] Certainly these charges were leveled against the New York dailies, and in all likelihood many were well founded, especially in the early decades of the penny press. Isaac Pray claimed, rather defensively, that the *Herald* "did not sell 'puffs,' or any part of the paper which the ordinary reader could not know was devoted to advertisements," and he maintained that by the mid-'50s most papers had abandoned the practice of "permitting agents and advertisers to occupy editorial space at a fixed rate."[31] But the substitution of disguised advertising for news was in many respects less significant than the deep interpenetration of the two categories. First of all, as newspapers became consumer commodities hawked competitively in an increasingly lucrative market, news items and editorials served (sometimes quite explicitly) as ads for the papers in which they appeared. Expanded headlines on the front page were attempts to draw readers into buying a particular issue, news stories frequently referred to rival journals, and editorials engaged in constant and often blatant efforts at self-promotion. The amount of space devoted to the personal disputes between different editors was astounding, and Bennett became notorious for exposing himself to beatings at the hands of his enemies in order to convert the events into sensational copy in the next mornings' papers.[32] Less spectacular examples abound as well. In January 1836, shortly before the *Herald* expanded to five columns, Bennett announced in true Barnumesque fashion that advertising patronage had increased so that "on many occasions we have had to leave out advertisers for several days, in order to make room for the crowd asking admission." A week into the life of the *Tribune*, Greeley subtly merged the ideology and the finances of his journal when he praised "the character of our circulation, being mainly among the active and substantial Middle Class of our citizens—those who live by their labor or their business, and are neither above the necessity nor devoid of the ability to buy and sell to the best advantage."[33] In these and other frequent boasts, spread throughout the editorial pages of all the major dailies (not only the cheap ones), the question of what is news and what is advertising becomes completely moot.

For their part, advertisements were not without a certain value typically associated with news. Commercial notices provided important information, practical and otherwise, about the communities their readers inhabited and offered, sometimes inadvertently, valuable accounts of life in the city.[34] Moreover, cheap papers initiated a revolutionary change in the pattern of advertising that enhanced its news status. Breaking with the tradition of selling advertising on an annual basis, the penny press encouraged shorter-term notices, and after 1847 most of the cheap papers followed the *Herald*'s lead in requiring advertisers to renew their copy every two weeks.[35] Pray explained the policy as an effort "to have new advertisements as a matter of interest both to readers and to advertisers, and thereby secure a kind of public curiosity."[36] If they changed often enough (a strategy employed to great renown and profit by Barnum), advertisements could stimulate "public curiosity" as effectively as crime stories or social gossip. In the columns of the penny press, advertising entered into the category of the "current intelligence of the day"—the category of the news.

In addition to these substantive continuities among the newspaper's ostensibly disparate contents, the printed space of the metropolitan press had its own powerful homogenizing effect on the information appearing in its columns. To begin with, the very juxtaposition of items on the same newspaper page tended to deny (or at least to suppress) their differences. And the rigidity with which antebellum dailies adhered to the rectilinear layout, hardly ever allowing headlines, stories, or advertisements to transgress the divisions between even columns, reinforced the implied precedence of form over content, of the uniform space over the particular message.[37] In New York's newspaper revolution, though, these general structural effects were magnified and focused significantly. First of all, the cheap dailies revolutionized the status of print space by transforming the way advertising was sold. Traditionally, advertisers in the city's journals had signed on for a year, paying the same price irrespective of the size of their notices. By selling advertising for shorter terms in measured lines and squares, the penny papers made explicit not only the fact that newspaper space was available for purchase, but also, more fundamentally, that newspapers (like real estate) consisted, ultimately and entirely, of such divisible and exchangeable units of space. By creating a newspaper composed of quantifiable space, the cheap press stripped away some of the privileges attached to particular voices and called attention to the homogeneous character of the printed news page.

What made the new newspaper's homogenizing tendency conspicuous, moreover, was the striking degree of typographical uniformity that prevailed in its columns. To a modern eye, the antebellum newspaper appears as a dense and underdifferentiated mass of tiny newsprint, with few large headings, rare variations in font and type, and minimal use of lines or illustrations to disrupt the steady streams of text. A page often consisted entirely of unbroken columns of minuscule copy, with each column holding as many as 120 lines in some of the blanket sheets.[38] Even the exceptional map or illustration tended to conform to visual patterns set by the printed words. In 1845, for example, the *Herald* printed a five-part wood engraving of the funeral procession of Andrew Jackson. Perhaps the most interesting feature of this pictorial collage, which has been called "the first full-page cover devoted to pictures ever to appear in a daily newspaper," is the way the five stacked, captioned segments of the procession resemble horizontal columns of newsprint, arraying the miniature figures in the procession along a different axis.[39] Like the mid-century trade cards, antebellum daily newspapers were, by later standards, visually drab documents dominated by words. Article heads were often the same size as or only slightly larger than the text that followed, editorials appeared in the same type as excerpts from rival journals, and advertising copy tended to be typographically indistinguishable from serialized fiction. Though virtually all newspapers used horizontal lines to separate individual advertisements, and though several used bold type to mark off the opening words of new items, substantive textual indications—rather than graphic clues—formed the dominant code for categorizing the contents of the antebellum daily newspaper in New York.

Advertising is an especially interesting case of visual homogeneity, since subsequent generations of newspaper readers came to expect lavish illustrations, striking variations in print size, and distinct conventions of typography and iconography. The 1870s witnessed the introduction of many of these innovations, most notably the inclusion of color illustrations, but newspaper advertisements before the Civil War were more prosaic and visually monotonous. Though the practice of using icons of ships or hats to mark ads generically persisted in some of the six-cent journals, most notices in dailies more nearly resembled their predecessors from the first quarter of the century, which Frank Presbrey, in his classic 1929 study of the history of advertising, labels "the legal notice period in display."[40] And while it is tempting to think of antebellum journal advertisements as primitive precursors of the more technically and creatively sophisticated productions of the later era (as Presbrey implies), this misconstrues the significance of the typographic homogeneity by suggesting that it was determined by economic or technological constraints. To begin with, newspaper advertisements were confined, for the most part, to small and uniform type at the same time that outdoor advertisements were flirting with new possibilities of graphic variation and elaborate display.[41] Barnum, for example, kept his newspaper ads in simple agate type even as his legendary handbills and posters pushed the printed word to tortured and exaggerated extremes. In addition, the leading figures and developments in New York's newspaper revolution reinforced, rather than resisted, this tendency toward typographical homogeneity. In 1847, the same year that the *Herald* instituted its historic requirement that advertisers vary their insertions, Bennett imposed a ban on all advertising display and all nonagate type, a move that precipitated a general decline in illustrated advertising. Though it may have been motivated by a variety of economic pressures and considerations, the agate-only rule was a conscious attempt to preserve and bolster a certain style of newspaper presentation, not a shortsighted failure to exploit the potential of the rising advertising craft.

Whatever his intentions, however, Bennett's policy helped confer upon the uniform newsprint the status of an official language, a standard mode of address that glossed over differences of perspective and interest—not only in the ideologically significant (that is to say hegemonic, manipulative, mystifying) manner Terdiman has ascribed to the Parisian press, but also in the more general sense that it enhanced the claims of the newspaper to be a public text. Discrete news stories, tendentious political commentaries, competitive commercial claims, and ostensibly unrelated bits of information blended together in the print columns of the metropolitan press in a characteristically urban juxtaposition of unlikely neighbors that also imbued all of the texts with the appearance of sharing a single, impersonal authority.

This effect is most visible, ironically, in several notable efforts by advertisers to get around the restrictions on display. Advertisements appeared in the cheap daily papers using standard type to form larger patterns (fig. 5.2), icons (fig. 5.3), or characters (fig. 5.4). In the mid-1850s, Robert Bonner, the bold and highly successful editor of the New York *Ledger* who became a canonized figure in the history of advertising and journalism, pioneered a tactic known as iteration copy, in which the same brief message would appear over and over again for an entire column (fig. 5.5).[42] These devices, which became increasingly common by the end of the period, did not simply circumvent the rules to create

FIGURE 5.2 Dr. Swayne's Compound Syrup. Advertisement
in New York *Tribune*.
FIGURE 5.3 Morse's Compound Syrup. Advertisement in New York *Tribune*.

• • •

major impressions in a sea of undifferentiated copy; they ventriloquized
the newspaper itself, drawing power from the official, uniform typography that it was manipulating—almost in the fashion of a collage.

An entrenched rectilinear grid and increasingly uniform typography
helped to shape the public space that New York's newspapers created
during the era of their explosive proliferation. And although pervasive
practices and policies discouraged some of the more glaring techniques

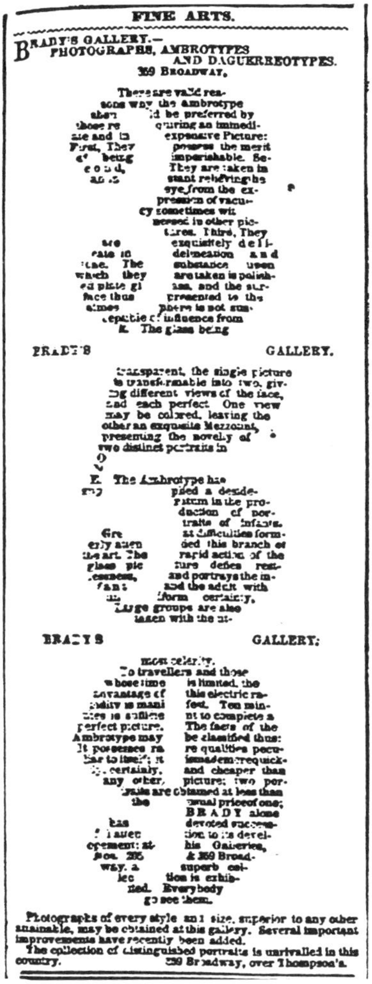

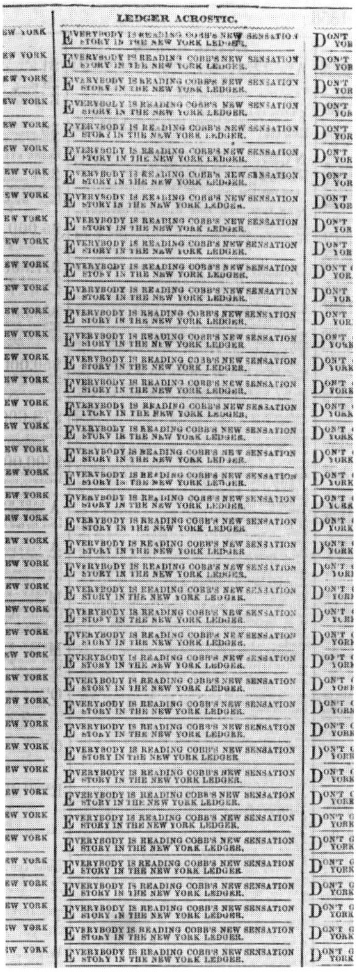

FINE ARTS.

BRADY'S GALLERY.—PHOTOGRAPHS, AMBROTYPES AND DAGUERREOTYPES. 359 BROADWAY.

LEDGER ACROSTIC.

FIGURE 5.4 Brady's Gallery. Advertisement in New York *Herald*, 1856.
FIGURE 5.5 New York *Ledger*. Detail of full-page advertisement
in New York *Herald*.

* * *

and styles of print communication characteristic of store signs and broadsides, the newspaper was a forum for public display. The history of the antebellum daily paper is in a sense about the developing consciousness of the implications of its publicness. There was, of course, nothing novel in the association between print and the public. As early as 1771, for example, the *Oxford English Dictionary* had acknowledged the modern meaning of the word "publish" as "making public exclusively by means of print."[43] Still, the newspaper only acquired its peculiar and privileged public status when its consumption became sufficiently regular, widespread, and simultaneous and when the community it described and addressed became sufficiently expansive and unwieldy. As New York's unprecedentedly large and heterogeneous population spread up the island of Manhattan, and as the daily newspaper improved its ability to describe events taking place in the city and elsewhere with speed and authority, the newspaper became a central site in the city's public sphere and, moreover, a dominant force in the construction of the city as what Benedict Anderson has called an "imagined community."

In his study of the cultural origins of nationalism, Anderson emphasizes the role of the newspaper as the center of a mass ceremony in which the coherence of a particular community-in-time emerges both in the text and in the act of reading. Crucial to Anderson's analysis is the fact that newspapers are consumed simultaneously by countless abstractly related individuals. While the paper is read in what Anderson calls "silent privacy, in the lair of the skull,"

> Yet each communicant is well aware that the ceremony he performs is being replicated simultaneously by thousands (or millions) of others of whose existence he is confident, yet of whose identity he has not the slightest notion. Furthermore, this ceremony is repeated at daily or half-daily intervals throughout the calendar.[44]

The public power of a medium whose readership was both shrouded (the *Herald* bragged of being "entirely ignorant, speaking individually, who are our readers, and who are not"[45]) and yet eminently conspicuous within the text was not lost on New York's journalists and editors. Nathaniel Parker Willis, editor of the *Home Journal*, described the newspaper as the wonder of the age, "opened at the same moment, by thousands, and . . . filling them all, on the instant, with the self-same thought."[46]

To be sure, the mass-circulation dailies of the antebellum era were not the first texts to incorporate an awareness of a larger, abstract readership. As Michael Warner has argued, the pivotal connection between print and the public sphere in the political culture of the Revolutionary period hinged on this powerful development.[47] What distinguished the public sphere created by the antebellum metropolitan press was its radically new spatial character. While in the beginning of the century New York's newspapers had functioned as sites of public opinion and critical discussion of public affairs, their connection to the public space of the city was at best abstract. In striking conformity to the model proposed by Jürgen Habermas, newspapers of the 1810s and 1820s evoked broad networks of international shipping and commerce and reproduced a mode of discourse associated with the salon. The symbolic center of this world was New York's famous Tontine Coffee House at the corner of Wall and Water Streets. In a travel record published after his journey to New York in 1819, German visitor Ludwig Gall offers a glimpse of the relationship between newspapers and the public sphere in this period. While dining at a hotel shortly after his arrival, Gall had taken interest in a dinner-table debate in which radically opposing views of Governor DeWitt Clinton and his Erie Canal project were exchanged. "Amazed" by the calm and civil tone of the debate, and "eager to learn more about a man and an undertaking that could cause such contradictory opinions," Gall went to the Tontine—a "municipal bourse," as he described it—where he could consult a wide range of journals. "I paged New York newspapers," Gall recalled, "searching for something on the Canal or the Governor. To my amazement I found *for* Clinton in *The New-York Columbian* and *against* Clinton in the *National Advocate* the same language my dinner companions had used." In the end, a perplexed Gall left the coffeehouse and consulted with a savvy French officer he had met aboard his ship, who offered the following sound republican principle: "Believe nothing a newspaper or an individual says that in any way might support a party or a person."[48] Though threatened by a creeping partisanship against which the Frenchman's skepticism struck Gall as a necessary bulwark, newspapers appear here as a centerpiece of a bourgeois public culture whose influence extended to the respectable hotels. Both stock exchange and salon, the Tontine had an interesting and ambiguous relationship to the outside world; it was a bridge to distant lands and at the same time a haven from the mounting din of the city. Newspapers bearing foreign postmarks and listing the latest price fluctuations were available in what Gall called a "beautiful reading room [where] solemn silence reigned." Such papers certainly belonged to the public sphere, but not necessarily to public space.

The Tontine Coffee House closed in 1834, just one year after the appearance of the first penny daily, and with it ended a chapter in the history of New York journalism and public life. The new metropolitan press brought about a profound shift to a type of imagined community and a model of the public sphere located in the streets rather than the salon. The public character of the modern urban newspaper is confirmed in daily encounters that connect print spaces to city spaces on a regular basis. "The newspaper reader," as Anderson remarks and as we have seen in our sources, "observing exact replicas of his own paper being consumed by his subway, barbershop, or residential neighbours, is continually reassured that the imagined world is visibly rooted in everyday life."[49] But newspapers did not simply circulate in urban public space; they also constructed an urban public space in which relations between strangers could be imagined and represented.

This crucial development in the history of the city had unique force, novelty, and meaning. As the traditional journals consulted by Ludwig Gall at the Tontine gave way to mass dailies crammed with local advertisements, attuned to the life of the city, addressed impersonally to unprecedented numbers of people, and circulated visibly in the streets, the newspaper became a special site of access and exposure. The process by which newspaper writers and readers adjusted to the nuances and implications of the material space they were shaping was gradual and uneven. Exactly what kind of forum for public communication and display was provided in the columns of the mass-circulation daily metropolitan press was not always obvious. Did the appearance of an item in the *Tribune*, for example, function like a letter sent by a particular author (Horace Greeley, a commissioned reporter, a paying advertiser) to numerous, generally intended subscribers and patrons, or was it more like an anonymous broadside placed on the side of a public building for all to see?

Especially in the early years of the penny press, advertisements suggest a good deal of awkwardness in the use of the daily paper as a medium for display. One ad for Hardy and Roche's Self-Setting Saw Mill Dogs included the request that "persons receiving this advertisement will please cut it out of the paper and put it securely in Mills, Stores and their Hotels."[50] Such an unusual request is striking not only for its quaint and ingenuous expectation that readers will cooperate with the company's promotional campaign, but also for the way it figures the complicated relationship between handbills and newspaper advertisements. After the Civil War, advertising experts made the case for the superiority of newspaper publicity over modes of display and communication that treaded more obviously into public space. "The handbills are thrown away and the posters not read," the 1870 advertising manifesto of George P.

Rowell and Company declared, "and it is safe to say that an advertise-ment costing five dollars will reach twice as many people and be read by twice as many as the same money put into a handbill."[51] It may still have been hard to accept that an ad in the print columns of a daily with a cir-culation of more than fifty thousand (a figure exceeded by several of the morning papers by the Civil War) attracted more public notice than an ad in the streets, and that contrary to the assumptions of Hardy and Roche (but consistent with those of P. T. Barnum), it was cleverer adver-tising strategy to produce a handbill that would attract press attention than to design a journal ad that would achieve a second life as a poster. Numerically, sheets were often more public than streets, a point drama-tized by Bennett's sensational narration of his fight with James Watson Webb. Webb attacked him in the streets, perhaps enacting the tradition of calling someone outside to humiliate him publicly, but Bennett raised the public stakes of their contest considerably by printing an account of the incident in his editorial column, in which the beating appears almost as a private event that is being exposed to general view.

The point is not that the daily newspaper replaced the street as the stage for public interaction, but rather that the press became another such stage, resembling the street in significant ways even as it encouraged different gestures of communication and extended the power of differ-ent members of the community. In many respects, perusing the columns of the major dailies resembled and paralleled walking down the city's major thoroughfares, and while the process did not always require that the reader present himself or herself to others, it did invoke a similar set of expectations about the contents of the paper. The "Moral War" waged against the *Herald* in 1840 was, in a sense, an attempt to restrict the scandals described or contained in Bennett's paper from invading the public sphere by reminding New Yorkers that it was their decision to patronize the journal—that newspapers were private commodities after all. The failure of the boycott signaled the fragility of that distinction between public and private in the new era of the metropolitan press. The *Herald* could not be effectively regulated by a taboo against its consump-tion; like a sketchy neighborhood, it could, at most, be avoided. By the end of the antebellum period the claim of a major daily newspaper to being a public space was hard to refute.

The relationship between streets and newspapers as linked urban are-nas of promiscuous contact between strangers is captured neatly in the rise of a certain type of personal ad familiar to modern city dwellers that became popular (though controversial) toward the end of this period. Sometimes these ads would connect two acquaintances who were unable to locate each other, or who needed to exercise particular discretion. Other notices sought to re-create the circumstances of a public meeting between strangers.[52] An item would announce, "If the young lady who, on Monday afternoon, at about four o'clock, took a Sixth Avenue small car at the corner of Varick and Water Streets, and left it at the corner of Waverly Place, and wore a black and white check dress, trimmed in front and below with black silk, edged with crimson, fur cape and muff and black bonnet with green velvet behind, desires to become acquainted with one who admires her very much," and a postal address would be provided. Other personal ads referred explicitly to meetings, glances, and acknowledgments exchanged in public, optimistically invoking a private conspiracy but displaying it in full view.[53] Like streets, news sheets were spaces in which anonymous strangers could gain easy access to information, make quick public impressions, expose themselves to the gaze of others (a gaze that is itself implicated obliquely in the scandalousness of the gesture), and expect to meet one another again. Of course, different public constituencies might favor one daily newspaper over another, much as different groups and classes might favor one neighborhood over another. Significantly, however, many New Yorkers read several journals, moving promiscuously from paper to paper much as they passed fluidly through different parts of the city. Each of the big morning or evening journals (the *Times*, the *Herald*, the *Sun*, the *Tribune*, the *Evening Post*, the *Journal of Commerce*, the *Commercial Advertiser*, and—until its death during the Civil War—the *Courier and Enquirer*), like a major street, avenue, or intersection, was a site of public discourse and encounter that at times seemed synonymous with the public itself.

The slippery and complex relationship between the publicness of streets and the publicness of news columns surfaced frequently. Newspapers played a special role as organizers of—and even sites for—the parades and processions discussed in the previous chapter. The visit of Hungarian nationalist Lajos Kossuth to New York in 1851, to enlist American support for the beleaguered cause of Hungarian independence, provides an illuminating example of how the newspapers came to represent the urban public. From the perspective of individual journals and editors, the Kossuth visit was an occasion for political contention.

Most papers, including the *Tribune* and Henry Raymond's newly founded New York *Times*, celebrated the exiled leader as a republican hero, while Bennett was cooler in his reception and James Watson Webb of the *Courier and Enquirer* was positively hostile to Kossuth and his cause. The impact of these editorial debates paled utterly, though, before the collective role of the press in staging and constructing the enormous spectacle that Kossuth's visit to the city would become.

During the weeks prior to Kossuth's delayed arrival, as he traveled from Marseilles to Gibraltar to Southampton stirring up crowds of supporters, the New York papers drummed up a swelling crescendo of excitement and speculation fueled by daily reports of his whereabouts and speeches. Much as they had during the tour of Swedish opera singer Jenny Lind the previous year, the city's newspapers mythologized a foreign visitor (despite the fact that most New Yorkers knew little of the history or geography of Hungary), creating a frenzy that led tens of thousands to greet the arrival of his ship and inspired the proliferation of Kossuth boots, Kossuth cigars, and the extremely popular Kossuth hats, all of which were duly advertised in the dailies. Throughout the visit, newspapers remained central in Kossuth's reception, both as vehicles for spreading his message and, more subtly, as the principal embodiments of a public whose support the Hungarian leader sought in winning aid from the U.S. government. Originally a journalist himself, Kossuth recognized the press as "that great controller of every word spoken by a public man," and conceded that "whenever and wherever I publicly speak, it is always chiefly spoken to the Press."[54] Perhaps for this reason, when Kossuth found it too noisy to deliver his prepared speech upon his arrival, he simply submitted it to the newspapers.[55] Though the outdoor hoopla attending Kossuth's appearance in New York was street theater, and though Kossuth was widely celebrated as a magnificent orator, the events of 1851 cannot be understood outside of the new print public created in and around the metropolitan press. The speeches and the crowds were products and extensions of the city's print culture, not vestiges of a now-romanticized era of politics unmediated. Four years later, Isaac Pray confirmed this relationship between oratory and print. "When the public Press did not report the speeches of citizens," he maintained, "there was little incitement to address audiences."[56]

Moments of collective celebration, such as the Kossuth visit, depended not only on the newspapers' advertising and coordinating events involving unwieldy numbers of city residents, but also on their construction of an intelligible and broadly inclusive public identity of New York. The phrase "public papers" thus alluded to the capacity of the newspaper to provide an identity for as well as access to the public. In other words, the metropolitan press created a space in which an increasingly diverse, dispersed, and contentious urban population could appear as a collective entity whose members' shared status as potential readers was inscribed into the columns of the daily papers.

All of this is not to suggest that newspapers embraced all perspectives and ideologies, accommodated the voices of all their readers (not to mention the minority who did not or could not read them), or faithfully represented all the conflicts endemic to life in an economically, socially, and culturally heterogeneous city. Despite the plethora of weekly journals dedicated to marginal constituencies and causes, the short-lived dailies addressed explicitly to women and to working men, the daily papers published in French and in German, and the rhetorical allusions, especially in ostensibly nonpartisan penny dailies such as the *Herald* and the *Sun*, to "every man and woman," the world of mass-circulation daily journalism was not an inclusive democracy. Running a successful daily became prohibitively expensive for most New Yorkers soon after the cheap papers arrived on the scene. Bennett claimed to have started the *Herald* with $500 in 1835; three years later the *Sun* was sold for $40,000, and by 1855 one informed observer estimated that it would require one or two hundred thousand dollars just to get a daily paper going in New York.[57] The most popular papers were controlled by a handful of men who belonged, almost by definition, to an elite social stratum. Most New Yorkers could express themselves in these public spaces only as advertisers (a mode of access and authorship not to be taken lightly), and many of their experiences were only dimly reflected in the mirror these papers held up before their readership.

The larger periodical press in antebellum New York included a striking range of New Yorkers, reflected much social, political, racial, and linguistic difference, and revealed the possibilities of using the press to create and solidify subcultures and subgroups. Foreign-language weekly newspapers (catering to immigrants from Ireland, Great Britain, France, Scandinavia, Italy, Latin America, and Central Europe) appeared throughout the late antebellum era alongside a range of specialty publications. Papers like the *Man*, the *Woman*, the *Ladies' Morning Star*, the

Courrier des Etats Unis (which began in 1851), and the more successful *Staats-Zeitung* even suggest a kind of fractured public, a starker and more extensive version of the social taxonomy Junius Browne attached to the newsstand.[58] Few of these papers thrived as dailies, however, and the best evidence suggests that the vast majority of New Yorkers relied upon mass-circulation papers that reflected a less differentiated picture of the urban public. The grand institution of the daily paper was thus actually narrow in perspective and unusually broad in public influence and symbolic function. Smaller, less successful, and less frequently published journals acquired an aura of publicness by virtue of their affinities with the larger ones, but the power of the metropolitan press was grounded in the regular appearance of widely read newspapers. And the major dailies were public not because they were responsive in all ways to everyone but because they projected meaningful notions of the public and of public access within their columns. This they did through exclusion as well as inclusion. The mass daily concealed political fractures and silenced alien voices that might have undermined the assumption that the city was a coherent subject of inquiry. At the same time, the juxtaposition of disparate elements offered a model for imagining such a subject.

As Anderson argues, the act of imagining a community always involves creating a fiction, positing relationships among people and events that may not be visible or recognizable without fictive techniques and tropes. For him, the newspaper, like the modern novel, connects events and people by presenting them as simultaneous. We might add that in the case of antebellum New York, the daily newspaper connected its subjects by presenting them as contiguous. The metropolitan press organized a community (and a public) around metaphors of space as well as metaphors of time, depicting people, events, products, and ideologies as sharing a crowded public space strikingly evocative (but not accurately reflective) of the city itself.

Largely because daily newspapers still enjoy this association with the public sphere, it is difficult to disentangle this inextricable link with the category of the public (a privilege more widely dispersed in the age of electronic media) long enough to reconstruct its formation. It is impossible to trace the various webs of association and identification through which residents and strangers in antebellum New York internalized the publicness of the daily paper, calibrated themselves to its rhythms, and naturalized its relationship to public space. Undoubtedly, New Yorkers brought countless divergent interests and tactics whenever they traversed the spaces of the newspaper and supported its claim to be a public document. Still, it is illuminating to explore the way one New Yorker used the papers in the construction of his own diary.

Edward Neufville Tailer Jr. was hardly a typical New Yorker. A highly successful import merchant and bank director, Tailer hobnobbed with the social elites and took extended trips with his wife to Europe. More singular still was the diary he kept, a sprawling multivolume document compiled over the course of sixty-nine years. Tailer's "Journal of Some of the Events Which Have Occurred in My Life Time" stands out among the nineteenth-century diaries collected by the New-York Historical Society not only for its length and ambition, but also for its extensive and elaborate use of newspapers. The early volumes, which begin in 1848 when Tailer was eighteen, include fairly typical accounts of how the author spent his time, describing lectures, social engagements, sailing expeditions, and fishing trips. During the early 1850s, Tailer shifts his attention a little toward politics and current events, as one might expect from the title of his journal, but most of the entries deal with developments in his business and quotidian details, such as the weather. Toward the end of the decade, however, newspaper clippings begin to appear alongside and within Tailer's text.[59]

At first, Tailer's clippings consist primarily of references to himself in the daily press (connections to the newspaper that would certainly have distinguished him from the average New Yorker), such as an 1857 list of passengers on the ship Persia, among them "Mr. & Mrs. E. N. Tailer, jun." Tailer's text also includes pasted-in articles describing charity banquets he attends, marriages of his friends, his acquaintances registered in Parisian banking offices, and similar points of contact between his daily life and the public record.[60] These sporadic excerpts from the daily papers serve to illustrate or spice up Tailer's personal narrative, but in the late 1850s the diary begins to invert this relationship, increasingly presenting newspaper clippings as the centerpieces of the text. Often the articles pasted in have little or no apparent relationship to Tailer and his daily affairs. A clipping included in a January 1858 entry marvels at the number of people who have died that month, a group large enough to form "a moving column of more than thirteen hundred to every mile of the circumference of the globe." Tailer's observation appears alongside the article, carving a circuitous path around the clipping: "Ladies are admitted to witness the Gentlemen exercise at Wood's Gym—& several of the fair sex were present this evening when I exercised."[61] The juxtaposition, perhaps motivated by some consciousness of his own mortality, is left unexplained (much in the spirit of the metropolitan press), as are many of the clippings over the next few years: *Times* accounts of nautical disasters mix freely with periodic articles from the *Journal of Commerce* detailing "the history of the Dry Goods trade for the past week."[62]

News clippings come to dominate Tailer's diary in several interesting ways. First, they proliferate markedly, turning the journal into a scrapbook. Tailer's collage of news extracts (often lengthy, sometimes multipage) from various dailies projects an evocative image of a man constructing his self-presentation out of a particular and privileged set of cultural artifacts. Within this self-presentation, moreover, the focus moves from how his daily life occasionally drifts into public view toward a construction of that daily life in relation to the public sphere, organized around Tailer's regular reading of the daily newspaper.[63] As the clippings multiply with the approach of the war, Tailer's diary becomes both a mock newspaper and a record of his daily reading habits.

Significantly, as the news pages grow more numerous and bulky, they become less conspicuous within Tailer's text, blending unobtrusively into one another and into the author/redactor's own contributions. Some entries (especially in the early 1860s) consist almost entirely of clipped war articles, obituaries, and miscellaneous news items. Clippings are often included without citations or other paratextual comments, and Tailer's handwritten entries increasingly resemble—in both tone and subject matter—his print sources. At certain points, the boundaries between original and appropriated texts appear deliberately unsettled. On July 2, 1858, Tailer notes in his characteristically journalistic style that "the removal of the remains of President Monroe from their long resting place in the Second st Cemetery took place this AM in N.Y."[64] A lengthy press description of the event appears on the opposite page of the journal, but where the article begins "Shortly after 2 o'clock yesterday afternoon," Tailer has crossed out the last two words so that the clipping can function within the diary's temporal framework. These continuities, though, do not quite obliterate the distinction between public and private writing; rather, they confer upon Tailer's diary as a whole the value associated with the newspaper. Whenever possible, Tailer employs news copy to describe the events that figure in his narrative, even when they relate to him personally and even when he has witnessed them himself. In the entry for Lincoln's inauguration, Tailer writes: "The accompanying letter, which I have cut from the Sunday Herald, will give the reader a capital idea of the inauguration ceremonies as I saw them in Washington."[65]

Such gestures seem calculated to enhance the public character of Tailer's own text, of which he is explicitly aware.[66] Throughout this period in his diary, the newspaper is clearly the model for the kind of public record Tailer is trying to create. Playing the role of editor, he clips larger and more numerous articles for events he considers notable—the death of Washington Irving in 1859, the visit of the Prince of Wales in 1860, the Draft Riots in 1863, the end of the war in 1865—and his summary remarks ("The year 1862 has drawn to a close, and to thousands has been a sad one, as the demands of a cruel civil war have summoned many a loved one to other than earthly scenes"[67]) have all the self-consciousness and ponderousness of a lead editorial. Tailer's diary aspires to the status of the newspaper, evoking the double meaning of the word "journal." But the fantasy is not solipsistic; at every turn it registers consciousness of being a public performance.[68]

What is most notable here is not that Tailer wrote for a public and to record the public events of his lifetime, but rather, first, that the clipped newspaper enjoys a monopolistic privilege in the construction of such a record, and second, that this public record can function at the same time as a personal diary. Of course, what allows for the dual status of the "Journal of Some of the Events Which Have Occurred in My Life Time" is the fact that the New York daily papers Tailer appropriates (even when they describe events that take place outside the city) are also his daily reading fare. Like in other anthologies of quotations, reading becomes writing, or writing poses as reading, except that the clippings Tailer presents are understood to belong generally to a community of readers and thus can stand for both himself and his society—they can represent his "Life Time" in both the individual and the collective senses of that phrase. This fictional connection between his life and his time links the diary and the daily in an unusually felicitous manner within Tailer's text, but their compatibility underscores how the New York dailies became easily appropriated instruments in individuals' self-presentations, powerful symbols and vehicles for finding a place and a way in an expanding city.

Part of what made newspapers such important documents for Edward Tailer—and for countless New Yorkers who did not bequeath scrapbooks to posterity—was their presumed authority. The impersonal, uniform type of the metropolitan press formed a kind of official language, much like the sign discourse described in chapter 3. Even when identified with a political party (as was the *Tribune*) or with a high-profile editorial personality (as was the *Herald*), newspapers became a space of public access because they circulated freely in the streets and were beyond the kinds of personal accountability associated with speech or personal correspondence. Yet the removal of these mechanically reproduced print documents from the physical presence of their authors raised problems of credibility. Numerous residents questioned the reliability of the New York press, and Russian visitor Aleksandr Lakier observed in 1857 that the American "does not trust the printed word."[69]

This mistrust of statements made impersonally in print may have been especially acute among social elites, who felt most threatened by the destabilizing impact of mass culture and whistled in the dark about the impotence of the popular press. Philip Hone reassured himself and the readers of his diary that "there is little dependence upon newspapers in a record of facts, any more, than in their political dogmas or confessions of faith." In his sketches of life among "the upper ten thousand," Charles Astor Bristed observed that "it is a standing American joke to say of the biggest possible hoax or *canard* 'I read it in a newspaper, and it must be true.' "[70] But beneath the jocular dismissal of newspapers' claims to authority lay a nervous recognition of increased social and cultural dependence on this authority and a recognition that, in the words of Edgar Allan Poe, "words—printed ones especially—are murderous things."[71]

In their attacks on the newspapers' credibility, critics acknowledged that the metropolitan press enjoyed a powerful presumption of authority. Hone charged that journalists, in "their avidity to have something new and in advance of others," mistake "the slightly grounded impressions of their informers for grave truths, setting upon them the stamp of authenticity, and sending them upon the wings of the wind to fill the ears and eyes of the extensive American family of the *gullibles*."[72] What disturbed Hone was not simply the sloppiness with which newspapers rushed out their "slightly grounded impressions" but the powerful "stamp of authenticity" impressed upon them. Novelist James Fenimore

Cooper, who attacked newspapers severely in *Home as Found* (1838) and whose battles with the press culminated in several libel suits, echoed Hone's suspicion of the insidious fraudulence of the newspaper in a non-fiction critique of American democracy. Taking on the widespread assumption that something "stated publickly in print [is] entitled to more credit and respect than the same fact or argument presented orally," Cooper demurred loudly: "He who would hesitate about committing himself by an allegation made face to face, and as it were on his personal responsibility, would indite a paragraph, behind the impersonality of his editorial character, to be uttered to the world in the irresponsible columns of a journal."[73] The paradox, as Cooper implied, was that print's impersonality permitted unreliable statements precisely because the medium was widely invested with credibility. Impersonality was both a license for irresponsibility and a mark of legitimacy.

Compounding this dilemma was the fact that as the city grew, residents and strangers turned to printed texts like newspapers for protection against the fraudulence of confidence men and impostors, widely feared figures who haunted the antebellum urban imagination.[74] The daily newspapers set themselves up as foils to what Bennett's biographer called "men ready to engage in plans for the purpose of deceiving the public."[75] Significantly, the first page of the first issue of the *Herald* was devoted almost exclusively to the story of the notorious Matthias, the false prophet accused of swindling and corrupting his followers. In the postscript to the article, Bennett warned:

> There is every reason to believe that the incredible imposture of Matthias is not an isolated event. Who knows but this great city and this huge state may not at this moment contain within its bosom, impostures going on equal in atrocity and beyond in absurdity to that of Matthias? . . . We trust we shall be able to publish the second part of this curious biography in our next number.[76]

Newspapers thrived on the widespread perception of the city as a mystery in need of deciphering, a land of tricksters and liars. Yet they were also caught up in the net of suspicion that they cast. Newspaper frauds such as Richard Adams Locke's famous Moon Hoax in 1837 (which fooled numerous readers into accepting an account of life on the moon and captured the imagination of Poe) flaunted the authority enjoyed by the penny press even as they compromised its credibility.[77] Print authority was thus paradoxically and disturbingly crucial to the recognition and exposure of the fault lines in the ground upon which it stood.

Newspapers figured prominently in the confidence games of the antebellum urban culture because the rival claims of personal and impersonal authority clashed and mingled uneasily in the early decades of mass publishing. The meanings of authority and authenticity in the age of mechanical reproduction became especially unstable in connection with printed texts that claimed to represent and transfer wealth, such as the dollar bills discussed in the next chapter. Newspapers gave this instability a particular urban cast by linking impersonal print authority with the impersonality of a city of strangers. In describing grisly murders, listing employment opportunities, reprinting speeches, reenacting parades, exposing frauds, and testing the limits of their readers' credulity, New York's dailies were assigning meaningful, if indistinct, identities to countless unknown and anonymous neighbors. Within the rectilinear columns of undifferentiated print, citizens appeared variously as voters, advertisers, victims, and cheats, but always as consumers, spectators, and readers. The underlying authority of these papers was rooted in the larger story they were continually renarrating: cheap dailies were being read and relied upon by so many people who shared the spaces of the city.

6

Promiscuous Circulation

~

The Case of Paper Money

"Paper money is fingered by a great many hands," observed William Leggett from the editorial page of the New York *Evening Post* on August 6, 1834, "as may be easily perceived from the soiled and worn appearance of many of the bills." For a radical Jacksonian Democrat such as Leggett, banknotes were something of a *bête noir*, and few *Post* readers would have been surprised to find its assistant editor railing against the evils of paper currency. At the end of the editorial, however, Leggett put forward an unusual strategy for attacking this scourge of the workingman. "A cheap . . . and most effectual method of disseminating the principles of those opposed to incorporated rag-money manufactories," he suggested, "would be for them to write upon the back of every banknote which should come into their possession, some short sentence expressive of their sentiments. . . . 'No Monopolies!' . . . 'Jackson and Hard Money!' 'Gold before Rags!' "[1] There is no evidence that *Post* readers took Leggett up on his ingenious proposal to turn dollars into political leaflets, or that they succeeded in shaming uncurrent bills out of circulation with legends like "*Wages of*

Iniquity," but it is worth pausing to consider the image. Historians have studied paper money from the perspective of its producers, its accumulators, its detractors, and its long-term function in a complex economy, but rarely from the perspective of its everyday users. Leggett's invocation of the quotidian act of passing a bill around the city illuminates the shadow life of the banknote and complicates his larger argument. While his slogans sound the familiar refrain against rag money, Leggett nonetheless recognized that banknotes were texts to be read, part of a network of written and printed words proliferating across the New York cityscape, and that these texts derived special power and appeal from the fact that they could address a broad and impersonal readership anonymously. Banknotes, like street signs, handbills, sandwich-board advertisements, parade banners, and daily newspapers, offered new possibilities of public communication; they both facilitated and dramatized the promiscuous circulation of strangers in an unfamiliar urban environment.

Banknotes differed from other urban texts in several important respects. They never labeled buildings or street corners and were rarely exposed to sustained public view. They were neither monumental like signs and banners nor disposable like handbills and newspapers. They also worked best when they did not have to be read at all—when they functioned unproblematically as vehicles for the transfer and exchange of goods and services. Still, paper money, like these other texts, extended the written word into more arenas of urban experience and raised many issues about writing and print as mediators of urban encounters. Banknotes elevated the stakes of the dependence on impersonal print authority that the new metropolitan press cultivated and accentuated, and introduced slippery and destabilizing questions of confidence in that authority into everyday life. At the same time, banknotes reinforced the power of city texts to promote anonymous exchange. Leggett's ironic awareness of the bank bill as a handbill—which found echoes throughout antebellum culture—reminds us that in a growing city during the state banking era, paper money was not simply an economic issue; it was also an urban issue.

From the perspective of an age when the dollar bill has acquired a certain transparency, when paper money seems a tautologous description of real wealth, classifying banknotes as texts may seem perverse or pedantic. But while we are now accustomed to identifying paper money by a quick glimpse of a number or the distinctive coiffure of a familiar dead president, antebellum Americans faced a completely different situation. Before the introduction of a uniform national currency during the Civil War, paper money consisted primarily of the various banknote issues of a rising number of state-chartered banks (as many as 1,500 of them by 1860) located throughout the country and difficult to distinguish by name. In New York State alone, there were eight "Union" banks issuing notes in 1863, as well as seven "Commercial" banks, seven banks identified with "Farmers," and seven more designated as "Merchants'" banks.[2] Banknotes appeared in a wide range of denominations (including one cent, nine cents, twelve and a half cents, one dollar seventy-five cents, and three thousand dollars, to name just a few),[3] bore a host of different historical and mythological icons ("vignettes," as they were called), and even varied in size. With over five thousand different note issues, not to mention bills of exchange, grain elevator receipts, mercantile credit instruments, postage stamps, store vouchers, and various forms of scrip that were passed as currency, the nation's paper money system was no simple index of quantitative value. Though cash, like other urban cultural institutions, linked unrelated people and objects in networks of circulation and exchange, nonuniform paper currency reflected and created its own set of differences.[4] The circulation of antebellum money involved an exchange of precarious and potentially competing claims to authority, much like those of advertisements in the daily paper or signs on a crowded street. Banknotes thus required a fair amount of scrutiny. Looking back at the 1830s from the relative stability of the postbellum period, merchant William Dodge noted proudly that "*now . . . we never think of looking at bank-bills.*" Five decades earlier, he recalled, money was "a perfect nuisance"; it had to be read.[5]

If paper money before the Civil War was radically unstable by later standards, it also marked a departure from earlier periods. Nineteenth-century urban Americans did not invent paper money, of course. At least since Marco Polo's descriptions of Chinese currency systems had strained the credulity of his European readers, Westerners had been familiar with the possibilities and problems of methods for counting, storing, and transferring wealth that did not rely on (and were not constrained by the bulk and availability of) metal coinage. In colonial North America, where government-authorized paper currency had first appeared in the West, monetary notes had been in circulation since the late seventeenth century.[6] Paper currency became both a useful tool and the subject of considerable anxiety. Americans frequently found occasion to doubt both the value of particular bills and the fundamental stability of a purely representative medium of exchange. The possibility that a given banknote might be an unauthorized imitation of a more reliable issue was clear to the colonists. According to numismatic historian Eric P. Newman, both the counterfeiting of bills and the raising of their denominations were common problems in the eighteenth century, prompting most colonies to make counterfeiting a capital offense. With the expansion of paper money production during the Revolutionary period, counterfeit detector sheets began to appear. Both Pennsylvania and the Continental Congress issued colored sheets of paper bearing the likenesses of authorized notes to be used by Treasury personnel in comparing suspect bills.[7] All the while, statesmen voiced serious concern over the use of paper as money. Mindful of the notorious depreciation of Continental currency, and ideologically attuned to what James Madison called "the pestilent effects of paper money on the necessary confidence between man and man, on the necessary confidence in public councils, on the industry and morals of the people, and on the character of republican government,"[8] the framers of the Constitution codified this discomfort, explicitly denying states the right to issue paper money and implicitly stripping the federal government of that power as well.

It might seem, then, that the antebellum experience of paper money was simply part of a long process by which the West adjusted to the demands for representative currencies. The mid-nineteenth century could be framed as just another chapter in the millennia-long transition from money that embodied and presented the wealth it symbolized to money that is wholly abstract, what literary critic Marc Shell describes as the journey from the electrum of ancient Lydia to the electricity of modern America.[9] The Jacksonian era marked a crucial and distinctive moment in this larger history, however, as banknotes came to dominate the American economy to an unprecedented extent. The banking business underwent revolutionary changes as new laws facilitated the proliferation of state banks of different sizes and varying degrees of stability. In the two decades before 1830, 165 American banks closed, and in New York, which did not have its first bank until after the Revolution, twenty different banks were in operation by the time of Jackson's second term, ten in shouting distance from one another on the same downtown block.[10] The growth and volatility of banks were symptoms of revolutionary economic and demographic changes (including urbanization, westward migration, improved transportation routes to the hinterland, and real estate speculation), and their proliferation attests to the rising importance of paper money and other transferable tokens of credit in urban economic life.

The state of banking in the nineteenth century also introduced new problems. Banks had multiplied (from 3 in 1784 to 88 in 1811, more than 300 in 1820, more than 900 in 1840, and more than 1,500 in 1860), their notes were now being issued and used as money (as a substitute for specie) rather than as promissory notes, and the value of paper currency bore little relation to available quantities of gold and silver. By the time of the Panic of 1837, the total face value of banknotes in circulation nationwide was almost four times the total value of specie.[11] Dollar bills referred to banks from all over the country, often in obscure and remote locations, and were largely unconnected to networks of trust familiar to the people who used them. Notes that passed in one place were often turned away in another. In the 1830s, according to one account, a traveler "starting from New Orleans for New York would have to change his currency several times in order to get funds that would be taken for fares or hotel bills."[12] Relying on over five thousand different note issues representing banks of varying solvency, the nation's monetary system during the antebellum period was, in the words of economist John Kenneth Galbraith, "without rival, the most confusing in the long history of commerce and associated cupidity."[13]

With the Civil War, everything changed. A uniform national currency was established in 1863, and within three years Congress's prohibitive tax on state notes had granted the new currency the status of a monopoly. The bewildering array of banknotes gave way to a simpler, more stable system. Counterfeiting was still a problem, but responsibility for its detection shifted, for the most part, from clerks and consumers to federal law enforcement agencies, specifically the Secret Service, established in 1865 for this very purpose.[14] The decades leading up to the war thus form a kind of chaotic interregnum—banknotes had already become economically indispensable, but they had not yet been stabilized and streamlined.

What this currency chaos meant to the daily lives of different groups of Americans remains a difficult question. As President Andrew Jackson turned the proposed rechartering of the Second Bank of the United States into the central issue of his presidency, paper money and the banking industry in general became highly fraught symbols of social and economic change in the national political imagination. In the neo-Jeffersonian rhetoric of the Bank's opponents and in the socialist rhetoric of labor activists, the banknote itself came to represent such evils as monopolistic privilege, unearned wealth, social inequality, a loss of virtuous independence, and the dissolution of the republic.[15] For middle-class reformers and cultural critics, the banknote and its counterfeit evil twin evoked the dangers of the big city and the treacherous instability of an urban society rife with confidence men and swindlers. Still, it is hard to say precisely what the connections were between larger political and cultural obsessions with money and banking and the more immediate, quotidian encounters between individuals and the paper with which they paid their bills, measured their worth, impressed their friends, and lined their pockets. In all cases, however, the meaning and the experience of paper money cannot be reduced either to its various practical economic purposes or to its overall long-term economic effects. Living with banknotes in a bustling city during this distinctive period involved certain kinds of encounters mediated by paper money and situated within a specific social and cultural context.

Though there is no way of determining exactly who used banknotes in antebellum New York, paper currency was clearly not just the instrument of a privileged class. Leggett and other radical Democrats ("Locofocos" as they were commonly known) concerned about rag money focused on the fact that workers suffered disproportionately from their extensive dependence on paper money. Writing as a college student in 1837, George Templeton Strong disputed this widespread assumption, characterizing the Locofoco constituency as "dock loafers and scavengers to whom bankbills are a rarity and whose circulating medium consists of coppers and sixpences and 'such small beer.' No bills to claim specie with are to be found in their pockets, even if they have any pockets to put them in." Such rhetoric needs to be taken with a grain of salt, however. On other occasions, elitist opponents of the Jacksonians disparaged workers on precisely opposite grounds. That same year, interestingly enough, Philip Hone blamed the failures of two banks on "the poor and the labouring classes of the community, who constitute a large proportion of the depositors of those institutions."[16] Whether or not working-class New Yorkers were systematically victimized by a paper money system many of them held in deep suspicion, banknotes were important in their everyday lives. Much less clear is how access to banknotes broke down along lines of gender and could be used to regulate control of resources within a given household, but frequent references to women handling money (as wives, daughters, vendors, and criminals) preclude any possibility that paper money was a private pass system for the internal use of a specific sector of society. Banknotes were portable, transferable texts suitable for circulation among strangers. They referred to a realm of exchange that was inclusive and open-ended, though exploitative and unequal.

Thus while the use of paper money was becoming more widespread throughout the country and throughout the century, it had particular impact and meaning in antebellum New York. For residents and visitors in the center of both banking and printing in the United States, the resonance of paper money and the visibility of the currency chaos were especially acute. Manhattan was the headquarters of the three largest banknote manufacturers in the country, and remained the material and symbolic capital of counterfeiting activity throughout the nineteenth century. More important, the promiscuous intermingling of bills and people from all over the country and abroad increased both the variety of banknotes in circulation and the likelihood that a banknote would be the only thing to pass between two anonymous individuals. Paper money marked and constructed these fleeting, anonymous encounters in interesting ways.

On the surface, banknotes appeared to represent a personal agreement. Bank cashiers and bank presidents, whose signatures appeared on the bills, promised to pay a certain amount of money in specie (or current bills, in some cases). Often, a note would identify by name the particular party to whom the promise was made (see specimen of a City Bank one-dollar bill in fig. 6.1), so that no matter how widely the bill circulated, any subsequent use would commemorate and draw upon the original transaction, much in the manner of a personal check signed over to an unlimited number of third parties. The typography of banknotes reaffirmed this ostensibly personal character of the fiduciary commitments they encoded. The name and location of the issuing bank tended to appear in block letters and the promise to pay on demand was typically printed in cursive, while the authenticating signatures, the

FIGURE 6.1 Specimen bill, City Bank, New York, c. 1810.

• • •

name of the original bearer, and the number of the note would be
marked in idiosyncratic handwriting. The typographic regularity of
newspapers and store signs evoked impersonal authority, yet banknotes
seemed to represent some individual accountability within a city of
strangers. On occasion, a banknote could even serve as an identification
card for a stranger caught in the urban maelstrom. When a visitor from
Ohio in 1843 had his money snatched while in the embrace of prostitute Melinda Hoag, his ability to identify the banknotes he had been car-
rying helped convict Hoag and her male accomplice, both of whom
were in possession of incriminating bills.[17] More often, however, banknotes preserved few traces of their previous owners, simply transferring
a tenuous claim to value from one person to another. After extensive
efforts to collect money from a difficult client who claimed to be a min-
ister, cartman Isaac Lyon finally received his pay, but discovered to his
chagrin when he tried to pass the notes at a butcher's that the notes were
Canadian and worth only eighty-five cents to the dollar. Just when Lyon
thought he had overcome the miserliness of the hypocritical clergyman,
the banknotes revealed otherwise, eventually pointing Lyon to the con-
clusion that his client was an urban confidence man who ran a gambling
outfit and a shoplifting operation.[18] All rhetoric and appearances to the
contrary notwithstanding, paper money thus registered personal
absence; once bills changed hands, all access to and accountability of the
individual who passed them disappeared as well. And like other urban
texts, banknotes addressed their readers impersonally and indifferently.

They spoke to the bearer, who in principle could be anyone and therefore was no one in particular.

The ground underlying this system of impersonal urban exchange was especially unstable, since every encounter involving paper currency raised the possibility that a given bill was from a failed bank, from a fictitious bank, or utterly counterfeit. Several scholars have estimated that as much as 40 percent of circulating paper currency was fake.[19] More significant, both culturally and economically, than the extent of actual counterfeiting (which by its nature is hard to determine) was the extent of the suspicion. Here the picture is clearer. A survey of the counterfeit detectors for 1856 revealed 1,409 separate banks listed, of which only 463 were *not* cited as targets of counterfeiting. Another study, appearing six years later in the New York *Times*, estimated that "out of 1,300 banknote issues but one hundred are not counterfeited" and that every open bank issuing notes in New York City had been the object of imitation.[20] Against the backdrop of increased circulation and use of paper currency, a steady chorus of panic ran through the press during the antebellum years. In 1837 the *Journal of Commerce* ventured that "at no period, perhaps, were there ever so many counterfeits afloat, of every description, as at present. Scarcely a day passes without one or two cases of the kind coming before the Police."[21] In 1840 the *Sun* proclaimed: "We have never known counterfeiting carried on to a more alarming extent than at present. We were shown yesterday a one dollar bill on the Atlantic Bank of Brooklyn, altered to a ten in so ingenious a manner as to have deceived all but the most wary." With apparently unintended irony, the article urged caution "on the part of those who are in the habit of receiving money."[22] Early in the following decade, a magazine article claimed that "there have never been in the History of Banking, such vast quantities of counterfeit paper thrown upon the community as at this period."[23] By 1862, the *Times* was claiming that four fifths of the banknotes in circulation were fake and that the practice of counterfeiting was "undermining our morality as a nation."[24]

Still more common than fake bills were circulating banknotes that were no longer current and could only be redeemed for specie at a discount. Even notes that had not become dated were often subject to significant and fluctuating redemption discounts. Leggett reported that it was "common practice" for employers to pay workers their weekly wages in depreciated bills that had been purchased from brokers expressly for the purpose of cutting labor costs by reducing the real value of wages.[25] During periods of economic crisis, the status of banknotes was further compromised by widespread refusals to give specie as change for paper money, and the substitution of store vouchers and, increasingly, postage stamps. Novelist Frederick Marryat reported that after the collapse of the economy in 1837 many shopkeepers "had been obliged to turn away a hundred dollars a day" and that visitors from the South were forced to live like paupers despite having arrived with large supplies of bills.[26]

Occasionally, a fraudulent banknote might be glaringly obvious. A phony bill in Horatio Alger Jr.'s *Ragged Dick* (1868) is confidently and unhesitatingly recognized as such by both of the honest adults in the scene, and an 1842 publication describes a counterfeit Maine note as "so miserably executed that a blind man could detect it by the touch."[27] More often, though, the legitimacy or value of a bill was not immediately apparent to the uninitiated, whether or not counterfeiting was suspected. Arriving hungry in New York in the 1820s, English actor Joe Cowell had to trade in his silver coins, which had been rejected at a herring shop for being of foreign origin, to "an honest Israelite" in return for "three dirty, ragged one-dollar bills" that Cowell found utterly inscrutable, though the dealer assured him they were better than gold. Relating the incident two decades later with the benefit of superior knowledge, Cowell observed: "As all I wanted then was that they should be better than silver, my politics at that time didn't cavil at the currency, and I hastily retraced my steps to the red-shirted herring dealer." Much to his relief, the herring dealer considered "the dirty scraps of paper" to be "as *good* as gold," and Joe Cowell ate his first meal in the United States.[28] Subsequent encounters with this paper sign system were undoubtedly better informed (by politics, Cowell's remarks suggest, as well as by mere familiarity), but the nuances of an unwieldy banknote system highly vulnerable to counterfeiting could elude seasoned New Yorkers as well.

Paper money thus joined such texts as store signs, sandwich boards, and hawked dailies to form a system of urban hieroglyphics, part of the mystery of the city that could only be decoded by connoisseurs. One guide to appraising currency published in 1863 observed that "every one who has tried it, knows that when a note is handed to a banker, to judge whether it is good or not, he . . . looks at the bill itself, and answers you in a moment."[29] A reference guide published a year later describes the expertise of a bank teller in reading bills in a suitably mystifying way:

To stand by and observe him counting, it might be supposed that he could hardly get a glimpse of each, so rapidly do they pass through his hands. He looks as if he were trying how many times he could strike the ends of his fingers together in the twentieth part of a second; but you see a steady stream of bills issuing beneath them and gradually gathering into a pile. There goes one aside, without perceptible pause in the handling! He checks the item on the list, and with his right hand thrusts the pile into a drawer, whilst with the left he tosses the single bill back to the depositor.

"Counterfeit—five dollars off."

He makes the entry, deducting it from the list, hands the book to the dealer, and takes the next in order, in which there is a package of mixed denominations of several hundred dollars. He gives it a smack on the counter to loosen the bills, and a peculiar toss, which makes them fall over like leaves of a book, affording an instantaneous glance at their ends. His eye has caught in that instant an old acquaintance. . . . This is very curious to an inexperienced observer. But there are certain well-known spurious and altered bank bills, which are distinguished by a quick teller, as well as the countenance of said teller's landlord who approaches to ask for his quarter's rent.[30]

But while the knowing clerk became a privileged figure in urban mythology, many New Yorkers turned to other guides to help them decipher the distressingly opaque money-texts they carried around in their pockets. Between 1826 and 1866, an impressive array of counterfeit journals (primarily weekly, semimonthly, and monthly periodicals, though there were also annual "delineators" and "descriptive lists") offering information on discounted, counterfeit, and altered banknotes sprang up in several of the nation's largest cities, most notably New York, where well over a dozen different publishers produced them. New York's counterfeit detectors, such as *Dye's Counterfeit Detector and Universal Banknote Gazetteer*, *Sylvester's Reporter, Counterfeit Detector, New York Prices Current and General Advertiser*, and the *German Banknote Reporter*, were generally the height and width of the smaller daily newspapers, though most were substantially longer, often running sixteen or thirty-two pages. The most popular of these publications, the *Banknote and Commercial Detector* by John Thompson, appeared as often as six days a week and claimed a national circulation of 100,000 by 1855.[31]

At subscription rates generally running between fifty cents (per issue for a monthly) and twelve dollars (per year for a daily), periodical detectors were purchased primarily by merchants and people engaged in frequent exchanges of large quantities of money. Still, they did not lie beyond the reach and concern of more modest New Yorkers. Citing the fact that "considerable amounts, in small bills of broken banks or counterfeits, have been lost by the industrious poor throughout the United States," the editors of the *New Monthly Messenger* addressed their new banknote detector in 1842 to a readership that "cannot afford to subscribe even to a weekly city journal."[32] Even New Yorkers who never purchased or even perused these papers were bound to notice them in the possession and use of clerks, tellers, and other people with whom they had frequent interaction. Describing the currency chaos of the Civil War, for example, Charles T. Harris recalled the sight of "cashiers [wearing] out their thumbs pawing over Kemper's (I think it was Kemper's) Banknote Detector, to see which was good and which was in the discard."[33] One way or another, anyone who used banknotes was affected by the widespread availability of texts that could be used to undermine the value of his or her money.

Far from being obscure trade journals for the private use of experts, counterfeit detectors were, like the banknotes whose claims to legitimacy they adjudicated, a visible part of everyday city life. Their broader cultural impact, however, lay in the complex shadows they cast over the use of paper money, limned brilliantly by Herman Melville in his 1857 novel *The Confidence-Man: His Masquerade.* In one of the last of countless reading scenes in Melville's novel, an old man pores over a counterfeit detector he has picked up from a peddler boy making his rounds on the riverboat. Coming so late in the novel, the detector serves a double function. In one sense it is the classic confidence text, a climactic example of the complex way printed documents are used on board the *Fidèle* both to arouse and to combat suspicion of financial ruses and frauds, in which the novel itself is potentially implicated. At the same time, however, the counterfeit detector pulls the rug out from under all previous confidence games by calling into question the one printed document whose stability the reader has come to rely upon. As posted signs, stock transfer books, and Bibles are peddled about the ship, the reader learns one rule for spotting the con artist: watch for the man who walks away with the dollar bills. Yet with the introduction of the final text, the reliability of this sign system is called into question as well. There is no escape from the flimsy paper foundations of value in the world of Melville's novel. As the old man notices, examining his dollars in search of red spots, micro-scopic geese, and other authenticating signs listed in the detector, "there's so many marks of all sorts to go by, it makes it kind of uncer-tain."[34]

Melville's use of the counterfeit detector underscores the paradox of confidence and authority in printed words—an especially compelling theme in Melville's narrative, which is saturated with texts, from hand-bills of anonymous poetry to business cards to Roman histories.[35] Beyond the confines of this largely unpopular novel, these paradoxes of print reliability resounded throughout a middle class anxious about rela-tions among strangers in an acquisitive, market-oriented, urbanizing society. As historian Karen Halttunen has argued, the moral and episte-mological dilemmas posed by the confidence man motivated and under-wrote many of the codes and formations that constituted bourgeois cul-ture in the mid-nineteenth century.[36] Counterfeit detectors dramatized these dilemmas, reaching beyond middle-class journals and etiquette guides to the most mundane moments of commercial exchange. As Melville's text illustrates, counterfeit detectors brought paper money back into the realm of print culture by stripping the banknote of its priv-ileged status as a text that did not have to be read. The authors of a note (who want their bills to remain in perpetual circulation) sought to create a text so transparent, so identical with its referent, that a twenty-dollar bill could *be* twenty dollars rather than a paper promise from an unknown bank president to pay twenty dollars in specie (an aspiration largely achieved by the twentieth century). Counterfeit detectors, by con-trast, promoted an extremely careful, though potentially destabilizing, reading of paper money. For while they discouraged taking banknotes at face value, they nonetheless attributed significance to every mark appearing on the bills.

Most counterfeit detectors identified failed banking institutions, pro-vided rates of exchange on uncurrent bills, and gave prices of various commodities. The heart of these texts, though, was the list of reported counterfeits and the criteria to be used in identifying them. Most detec-tors distinguished three categories of phony currency. The term "coun-terfeit" was often used in a restricted sense to refer to unauthorized fac-similes of actual banknotes in circulation, whereas "altered" bills were notes whose bank name, bank location, or (most often) denomination had been changed. "Spurious" bills had no specific resemblance to any legitimate currency, and often bore the names of fictitious institutions. Breaking down their lists by state and frequently adopting typographical codes for distinguishing particular types of banks or types of fraudulence, a given issue might enumerate thirty pages' worth of suspect bills, labeling some as the issues of insolvent institutions, designating others as unsellable in New York, and providing criteria for picking out the counterfeits. Sometimes the identifying marks were reasonably clear and straightforward, such as signatures of wrong bank officers or words appearing on the wrong side of the bill. Frequently, however, they were as obscure and comical as those in Melville's fictional example. An early issue of *Day's New-York Banknote List, Counterfeit Detector and Price Current,* for example, instructed readers to examine a particular three-dollar bill issued by a Hartford bank for counterfeits marked by a "boat too wide— oxs tail too short—hole in post too distinct" and impugned the credibility of a Bank of New York note in which the "face in the vignette is not sufficiently expressive, and the eyes are too round and full."[37]

Counterfeit guides shifted attention away from a bill's intended purpose to its fine print, much like the parody of a five-dollar bill in fig. 6.2, in which the proprietors of the Mechanics' Bank promise *not* to pay the bearer—a small detail that might escape the notice of a careless reader. In an interesting enactment of the symbolic battle over how to read paper money that was being waged, willy-nilly, between the producers of banknotes and the vigilant detectors, John Thompson successfully sued the Union Bank of New York in 1836 for nonpayment of one of its $500 notes. A banknote broker at the time, Thompson was in the habit of bringing in bills for redemption, and the bank was giving him the runaround and delaying payment. In the jury instructions, the presiding judge emphasized the precise meaning of the words on the bill, requiring the bank to pay *on demand.* With the issue so neatly framed by the contractual terms printed on the note, the jury found for the plaintiff.[38] When Thompson embarked six years later on his first counterfeit detector, he parlayed this same insistence that banknotes should be read and not simply recognized as money—an almost Barnumesque reliance on literal readings of sparse, freestanding texts—into a lucrative and culturally significant publishing practice.

Though they were popular and influential, periodical counterfeit detectors had several significant deficiencies, as numerous critics were quick to point out—especially those who were promoting an alternative

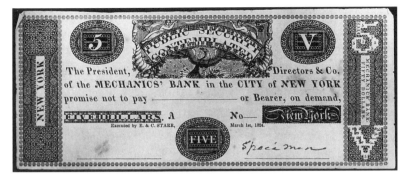

FIGURE 6.2 Bogus bill, Mechanics' Bank, New York, 1824.

• • •

genre of counterfeit detector, such as the nonserial guides that claimed to teach readers general principles in the identification of phony bills. First, critics claimed, counterfeit lists reported on bad money too late, only after substantial damage had been done. One 1863 text observed that for the victim of a successful counterfeit, "it would be better . . . if the Detector never came, as he might divide his loss by getting rid of a part of his bogus money."[39] Skeptics also suggested that these periodicals encouraged a false sense of security. By advertising certain betraying signs of imposture, the detectors concealed others; by marking a few notes as frauds, they implied approval of the rest. "If the dealers had not these false guides," one 1859 guide to spotting genuine currency declared, "they would be more circumspect in their operations of the money they take." Another publication pointed out that counterfeiters could manipulate the detectors to their own advantage for this reason.

> [A] forger will prepare his plate as perfectly as possible in every part but one, which is designedly left imperfect to attract notice. A horse, for instance, will be represented with but three legs. The Note will be immediately advertised in the Lists, as a dangerous counterfeit, with its imperfections specified. The Counterfeiter will now correct his plate, and forthwith print and circulate his Bills, with less chance of detection.

Even if "the Counterfeiter has not the ingenuity to do this by design," the argument continued, the result was the same, "for it is natural that the first thing he will think of after his fraudulent production has been noticed by the detector, will be, to alter his plate, so that it will not correspond to the description given."[40] More generally, policing individual counterfeits tended to shift attention away from the precariousness of paper money as a whole. S. J. Sylvester expressed understandable (if debatable) optimism that his banknote detector would "be a good medium of setting forth the stability of Monied Institutions."[41]

On the other hand, several observers worried about exactly the opposite. Overly vague distinguishing criteria tended to cast a wide net of doubt, which was likely to call legitimate notes into question as well. Typically, counterfeit bills were called "well done," "well executed," or, as in one 1837 example, "calculated to deceive such as are not familiar with the notes of that bank."[42] Such warnings, as well as the countless instructions dealing with shades of color, fullness of figures in the vignettes, or subjective assessments of verisimilitude could well have the general effect, as in Melville's text, of undermining the entire system of confidence on which paper currency was based. At the very least, this sort of listing would discourage anyone from accepting any version of the note in question, however authentic. "Detectors only serve to bewilder a common man, and make him afraid to take a good bill," averred an 1863 publication whose author claimed to have seen more than a hundred instances of unwarranted suspicion. Due to the impact of the detectors, "men are often compelled to carry a good bill for weeks before they can get it off, and then have to make a bargain to take it back if further refused."[43] Counterfeit detectors impeded the free circulation of paper currency by introducing a virus of suspicion into a medium that depended on confidence.

While periodical detectors were highly imperfect antidotes to the antebellum paper money crisis, anticounterfeit publications of all kinds faced an additional problem associated with print culture during this period. In publicizing the methods used to replicate or modify banknotes, these texts inevitably offered lessons in counterfeiting. Anticounterfeit tracts could have the same effect (however unintended) as the famous brothel directories that advertised the addresses and attractions of the city's various houses of prostitution under the thin guise of expressing outrage and arousing public opposition.[44] Counterfeit detectors and guides often included pictures of fake bills, specimens of counterfeit plates, or facsimiles of real ones, providing exemplary illustrations of the art of replicating currency. Moreover, in an effort to impress upon readers the ease with which banknotes could be altered, the text of these books would frequently demystify the process in a most instructive manner. An 1851 issue of *Thompson's* described the method of "pasting the figures 3, 5, 10, &c. over 1's and 2's, and the words expressing the value of the bill."[45] Others were more helpful. "A torn bank bill can be mended as strong as ever by straightening out the pieces perfectly level," one book pointed out, "and then wetting the edges with the mouth, and placing the pieces together just as it was before it was torn, then placing it between several sheets of paper and pressing down carefully, and then putting it in a book to dry." In the margins of the copy of this book held at the New-York Historical Society someone penciled "try this."[46] Like the bills themselves, counterfeit guides were thrust into a promiscuous circulation beyond the control of their authors and publishers, and were better positioned to advertise the abuses of the paper money system than to create a firm bulwark against them.

All these deficiencies underscored the Melvillean suspicion that there was no escape from the circular crisis of confidence as it played itself out in print culture. If the problem with banknotes is that they are just pieces of mechanically reproducible paper, then any attempt to create a printed means of judging their claims will be subject to the same suspicions. If shaky financial institutions or enterprising counterfeiters could put out bad notes, they could also issue unreliable detectors. The *Herald* urged readers in 1841 "to be careful how they put confidence in these 'Reporters' and 'Bank Detectors,' which inundate the community," charging that these texts were thoroughly implicated "in all the financial tricks of the age." The particular target of James Gordon Bennett's suspicion in this case was the Philadelphia-based *Bicknell's Reporter*, which had recommended the notes of a Michigan bank as accepted by a particular insurance company in Ohio. "This statement is now contradicted by the Ohio Life and Trust," the article claimed, "and no doubt the River Raisin Bank, is one of those impudent speculations which are got up in conjunction with such fraudulent prints as 'Bicknell's Reporter.' "[47] Though the *Herald* certainly had its own axes to grind in impugning particular counterfeit detectors, the article properly disabused readers of any expectation that banknote reporters lay somehow outside the networks of interest and speculation that had brought paper currency under suspicion. Many publishers of detectors were also dealers in banknotes and other speculative ventures. Like almost all of his New York colleagues (with the exception of Mahlon Day), John Thompson sidelined as a lottery broker, and some banknote detectors (especially that of S. J. Sylvester) devoted considerable space to lottery advertisements and results. Thompson's main business, though, was as a dealer in uncurrent banknotes; the banknote tables that were standard features in counterfeit detectors typically listed rates of discount at which the publisher-editor himself would redeem the notes in question.[48] Sylvester placed advertisements in his detector claiming to "continue to give the highest price for most Broken Bank Bills."[49] Though each detector stood to gain the greatest profit from acquiring a reputation as the most reliable public watchdog (a pose assumed often and volubly), there was no way to elevate the genre as a whole above the doubts upon which it was founded.

But if detectors were in one sense institutions of speculative finance, they were also journals; their claims became embroiled in the games of confidence associated with print culture as well as those particular to the paper currency market. The world of the counterfeit reporter merged significantly with that of the metropolitan press. While most of the individuals who produced detectors were also brokers, they were all (by definition) publishers. Some, like Mahlon Day (who in addition to pioneering the periodical counterfeit detector published numerous children's books), were involved in extensive printing ventures, many of which had little to do with banking.[50] Well-known detector publishers could also become embroiled in the lively interjournal disputes that spiced up life in both the streets of lower Manhattan and the pages of the penny press. In addition to his quarrels with editors of other bank reporters, Thompson frequently clashed with Moses Beach of the *Sun*, and won a libel suit against him. At the same time, the city's daily papers shared the territory claimed by the detectors. Traditional six-penny journals like the *Journal of Commerce* and the *Commercial Advertiser* retained an emphasis on mercantile news that regularly included information on banking and currency, and even cheaper papers like the *Herald* and the *Sun*, whose reputations were more often attached to sensationalized crime stories, devoted considerable space to such questions.[51] Bennett's money market columns were a central feature of the *Herald*, and were scarcely less detailed in their discussions of specific banks than many counterfeit reporters. The *Sun*, for its part, actually published a bank detector, which the *Herald* predictably characterized as "unworthy of confidence by the public."[52]

By engaging in disputes about the reliability of particular banknotes, the daily press called attention to the overlaps and interpenetrations between the confidence games of newspapers and those of paper currency. In 1841, to take a suggestive example, the *Herald* attacked the *Sun* for using its influence to puff the notes of two banks, the Jacksonville Bank and the Manufacturers' Bank of Ulster. Moses Beach himself had purchased the notes of the suspect Florida bank and, according to a Boston newspaper friendly to Bennett, the Manufacturers' Bank, "although nominally located at Ulster . . . is in reality located at the office of . . . the 'Sun.' " Beach counterattacked, accusing Bennett of trying to depreciate sound currency.[53] The conflict called public attention to the interests and predicaments shared by newspapers, counterfeit detectors, and banknotes themselves. Beach's efforts to raise the circulation of his paper and of his banknotes (redeemed at discount, of course) merge, just as Bennett's constant political attacks on "shinplaster" currency tangle inextricably with his struggle to promote confidence in his own paper. Bennett offers a glimpse of this muddled culture of suspicion when he quotes a characterization of the rival daily as "the advocate of rag banks, and the organ of quack doctors in general, and Madame Restell [the abortionist] in particular." Casting a typically wide and ironically self-referring net of skepticism over the world of published texts, Bennett then warns "the honest portion of the public [against] trusting in the integrity of such prints."[54]

Like the banknotes they evaluated on the one hand, and the daily newspapers they paralleled on the other, counterfeit detectors depended on public confidence in order to circulate and on circulation in order to acquire value. Threatening this confidence, however, was a profound fear of imposture that extended beyond paper money to pervade the entire print culture in which both the banknotes and the detectors were embedded. As S. J. Sylvester learned in 1838, even detectors could be counterfeited. "A paper having lately appeared in this city under the title of '*Sylvester's NEW Reporter*,' " he warned his readers, "I deem it advisable . . . to state that the name of my paper remains unchanged, and I am still at 130 Broadway, where I have been for *thirteen* years past—and of course have not removed therefrom."[55] The *Herald* also expressed anxiety over "various attempts, from many quarters, to impose fraudulent statements upon us, even to the forgery of our name and reputation."[56] Of course, warning against frauds and spurious imitations functioned as an advertising gimmick, an early attempt to link brand name identity with quality. An 1841 ad for Payson's Indelible Ink appearing in Day's detector cautioned that some competitors "have put up their counterfeits in the same style, and copied his name and directions word for word, so that many have bought a worthless article, under the name of Payson's Ink." But if advertisers co-opted the language of counterfeit detection for promotional effect, their strategies also reflected particular anxieties connected with the spread of print. For as the case of paper money illustrates, it was now easier to send the same message to a wide range of people but harder to assure the integrity of that message and to prevent others from replicating it. The possibility of making money or developing a reputation through the mechanical reproduction of printed messages also destabilized the grounds of personal identity upon which fortune and fame had previously been built.

Paper money and the widespread fear of counterfeits thus crystallized a powerful paradox endemic to the proliferation of print. More than other printed documents, banknotes relied on a particular interplay of replication and singularity. On the one hand, the notes' power to circulate came from their resemblance to other identical tokens for which they could be substituted. On the other hand, the notes' authenticity came from their relationships to specific authorizing banks. Paper money had to be both a perfect copy and, at the same time, unique. Moreover, visible resemblance had to provide the grounds for assuring both power to circulate and authenticity. Much of the confusion filling the pages of antebellum counterfeit guides stems from this paradox. Attempts to safeguard paper currency against unauthorized imitation leaned alternately (and sometimes simultaneously) on personal imprints and on the power of the machine for guarantees of authentic value.

As might be expected, counterfeit guides placed great emphasis on the personal signatures appearing on banknotes as authenticating marks. Since banknotes were promises to pay specie, the signatures represented acknowledgments of debt and invested the bills with individual authority. In colonial times, recipients of suspicious notes required payers to affirm additional personal responsibility for the debt expressed in the bill by inscribing their names on the backs (much as we do now when we sign over personal checks), a practice preserved for posterity by the appearance of several signatures on some old currency.[57] The use of signatures as stamps of authenticity was a feature of paper money that extended into other cultural arenas in which authenticity became an issue. In the example of Payson's Indelible Ink, customers were instructed to look for the owner's written signature, "as security against counterfeits."[58] Advertisements for the notorious Madame Restell's "Female Monthly Pills" from around the same time warned of "counterfeits and imitations" and offered Restell's signature on the corner of each box as a mark of the genuine article.[59] Such signatures, though, were still just written words, no more sacred than the word "confidence," which one of Melville's characters has "water-marked in capitals" as the guarantor of authenticity and efficacy contained on the boxes of his "Omni-Balsamic Reinvigorator."[60] Faith in the power of signatures to secure banknotes persisted, though, based not only on the notion of personal authority they conveyed, but also on the assumption that each signature bore the inimitable mark of its author. Graphic distinctiveness promised to restore to banknotes a visible trace of the unique. In addition to his *Banknote Reporter*, Thompson also published (and sent to his subscribers free of charge) an *Autographical Counterfeit Detector*, "containing fac-simile signatures of the President and Cashier of every bank in the United States" (see fig. 6.3). These guides, which may have been as useful to counterfeiters as to their intended victims, accentuated the subversive irony of producing facsimiles of the unique to prevent counterfeiting.

Both bankers and authors of counterfeit guides worried considerably about the threat posed by new print technologies to the integrity of paper money. Since visual resemblance remained the foundation of authenticity, advances in lithography and photography could have highly subversive consequences. George Lyman of the New York Clearing-House noted in 1857: "The wonderful art of producing and copying pictures . . . has recently been so perfected and simplified as to have seriously endangered all paper currency."[61] An anecdote circulating in the 1850s told of a banker who accepted a photographed counterfeit bill because it bore an incontrovertibly faithful reproduction of his own signature.[62]

In response to this challenge, many self-styled currency experts continued to invoke the notion of a personal imprint as security against fraud by shifting the focus to a different set of banknote authors. In an 1856 lecture, John Dye, publisher of a periodical detector as well as *Dye's Banknote Delineator*, explained that "the true way to detect a counterfeit is not always by the signatures, but by the workmanship." If signatures

FIGURE 6.3 *Autographical Counterfeit Detector*, fifth edition, 1853.

• • •

could be reproduced, Dye reasoned, the expertise of the engraver could not. "Most counterfeits can be detected by the imprint alone," he insisted.[63] Others pointed to various indices of artistic quality ("the hair on a genuine portrait always looks easy and natural . . . see if the faces look round, easy and expressive, having a natural expression of the eye")[64] as sure marks of legitimate currency. Former engraver W. L. Ormsby argued in 1852 that the ease with which banknotes were forged was the result of a patchwork system that stripped the bill of artistic unity. "The whole surface of the Bill should be covered with one unbroken and inseparable design," he contended, "with the lettering so interwoven by the hand of the Artist, as to form an integral part of the design." Describing the engraving process in a manner that echoed widespread cultural concerns over the deleterious impact of technology and labor reorganization on the skilled crafts, Ormsby envisioned a system of paper money in which "the security against imitation or alteration will be exactly in proportion to the ingenuity of the design, the talent of the Artist, and the amount of labor bestowed upon it."[65] Evidence of workmanship was, of course, a limited guarantee of a good banknote. As an 1859 guide published in New Hampshire pointed out, the engraver of a legitimate banknote at one time could be in the employ of a counterfeiter at another.[66] Ironically, Ormsby himself appears to have crossed over the line, producing plates for at least twenty-two separate banknotes for New York counterfeiter Joshua Minor.[67] Despite these limitations, however, the impulse to locate the sign of a genuine banknote in the impress of an individual author was powerful and pervasive.

While many guides sought to link authenticity with artistic distinctiveness and integrity, others looked to the technology itself to outpace the counterfeiters. The New Hampshire publication neatly inverted the relationship between the human hand and the machine, claiming that since much counterfeiting was done manually, bogus notes would lack the telltale signs of uniformity. No two lines, dies, or medallions would be exactly alike.[68] To prevent photographed counterfeits, defenders of the banknote turned first to colored currency and then to special green inks that could not be removed without defacing the paper or erasing the black ink underneath. "This important desideratum has . . . been attained in the 'green ink,' " an 1863 guide announced, "for the use of which the American Banknote Company holds the exclusive patent." The public would then have to learn exactly which parts of the bill were supposed to appear in the distinctive green color.[69] An 1858 text described a similar plan of defense, wherein "a banknote . . . printed in TWO PERMANENT INKS, would be protected against the possibility of imitation" by lithography and photography.[70] Characteristically, whereas writers like Ormsby had presented engraving as creating art

that could not be reproduced by assembling its constituent parts, counterfeit guides that downplayed the role of workmanship in favor of
mechanical uniformity explained the technology of banknote production in elaborate and demystifying detail. Relying on the possibility that
banks could gain privileged access to new print technologies, these pro-
posals accepted the inevitable limitations of the personal imprint and
hoped that, in the words of one proponent, science might "remedy the
evil which it had occasioned."[71]

These conflicting strategies for imposing order on the process of
inspecting paper money expressed divergent responses to the expansion
of print technology. At the same time, they reflected the dual status of
the banknote as both original and replica. Lurking behind this paradox,
of course, was the troubling fact that an original only existed as long as
a replica failed to be sufficiently faithful; upon close inspection, the
notion of the original disappeared altogether. Though the banknote
promised the reappearance of its author as redeemer, the one to recognize original intent in the paper copy, the real value of the note (even
when it was being returned to the bank for specie, which, after all,
required the same process of recognition) lay in its ability to pass unobtrusively as an identical copy. Frazar Kirkland's 1863 reference guide to
business relates the story of a businessman's unsuccessful attempt to
invalidate a check that bore his signature but of which he had no recol-
lection. Unable to identify visible signs of forgery and unprepared to dis-
own the signature under oath, he was forced to honor the check. Without
visible traces of difference, a bad bill was in fact a good bill, and (as the
banker confronted with his own photographed signature discovered)
there could be no privileged vantage point from which to challenge its
legitimate parentage.[72]

Paper money, in other words, obscured personal identity or, more precisely, bracketed it. While bills claimed to represent personal authority,
their successful circulation depended on their ability to transcend that
model. Like other urban texts, banknotes were beyond the control of
their authors. They bore the authority of the anonymous individuals
who had exchanged them previously and expressed the fragile promises
of countless others who might keep them in circulation. More important
than the personal imprint of a bank president, therefore, was the impersonal imprint of all those fingers whose rough handling of a banknote
symbolized both contempt and political possibility in Leggett's editorial.

The circulating banknote became a powerful symbol of the new impersonal way of life emerging in the big city at this time. For many politicians and cultural critics, the discourse of counterfeit detection slipped easily beyond the economics of representative currency to the semiotics of everyday life in New York—to larger questions about the city's dependence on free-floating print texts to mediate and regulate encounters among strangers. As counterfeit detectors attempted to police a chaotic currency system, the anxieties they reinforced called critical attention to other written signs as well. For while banknotes may have been uniquely precious to their owners, they were still signs. And in the absence of accountable authors or any solid ground on which to validate authors' claims to their own words, signs could be dangerous things.

What was an epistemological nightmare for counterfeit regulators and a source of concern for middle-class reformers was also an important and empowering feature of everyday urban life. In circulating money, as Leggett reminds us, everyday people were coauthoring the texts of the money they spent. Close reading of money was less a matter of recovering an original value than of mastering signs of a bill's prospective circulation, which was being constantly renegotiated in detectors, guides, newspapers, political tracts, and ordinary use. The authenticating marks of a dollar bill referred not to a holy grail of an engraving plate but to a network of print exchanges from which there was little possibility of escape in antebellum New York.

But this was not anomalous or paralyzing in the context of the nineteenth-century city. Compared with later monetary policies and practices, the thousands of state bank issues seem impossibly insecure and unstable. It is important to remember, though, that despite massive counterfeiting, widespread suspicion, speculative banking practices, and chaotic supervision the paper money system still functioned—banknotes still managed to represent and transfer wealth in antebellum cities. That this underregulated currency system wreaked havoc in the lives of many people testifies not to the utter worthlessness of the pieces of paper, but rather to the very fact that so many people took them seriously as money. The instability endemic to the system and the fears provoked by that instability did not stem simply from a disparity between the face value of notes in circulation and the value of specie in bank vaults (considerable though that disparity was). The precariousness of the economy dovetailed with other instabilities in the public life of a growing heteroge-

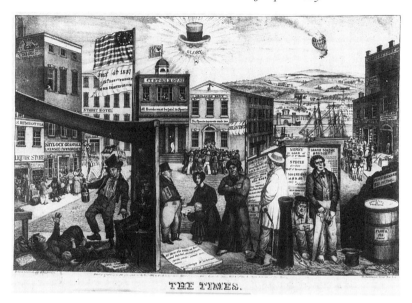

FIGURE 6.4 "The Times," 1837. Painting by Edward W. Clay.

• • •

neous city saturated with print. An 1837 illustration by artist Edward W. Clay entitled "The Times" (fig. 6.4) brings home the continuity between the currency crisis and the explosive growth of both urban spaces and written words in the middle of the century. To lampoon the speculative economy, Clay selects not Wall Street but the notorious Five Points slum district—perhaps the dominant pejorative symbol of urban intensification and social heterogeneity in antebellum America. Moreover, Five Points appears not as a site of filth, disease, and racial amalgamation, but rather as a collage of writing—a bazaar of spurious print claims covering a multitude of surfaces and even floating freely in the sky. Following the cues of Leggett and Clay, then, it may be worth reading the banknotes of the antebellum era alongside their contemporary urban texts rather than simply comparing them to specie or to the national currency that displaced them.

New Yorkers had good reason to be attuned to the analogy between dollar bills and other urban texts—to the newspapers that competed with one another for confidence and circulation, and, more strikingly, to the handbills and trade cards that were distributed in the streets. As mentioned in an earlier chapter, New York merchants reinforced this

FIGURE 6.5 Advertisement for "Lyon's Celebrated Kathairon."

• • •

analogy by designing advertisements to resemble paper currency. Many of these ads could pass easily for money at a quick glance, and several have even found their way into the currency collections of the American Antiquarian Society. In Alger's *Ragged Dick*, the ability to distinguish a dry-goods circular from the twenty-dollar banknote it resembles marks the novel's hero as an unusually savvy master of the ways of the city.[73]

Circulars modeled after money reflected playfully and self-consciously on the links connecting print, public circulation, and commercial exchange. The hair tonic ad shown in figure 6.5 promises to pay "on demand . . . *for* TWENTY FIVE CENTS" [emphasis added] one bottle of the product at the counter of any druggist. This bill, which was probably passed out on the streets of New York, mimics the banknote in elaborate detail, complete with mythological vignettes, signatures, a denomination marker (though the "50" in the upper left refers to nothing at all), and of course the ubiquitous pledge of security—in this case offering readers not the security of public stocks or real estate, as dollar bills often did, but rather the more crucial security of "public confidence." Melville could not have produced a more apt illustration. Figure 6.6 advertises a boot sale with an equally compelling copy of a banknote, and even identifies the New-York Savings Bank as the proprietor. This popular practice among the city's tradesmen concerned the producers and protectors of banknotes, as the handbills flaunted the ease with which someone could produce a realistic facsimile of paper currency.[74] More generally, money-ads underscored the threat posed by an expanding culture of

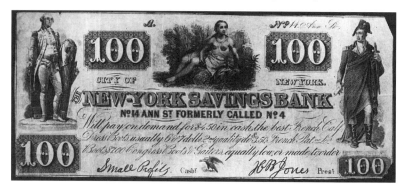

FIGURE 6.6 Boot advertisement, The New-York Savings Bank.

• • •

mechanical reproduction to the privileged status of paper currency. Never secure in this privilege, banknotes could only take their place, and their chances, within a confusing and contentious urban public increasingly organized around written and printed words.

Treating the banknote as a form of handbill—locating the complicated currency of antebellum New York alongside other urban texts—illustrates the ways in which city people experienced paper money as a vehicle and a symbol of a modern mode of human interaction emerging in the public. The volume and variety of bills circulating in the streets of Manhattan did not simply condition New Yorkers to the vicissitudes of the currency market or the instability of an inchoate banking system; it also conditioned them to the kind of impersonal relations between strangers that we now take for granted. Banknotes evoked both the frenetic anonymity of urban life and the highly fraught social and economic interdependence that such anonymity obscured. None of this changes the fact that money had a practical function in the transfer of goods and services, redistributed wealth within the economy, and mediated and symbolized real forms of social inequality. But banknotes had other functions, to which counterfeit detectors, enterprising advertisers, novelists, and everyday people were quite attuned. Like other texts circulating through the ever-changing spaces of the growing city, dollar bills facilitated impersonality and anonymity. The revolutionary tendency of paper money to bracket personal identity in economic exchanges was thus reinforced in New York by its affinity with similar trends in the wider world of city reading. Antebellum critics emphasized the anomie and alienation of such an urban existence, but for many city dwellers, especially but not exclusively white men, to circulate publicly with unencumbered and unmarked wealth, gaining access to new forms of commercialized leisure, popular culture, and mass politics, was to enjoy a striking degree of personal freedom.[75]

7

Epilogue

~

Words of War

Just days before the surrender of the Confederate Army, a short story appeared in *Frank Leslie's Illustrated Newspaper,* one of New York's most popular weekly magazines. Edward Spencer's "Number Ten" opens with a pedestrian encountering an innocuous-looking sign. The narrator-protagonist is struck by the words NUMBER TEN printed on the Manhattan sidewalk in chalk. Sensing immediately that these words are not simply "a dealer's sign, or his number, as doubtless most persons took them to be, who noticed them at all," but a revealing clue, the narrator does some detective work, discovers an apparently deranged man, and arranges to have him released from a military prison. The man turns out to be a certain James Leyford (a.k.a. Jack Ford) from Tennessee, a double agent in the Civil War and a cuckold bent on revenge. The protagonist learns most of this after Leyford has murdered his wife's seducer and then committed suicide, at which point it becomes clear that NUMBER TEN had referred to his room at an insane asylum, "and had become a sort of mystical symbol to him, and a means to the revenge he contemplated."[1]

Spencer's story strikes a number of cultural chords. A Civil War tale of betrayal, confused identity, and bloody catharsis, "Number Ten" is also an urban detective story in the tradition of Poe's "The Man of the Crowd" (1840) and Melville's "Bartleby the Scrivener" (1853). The protagonist, much like Poe's narrator, seeks to make sense of the changing city by finding meaning in the signs of everyday life. Though the appearance of words on the sidewalk seems normal to most people wandering the streets, Spencer's narrator is the classic urban connoisseur to whom inconspicuous marks on the cityscape disclose their secrets. This urban detective is blessed with "a magnetic sympathy" that allows him to penetrate the opacity of the chalked message to discover the individual drama lurking beneath its surface. He is, of course, also attuned to the process by which New Yorkers of the Civil War era had become, by necessity, city readers.

The specific text featured in Spencer's story is especially evocative of the anonymity of modern urban life. The representation of individual identity (and the individual's small place within the city) by a number stands as an appropriate metaphor for the emergence of a world of strangers in nineteenth-century urban America. Explaining his move from "a small but satisfactory house in the very heart of the city" to the quiet of rural Westchester, Horace Greeley wondered who would want "to grow old and die at No. 239, unknown to, and uncared for by, the denizens of Nos. 237 and 241?"[2] Urban numbering systems, as Walter Benjamin puts it, are attempts to compensate "for the fact that the disappearance of people in the masses of the big cities leaves no traces."[3]

Moreover, the enigmatic sparseness of the chalked sign allows it to drift ambiguously among several possible discourses and registers. Does it refer to commerce, politics, religion? Is it a slogan, a promotion, a premonition? Most city readers would mistake the words for a dealer's sign, Spencer's protagonist imagines, and not without reason. A couple of years earlier, New Yorkers encountered the mysterious word SOZODONT! on the sidewalk. After six months of titillating the urban imagination, the text turned out to be an advertisement for mouthwash. Shortly thereafter, a French visitor spotted the word BLOOD! written on the ground in red letters.[4] Detached from discursive context as well as from their authors, words like these became emblems of an expanding urban culture of transition, discontinuity, and disjointed spectacle.

Words in public also claimed particular attention in 1865, the end of a period in which New Yorkers had become increasingly and dramatically dependent on the public reading practices described in the previous four chapters. With the outbreak of the war, demand for up-to-date news about distant events focused unprecedented attention on the city's dailies. Several of the major papers enjoyed significant increases in circulation, and reports from the battlefield appeared in countless extras hawked in the streets at all hours of the day. Anticipating or responding to new bits of information, crowds would gather around the newspaper offices to read the latest editions and bulletins. After the firing on Fort Sumter, the *Times* reported, news offices "were besieged from an early hour in the morning" and "mass meeting[s]" sprang up at "each corner where bulletins were posted." The following day, "anxious crowds continued to surround the newspaper bulletins."[5] Such scenes of public reading continued throughout the war, endowing the reception of news with a striking (though not altogether unfamiliar) degree of urban pageantry. Though newspapers may have been inclined to exaggerate or mystify the impact of their medium, the following *Herald* account of the arrival of reports from the Seven Days' Battle in 1862 highlights the public role of the news buildings during the war:

> As soon as the bulletin of "Good News" was posted on the board outside the HERALD office an immense crowd of people was almost spontaneously summoned to the spot. Thicker and thicker grew the mass of anxious people, until it was impossible for a quarter of them to gain sight of the pleasing transcript. One individual, with the lungs of a Stentor, ventured to act as telegraphic medium to the multitude, and read aloud the following words:
>
>
>
> GOOD NEWS FROM GEN. MCCLELLAN!
>
> THE REBELS BADLY BEATEN.
>
> ONLY ONE GUN LOST[6]
>
>

Characteristically, shouts and cheers accompanied the reception of the written words, but the posted bulletin remained the centerpiece of the event. Though a relatively new technology, telegraphy had become sufficiently fundamental to the spread of information in the city that the stentorian reading of the news is represented, significantly, as a makeshift substitute. Just as Walt Whitman discovered that the war had begun, just as George Templeton Strong discovered that it had ended, New Yorkers throughout the Civil War period gathered news in a strikingly public setting dominated by the written word. When President Washington died in 1799, word reached New York seven days later and spread unevenly, and orally, through the population. When President Kennedy died in 1963, most New Yorkers knew within the hour, having heard the news on the radio, on television, or from others (in many cases via telephone) with access to those media. When President Lincoln died in 1865, however, New Yorkers learned about it through the network of information exchanges built in and around the newspaper. "What can one do?" Caroline Woolsey wrote to her relative Eliza Howland. "We are all dumb with grief. The extra has just been cried giving the awful moment of his death. What a moment for America! . . . The papers were brought up while we were in bed this morning."[7] Woodward Hudson, a journalist, learned of the tragic event when his early-rising seven-year-old son asked why there were black borders around the front pages of the city's dailies.[8]

The information posted on bulletins, printed in extras, or shouted by newsboys was not always reliable. The outcomes of many battles were prematurely celebrated on the basis of false reports.[9] Though the dailies presented themselves as privileged authorities, they had no more protection against forged press releases or bogus telegrams than their readers. At a loss to explain the barrage of contradictory news from South Carolina dispatched through its own offices, the *Herald* suggested that "the rebels were using the telegraphy, like everything else, for their own purposes," an apt reminder of the dilemmas and paradoxes endemic to the new print culture.[10]

Despite their fallibility, newspapers were essential to the experience of the war in New York City, offering not only battle accounts and contentious editorials on Lincoln's war policies, but also casualty listings—a seemingly endless catalogue of names scanned with dread by friends and relatives of Union soldiers. These lists were powerful documents, simultaneously depicting the magnitude of the carnage, offering public recognition of individual sacrifice, and glossing over the loss of human life with ordered rows of monotonous newsprint visually indistinguishable from currency listings or classified ads. In a disturbing parallel to the casualty rolls, the *Herald* would periodically print a "List of Letters Remaining in the New York Post Office," a compilation of "dead letters"—the metaphor Melville employed for the lonely and tragically illegible life of Bartleby—filling several columns of minuscule type.[11]

New Yorkers confronted all kinds of public texts during the Civil War, many of which were achieving new heights of power and prevalence. The war was a time of frequent public celebrations, mournings, rallies, meetings, and confrontations, and, as we have seen, banners and placards played a central role in the planning, presentation, and interpretation of all these events. Writing and print were ubiquitous in the political theater of the war era, even in those scenes we tend to imagine as most spontaneous, rowdy, and beyond the reaches of literate communication. During the Draft Riots of 1863, for example, rioters strung a blinded black man to a lamppost and covered his chest with a sign reading: "We will be back for you tomorrow." Upon seeing the sign, former Navy Captain George Blunt went to the newspapers to have them issue a personal challenge to the rioters, a challenge that went unanswered. Though Blunt understood the link between signs in the streets and advertisements in the daily press, the anonymous placard resisted the kind of personal accountability he was invoking.[12] Riot placards sought to attract notice and communicate messages within a large, print-oriented urban community, and this particular one took full advantage of the ironies associated with the ambiguous readership of a posted sign. The written slogans lofted at rallies, processions, and meetings may also have shaped political rhetoric by publicizing a set of pithy aphorisms (the most common being "the Constitution as it is, the Union as it was") that became campaign shibboleths. In the hands of pioneers of advertising (a profession that emerged around the time of the war), wartime slogans were also adopted for private interests in newspapers, on parade floats, and throughout the commercial print culture of the city.[13]

Advertising continued to flourish during the war, both on retail storefronts and on the showbills and sandwich boards through which entrepreneurs like P. T. Barnum sought to create commercial sensations. Barnum played a significant and self-promoting role in the public reception of war news,[14] but his big splash came in 1863 with the wedding of General Tom Thumb to the thirty-inch-tall Lavinia Warren, whose "cartes de visite" netted the impresario about $300 a day. Around the same time, more official signs were sprouting up, not only at army recruitment centers but also in the new public spaces being created in Central Park, where Frederick Olmsted's vision of a well-ordered counterpoint to the frenzy of the city called for an elaborate system of freestanding public regulations visible to all park visitors.

In addition to restrictive signs, commercial ephemera, political banners, and daily journals, New Yorkers had to be sure to read their money during the Civil War. Massive inflation and constant shortages of specie destabilized an already chaotic currency system and wreaked havoc in daily life. Because silver coins were being hoarded, just making change was a challenge. According to one *Times* reader in 1862, "We are in a great strain for change. Wife complains terribly. A $5 bill is good for nothing, unless a dollar's worth is wanted." Worrying about "the shinplaster deluge that will soon overwhelm us," the author of the letter proposed that government issue notes for incredibly specific denominations.[15] Stores gave change in scrip, adding their own new and doubtful notes to the paper cornucopia of the state banking era, or else in postage stamps. Though an unconventional form of currency, stamps retained their value, and their frequent use suggests how broadly entrenched the mail system had become by the 1860s. By 1862, the substitution of postage stamps for specie change grew so widespread that a new fractional paper money—a national "postage currency"—was created.[16] Adding to the trouble, of course, were frequent reports in the papers of counterfeit notes circulating around town. A particular set of spurious bills, noted the *Times* in July 1862, "are so well executed that some of the best judges in New-York have been deceived by them."[17] Counterfeit detectors were peaking in popularity when Salmon Chase devised a plan for a national currency which by 1866 (when state notes were subjected to a prohibitive tax) would radically simplify the reading involved in using paper money. When greenbacks were introduced in 1863, though, they were fragile, experimental, and quickly depreciating tokens of a shaky federal government.

Everyday life in New York during the war entailed countless acts of reading, many of which took place in public and involved some renegotiation between individuals and the urban community. In a time of intense demographic mobility, economic instability, political ferment, and sudden changes in the physical appearance of the city, New Yorkers turned, liked Edward Spencer, to the verbal cityscape for clues. Some were minute details of great significance, such as a telltale mark on a counterfeit banknote or, more tragically, a name on a casualty list in the newspaper. Others were bold and glaring but somehow more suspect, like a posted news flash from the front or a showbill for the American Museum. These myriad urban texts greeted their readers in a special kind of public space where strangers mingled and habituated themselves to a specifically urban form of reading.

By 1865, city reading had become a dominant mode of interaction in New York City. In less than half a century, face-to-face contact, coffeehouse gatherings, and mercantile newsletters had given way to a collage of imposing signs, flashy posters, daily extras, worn dollar bills, and enigmatic inscriptions stretched across a growing and ever-changing metropolis. But what were the consequences and implications of this broad development? Writing and print assumed so many forms and served such a wide range of purposes that it is easy to overlook their general impact. Despite important differences among the various genres and instances of urban text, a few central effects were clear by the time of the Civil War. To begin with, store signs, posters, newspapers, and banknotes produced and reinforced a profound democratization of authority in the city's public life. With so many different voices and messages appearing in the streets of Manhattan, the range of public communication had grown impressively inclusive. Though it was constrained in certain important respects by the rising costs of starting a newspaper and by the disproportionate advantages of those with access to expensive real estate, we should not underestimate the revolutionary significance of this democratic collage. Striking workers, small business owners, parvenu entrepreneurs, foreign dignitaries, employment seekers, graffiti artists, confidence men, sentimental novelists, prostitutes, beggars, boxers, bankers, and the municipal corporation all took to the streets, availing themselves of the opportunity to address unknown readers circulating about the city.

At the same time, this dispersed authority was being subtly destabilized. Though words appearing in large gaslit letters on the front of a building or in the homogeneous agate type of a daily newspaper claimed an aura of official discourse, others simply floated freely and mysteriously in the contested public spaces of the changing city. Throughout the verbal cityscape, as countless private interests and spurious claims competed for public attention, freestanding words had to be read selectively and critically. Detached from the identities of their authors, they aspired to ventriloquize some impersonal print authority (often associated with the public or the city). But this detachment allowed the kind of free play of signs exemplified by mysterious inscriptions on sidewalks and dramatized by the chaotic attempts to regulate the authenticity of paper currency. So while city reading marked the creation of a more open arena for the elaboration of authority in public, that very openness suggested a redefinition of public discourse. Urban words were not controlled speech acts, nor were they the putative expressions of some holder of political power. They were bits of text made meaningful and powerful by their readers, not their writers—by the unknown masses of people concentrated in the city.

Habituating themselves to this reality, New Yorkers learned a mixed lesson about mass democracy and the mass public. To distribute authority among the people was not, as much eighteenth-century republican theory represented it, simply to unite those people around shared public interests, but rather to disperse authority among them, beyond willful control. Even when it projected fictions of community, such as those represented in the columns of the metropolitan press, the legible city still stressed sheer mass and reflected unwieldy diversity, impressing urban readers with how small a part each of them played in the activities and pursuits that made up public life.

A second major development encouraged and epitomized by the spread of city reading was the creation of a culture in which politics, entertainment, and commerce shared a common stage and common modes of appeal. On crowded thoroughfares, in parade processions, in Barnum's playbills, on mechanically reproduced dollar bills, and in rectilinear columns of homogeneous newsprint, discrete pursuits and practices blended in a common language of publicity. Like the overlapping bills in the 1862 lithograph featured in chapter 4, urban texts called attention to the continuities between the (otherwise) mutually indifferent activities of the city's heterogeneous population. An election, an auction, a riot, a preacher, an opera singer, and a cough medicine could all be publicized in the same spaces, and moreover could belong to the same culture by virtue of their juxtaposition in those spaces and their common quest for popular patronage and support. The expanding media and institutions of the new urban print culture thus contributed to the formation of a modern consumer society.

The third major consequence in the history of city reading was the extension of connections among urban dwellers. As buildings donned labels, directories publicized store façades, streams of paper littered the streets, newspapers drew wider readerships, and unprecedented numbers of people became dependent on a diverse and fluctuating paper currency, the rate and range of information exchange increased substantially. By the time of the war it was clear that posted signs and mass-circulated dailies could be used to mobilize or to regulate large numbers of people without recourse to regular, face-to-face contact between civil subjects and the personal embodiments of power. The implications of this development in the lives of everyday people are profoundly polysemous. Urban texts were used during the Civil War era both to undermine and to enlarge government authority, both to organize popular riots in the streets of the city and to keep people off the grass in Central Park. Then, as now, there were costs as well as benefits to being plugged into channels of publicity. Nonetheless, city reading cemented assumptions and expectations of interaction and interdependence that lie at the heart of modern notions of a shared society.

Perhaps the most important and the most elusive historical implications of city reading lay in the capacity of writing and print to facilitate anonymous circulation in the city. Signs, placards, newspapers, and bills represented, among other things, a set of agreements and cues that obviated the need for personal acquaintance and identity. Public spaces marked with signs and littered with paper made it possible to find one's way, pursue a livelihood, negotiate a range of private and public pleasures, and forge a new identity without having a long history in the community and without relying on traditional institutions of social control. That many New Yorkers continued to tether their identities to, and plot their itineraries in keeping with, older ties and allegiances does not minimize the impact of these new maps appearing regularly in public view. And while residents and strangers may have been alienated by the way public reading kept them at bay—enforcing anonymity as well as offering it—the verbal cityscape was there, subject to casual browsing, criticism, reappropriation, dismissal, or, as in Spencer's urban detective fiction, profound investigation.

Access to the verbal cityscape facilitated anonymous access to urban life, a point that strikes us as unremarkable largely because we have grown accustomed to the kind of city that was emerging in antebellum New York.[18] Although cities had long been associated with the lures and dangers of anonymity, a city with little public signage, without mass-circulation newspapers, and less accustomed to paper currency required more personal forms of self-presentation. Urban texts institutionalized the presence of the stranger in new and fundamental ways. Confronting such texts as anonymous subjects of an impersonal public, city readers cultivated more flexible selves and forged more fluid relationships to public space.

Taken together, these developments suggest a powerful connection between the rise of public reading in the city and the emergence of modern ways of voting, shopping, moving, participating in popular culture, and forming public opinion. And there are some affinities between the world of city reading and the darker sides of mass democracy and competitive consumer capitalism in the United States. How significantly this impersonal urban print public has contributed to the (overdetermined) historical processes yielding a society dependent on mass consumption, a disengaged electorate, a largely nondeliberative political culture, or a narrow popular understanding of the public good is difficult to trace, of course. But as with many other forces and symptoms of modernization, we can recognize in city reading embryonic stages in the development of our own forms of alienation. What makes this story distinctive, though, is that at its core, the culture of city reading in the nineteenth century organized and imagined social relations around an experience of public space rather than an ideology, a set of class interests, or a fiction of an abstract community.

In that sense, the most compelling evidence for the advent of city reading in the era of the Civil War comes not from the lofty parade banners or the new authoritarian signs in Central Park, but from the new personal ads appearing in the *Herald*. These scandalous notices posited a symbiotic relationship between print culture and street culture, and marked the normalization of a space of promiscuous circulation in which anonymous and pseudonymous strangers met one another's quick but scrutinizing gaze. New Yorkers knew where to look to discover that "John L. Mason will find a letter in Station D from J.L.W." or to see the following message repeated for several days:

> Jabie is still faithful, but hope deferred is having its effect. "We, I trust, understand each other too well to require words expressed on paper." But why so long a silence? Write immediately, either direct or as before.

Other notices alluded more explicitly to public encounters, addressing the anonymous stranger "I saw yesterday in City Hall Park" or arranging a meeting: "Bull Run—Will call on you to-day at three o'clock. Let me know if you are at home by showing yourself at the window. Bull

Run." Another item represented public space more elliptically, address-ing itself to "27th street—Where have you kept yourself this long, long time?" A fairly typical 1862 personal ad ran: "If the young lady (one of two sisters) who sat on the end and back seat at Wallack's last evening will honor the gentleman with whom she flirted . . . please address Montgomery Peyton, Union square post office."[19]

Of course not all New Yorkers wrote, answered, or even read these impersonal personal ads. But they testify to expectations and assump-tions about the stakes of circulating in a city of stranger-readers. This was a city of individuals pursuing private pleasures and interests, but pursuing them on an inclusive and exposed public stage. The sensibili-ties of everyone implicated in these print exchanges—from the author to the addressee, from the avid reader to the scandalized detractor—were being shaped by modes of authority and interaction particular to this public stage.

Though urban literature of the period presented the city as a veiled mystery to be decoded, unraveling the legacy of nineteenth-century urban life requires an appreciation of what was rendered visible as well. Like the words "Number Ten" in Spencer's story, each of the personal ads provides a clue to a larger individual drama unfolding somewhere in the mysterious city. What is most striking about these clues, though, is not their opaque sparsity but rather their brazen visibility: they stand squarely in public space, rubbing up against cigar ads and foreign news items. The chaotic and often anonymous promiscuity of urban life was not a matter of dark secrets lurking underground; it was a prominent fea-ture of the city in which strangers presented and interpreted public selves for a variety of purposes and effects. Personal ads reminded New Yorkers how useful, how necessary, how familiarly scandalous, and how socially explosive the written word had become within this public life.

Notes

1. Introduction: Public Reading, Public Space

1. Allan Nevins and Milton Halsey Thomas, eds., *The Diary of George Templeton Strong* 3:574 (April 3, 1865).

2. Lewis Mumford, *The City in History*, 99.

3. Since most recent urban history focuses on quantifiable data, urban reading practices have been buried by an avalanche of demographic and economic statistics. Moreover, many urban histories are primarily concerned with issues such as economic mobility, class formation, or government organization, for which the city simply provides a coherent research sample and within which the experience of the city is simply a contingent condition. The reasons why historians of reading and print culture have neglected crucial aspects of the nexus between the written word and the urban public are more complicated, as I suggest later. Structurally, though, the history of reading tends to fall into one of two general categories: the history of the acquisition and diffusion of literacy or the history of the reception (and in some cases interpretation) of books. The first category either assumes a link between literacy and some other fixed point of socioeconomic status (and uses literacy as a convenient and ostensibly quantifiable index of that status) or concerns itself with the history of education and educational philosophy. The second category often focuses on the ideas and values that books express and popularize, and positions itself as a branch of intellectual or literary history. Thus while there has been a torrent of recent work in the history of reading (many of the titles appear in the bibliography), the field is still organized in such a way that inquiries into the urban texts analyzed here appear out of place. For a good summary and taxonomy of the field, see David D. Hall, *Cultures of Print*, 169–187. Ronald J. Zboray's *A Fictive People* bridges some of the disparate thrusts in the history of reading and broadens the subject by demonstrating the roles of such diverse phenomena as railroads, bookstore organization, marketing strategies, and the rise of corrective lenses in the experience of reading in nineteenth-century America, though here too there is a tendency to equate a reading public with a novel-reading public and to ignore the specifically urban character of much reading.

4. In *The Image of the City*, Kevin Lynch discusses the nodes, landmarks, and

lines through which urban dwellers imagine their relationship to city space, but underplays the role of written words in this process.

5. Mary P. Ryan, "The American Parade: Representations of the Nineteenth-Century Social Order," 139; John F. Kasson, *Rudeness and Civility*, 70.

6. Peter Fritzsche, *Reading Berlin, 1900*.

7. Elsewhere, I deal at length with the mythology of the private reader. See David Henkin, "City Reading," 18–38. For a representative articulation of many of the theoretical premises of this pervasive mythology, see Walter J. Ong, *Orality and Literacy: The Technologizing of the Word*.

8. Elizabeth Long, "Textual Interpretation as Collective Action," 193.

9. As Geoffrey Nunberg points out, most printed documents today have little to do with the cultural functions associated with "the book." "The Travelers Insurance Company produces printed output at a rate of roughly a billion impressions a month, enough to fill all the shelves of the new Bibliothèque de France every six months or so. The printed documentation that accompanies the delivery of a single Boeing 747 weighs about 350 tons, only slightly less than the airplane itself." See "The Places of Books in the Age of Electronic Reproduction," 14. In sheer volume, the antebellum case is less dramatic, but the disproportionate attention paid to novels among historians of reading is scarcely more warranted.

10. Isaac Lyon, *Recollections of an Old Cartman*, 5; Graham Russell Hodges, *New York City Cartmen, 1667–1850*, 160.

11. *Squints Through an Opera Glass*, 17. See also the 1853 cartoon of a book-holding breastplate, designed so that "those who run may read," both in Zboray, *A Fictive People*, 125.

12. Catherine Elizabeth Havens, *Diary of a Little Girl in Old New York*, 19–20.

13. Charles Dickens, *American Notes*, 80.

14. Jürgen Habermas, *The Structural Transformation of the Public Sphere*, 27.

15. Paradoxically, while a strict separation between public and private interests maintains the integrity of all critical deliberation within the sphere, the creation of the sphere itself rests on the marketplace, through which educated and property-owning citizens gain access to one another and acquire collective identity. Only through the market do affairs, products, and events become objects of public discussion. In many ways this paradox is characteristic of Habermas's approach, which acknowledges complex and unwieldy cultural factors in the *origins* of the bourgeois public sphere. Once the sphere is formed the categories become more rigid and a whole host of cultural factors, consumer desires, slippery metaphors, and irrational actions become delegitimized as corrupting influences.

16. A fuller description of the subjectivity associated with this notion of publicity (and an excellent discussion of its implications) appears in Michael Warner, *The Letters of the Republic*, and Warner, "The Mass Public and the Mass Subject," in Craig Calhoun, ed., *Habermas and the Public Sphere*, especially 378–380.

17. Warner, *Letters of the Republic*; Benedict Anderson, *Imagined Communities*.

18. See for example Seyla Benhabib, "Models of Public Space: Hannah Arendt, the Liberal Tradition, and Jürgen Habermas," in Calhoun, ed., *Habermas and the Public Sphere*, 73–98.

19. The meaning of this spectacle varied, naturally, depending on the kind of text. It is one thing to be seen reading a signboard that is itself broadly visible, another to be seen reading a generally familiar daily newspaper, and yet another to be seen reading a small and unidentifiable book. Still, all of these acts become part of the cityscape. There were other modes of publicity at work in American society at the same time, including the powerful legacy of an impersonal print public that had developed in what Warner characterizes as a process of mutual clarification with republican ideology during the previous century. Urban publicity, however, was something more specific. Most texts and most acts of reading in antebellum New York were public in one sense or another. Sentimental novels consumed in domestic isolation, intimate correspondence between lovers, and even personal diaries all participated in some conventions of publicity that belied their claims to be private texts. See Zboray, *A Fictive People*, 115–119.

20. Jean-Christophe Agnew, "Banking on Language: The Currency of Alexander Bryan Johnson," in Thomas L. Haskell and Richard F. Teichgraeber III, eds., *The Culture of the Market*, 231.

21. Thomas Haskell has associated the spread of the market with the creation of autonomous, reliant, rational, and humanitarian subjects that fit better into Habermas's bourgeois public sphere than into the promiscuous reading public of the modern city. Without insisting too forcefully upon the way nineteenth-century economic developments complicate Haskell's analysis, one needs to distinguish carefully between the tendency of the market in the early modern era to promote promise-keeping and long-term planning, and the tendency of a more complex market to depersonalize and mystify human relations. See Haskell, "Capitalism and the Origins of the Humanitarian Sensibility," in Thomas Bender, ed., *The Antislavery Debate*.

22. As Warner has argued, the negative relationship between the capitalist mass subject and some more differentiated, whole sense of self is central to the logic of the eighteenth-century print public sphere. Warner, "Mass Public and Mass Subject" in Calhoun, ed., *Habermas and the Public Sphere*.

23. Racial difference figures powerfully in the history of reading in nineteenth-century America. Severe restrictions on the education of slaves, especially after Nat Turner's 1831 revolt, raised the specter of African American literacy in a way that shaped the meaning of reading and writing on each side of both the color and the Mason-Dixon lines. While white America was approaching universal literacy, only 7 percent of the nation's black adults knew how to read at the time of emancipation. The South's ideological and economic investment in the illiteracy of blacks was captured best in the pass system, which relied

(often uneasily) on writing as a code among white people to be borne on the bodies of chattel slaves. At the same time, African American access to writing and print proved central to the experience of limited liberation in the North—or at least to its representation—as the writings of Frederick Douglass, Harriet Jacobs, Harriet Wilson, Frances Harper, and others highlight. In antebellum New York, both sides of this coin shone conspicuously. Black New Yorkers were far less likely to be able to read books and newspapers than their European counterparts (though far more likely than southern slaves), yet New York was also the center of a burgeoning African American press. See Janet Duitsman Cornelius, *"When I Can Read My Title Clear"*; Eugene Genovese, *Roll, Jordan, Roll*, 561–566; Lawrence Levine, *Black Culture and Black Consciousness*, 155–157; Hazel Carby, *Reconstructing Womanhood*; Henry Louis Gates Jr., *Figures in Black*, 11–17; Shane White, *Somewhat More Independent*, 116–119.

24. Lynch, *Image of the City*.

25. Randolph Starn, "The Republican Regime of the 'Room of Peace' in Siena, 1338–1340," 8. See also Michael Fried, *Realism, Writing, and Disfiguration*. For an extensive treatment of the theoretical grounds for distinguishing images and words as signs, see W. J. T. Mitchell, *Iconology*.

26. Armando Petrucci, *Public Lettering*, 74.

27. Such diverse phenomena as the migration of young, single men from family farms to the growing towns, the commodification of land, and the rise of paper money served to create and epitomize what might be labeled a "crisis of immanence"—a confusion of real and represented values—in which mass literacy and the proliferation of print and writing figured heavily, if somewhat paradoxically. Underlying contemporary concerns about the deceptive disguises of confidence men, the fraudulent foundations of speculative wealth, or the false values of the new parvenu commercial class lay a profound suspicion that urban society had become a mask of paper appearances in which authority and reputation were being replaced by their representations. Reading and writing were seriously implicated in this cultural indictment of representation, but of course it was through print that the indictment was promulgated and through books and paper that deceptive and fraudulent representations would be exposed. See Larzer Ziff, *Writing in the New Nation*; Karen Halttunen, *Confidence Men and Painted Women*.

28. William Alexander Caruthers, *The Kentuckian in New-York*, 162–163.

29. Margaret Spufford, "First Steps in Literacy"; Robert Darnton, *The Kiss of Lamourette*, 174–175; Carl F. Kaestle et al., *Literacy in the United States*, 22–23.

30. Lee Soltow and Edward Stevens, *The Rise of Literacy and the Common School Movement in the United States*; Harvey J. Graff, *The Literacy Myth* and *The Legacies of Literacy*, 260–372; Kaestle et al., *Literacy in the United States*, 19–32; Carl F. Kaestle, *The Evolution of an Urban School System* and *Pillars of the Republic*.

31. Quoted in Marilynn Wood Hill, *Their Sisters' Keepers*, 13–14.

32. Michael Schudson, *Discovering the News*, 37.

33. It is also important to resist the temptation to see the rise of mass literacy as the prime mover in this story. Like contemporary advances in printing, paper making, and telegraphic communication, mass literacy can be seen as a necessary condition for the full flowering of the network of urban texts and reading practices analyzed in this study, but the causal links are hard to determine. More reading was as much a cause as a consequence of expanded literacy skills and improved print technology. It is fairer to describe these developments as mutually reinforcing. In this connection, see Schudson's discussion of the rise of the penny press in ibid., 31–43.

34. More generally, one can detect in the 1820s the beginnings of various developments with which antebellum American culture is associated. The election of Andrew Jackson and his new party in 1828 ushered in the era of mass democracy; James Fenimore Cooper's *The Spy* (1821) became the first commercially successful American novel; the revivals of Charles Grandison Finney (from 1825 onward) inaugurated the religious movement known as the Second Great Awakening. Insofar as the story told here belongs to the broader narrative of social and cultural change before the Civil War, it seems apt to integrate the study into the rough periodization marked by the term "antebellum."

35. Allan Pred, *Urban Growth and City-Systems in the United States, 1840–1860*, 147–149, 223–224; Stuart Blumin, ed., *New York by Gas-Light and Other Urban Sketches*, 14.

36. Fritzsche, *Reading Berlin, 1900*, 1. While Fritzsche pays similar attention to the phenomenology of public circulation and to the role of city words in guiding strangers, producing visual pleasure, projecting abrupt discontinuities, and obscuring social differences, there are several important differences between his approach and the one presented here. In addition to the fact that he sees Berlin largely through the eyes of artists, philosophers, and poets (Walter Benjamin, Jakob von Haddis, Alfred Döblin, Hans Ostwald, and others), Fritzsche treats Berlin's urban texts (principally the newspaper) as a textual map and a narrative analogue for modern urban life rather than as a primary feature of the cityscape.

37. Simmel, "The Metropolis and Mental Life" in *The Sociology of Georg Simmel*, 409–424; Dana Brand, *The Spectator and the City in Nineteenth-Century American Literature*; Richard Terdiman, *Discourse/Counter-Discourse*.

38. M. Christine Boyer, *The City of Collective Memory*, 28.

39. Sven Birkerts, *The Gutenberg Elegies*; Neil Postman, *Amusing Ourselves to Death*; Geoffrey Nunberg, ed., *The Future of the Book*.

2. Brick, Paper, and the Spectacle of Urban Growth

1. *American Magazine of Useful and Entertaining Knowledge* (April 1836).

2. Ira Rosenwaike, *Population History of New York City*, 32–54. Extensive treat-

ments of the city's growth during this period appear in Edward K. Spann, *The New Metropolis*; Richard B. Stott, *Workers in the Metropolis*; and several other important works cited in this chapter.

3. See Spann, *The New Metropolis*, 152–153; John A. Kouwenhoven, *The Columbia Historical Portrait of New York*, 245.

4. Spann, *The New Metropolis*, 182–189.

5. Lydia Maria Child, *Letters from New York*, 94.

6. Of course then, as now, urban residents had recourse to a variety of social stereotypes through which strangers could be coded. The growth of cities in the nineteenth century, however, marked a point of crisis in this process of human typology. Indeed, as Poe suggests in his famous story, "The Man of the Crowd" (1840), the camouflaging of legible social types constituted a central feature of life in a big city. See Kasson, *Rudeness and Civility*, 70–111; Halttunen, *Confidence Men and Painted Ladies*, 33–40; and Eric Homberger, *Scenes from the Life of a City*, 220–222.

7. Stott, *Workers in the Metropolis*, 70–73; Rosenwaike, *Population History of New York City*, 42. Hidden beneath these figures are countless immigrants who left New York after brief stays, opting to try their luck farther west or returning to Europe. A few days after John James arrived in New York from Britain in 1829, he wrote to his brother of a member of his travel party who "is going home, without having seen more than half of New York." James speculated that "it is through such men as these that lies and prejudice are built up among the ordinary English people." Alan Conway, ed., *The Welsh in America*, 77. Although out-migration statistics are not available, there is good reason to suppose that the proportion of New Yorkers of foreign nativity over a period of time was considerably higher than it was at any given census date, and that the role of immigration in creating a world of strangers was even more powerful than these numbers imply.

8. See for example the anti-Semitic reflections of Charles Harris quoted in chapter 3 of this study.

9. Meryle R. Evans, "Knickerbocker Hotels and Restaurants, 1800—1850," 377–378.

10. Kenneth A. Scherzer, *The Unbounded Community*. Though Scherzer claims to be charting the process by which residential patterns in New York "fitfully moved from heterogeneity to homogeneity" between 1830 and 1875, his evidence supports the adverb of that thesis more convincingly than the verb. Scherzer stresses how partial and incomplete residential segregation was, and how abstract and porous nineteenth-century neighborhoods were by later standards. Even historians who have stressed the role of spatial differentiation in antebellum New York have acknowledged its limits. Elizabeth Blackmar writes of the gradual formation (before 1820) of "neighborhoods of propertied and propertyless New Yorkers," though she is clear at the outset of her work that

these neighborhoods were often areas no larger than a block or two, vicinities rather than insular communities. See *Manhattan for Rent*, 11–12, 76. Even Stott, who goes farther than most in depicting "strong neighborhood localism," especially among workers, concedes that traveling between different neighborhoods was "a fact of working-class life." *Workers in the Metropolis*, 210. See also Spann, *The New Metropolis*, 106–109 and Amy Bridges, *A City in the Republic*, 43. This is not to deny that there were serious differences in living conditions (including striking variations in mortality rates) between different wards. Still, it is important not to use such data to obscure the broad impact of transience and mobility on the experience of living in antebellum New York. On May Day, see Seba Smith's fictional account in *May Day in New York*; Child, *Letters from New York*, 283–288; Bayrd Still, *Mirror for Gotham*, 114; Nathaniel Parker Willis, *The Rag-Bag*, 101. For broader discussions of the Moving Day phenomenon, see Blackmar, *Manhattan for Rent*, 213–216, and Scherzer, *The Unbounded Community*, 19–48.

11. Even the famous case of *Kleindeutschland*, the neighborhood east of the Bowery between Houston and Twelfth Streets, was more a center for cultural and commercial life than a closed ethnic neighborhood in which most of the city's German immigrants resided. Scherzer, *The Unbounded Community*, 36–39, 52–65.

12. Spann, *The New Metropolis*, 285–294.

13. Bridges, *A City in the Republic*, 44; Hill, *Their Sisters' Keepers*, 177.

14. Robert Greenhalgh Albion, *The Rise of New York Port*, 55–75, 392–393, 401.

15. Stott, *Workers in the Metropolis*, 289; Diane Lindstrom, "Economic Structure, Demographic Change, and Income Inequality in Antebellum New York," 9; Sean Wilentz, *Chants Democratic*, 403–404; Bridges, *A City in the Republic*, 45.

16. Wilentz, *Chants Democratic*, 107

17. Spann, *The New Metropolis*, 126, 205–207; Scherzer, *The Unbounded Community*, 86–87. By 1845 1 percent of the population owned 40 percent of the total noncorporate wealth in the city, and 4 percent of the population owned two thirds of the total. Edward Pessen, *Riches, Class, and Power Before the Civil War*, 33–35.

18. Stott, *Workers in the Metropolis*, 3, 58–63, 72, 96–102. On the transformation of crafts, see Wilentz's highly influential chapter on "metropolitan industrialization" in *Chants Democratic*, 107–142; On rising costs of housing and "the power of property to reduce the value of labor," see Blackmar, *Manhattan for Rent*, 104 and throughout; Christine Stansell, *City of Women*.

19. Rosenwaike, *Population History of New York City*, 48–49; Spann, *The New Metropolis*, 103. The northward drift of the population and the conquest of rugged terrain by urban settlement formed the starting points of most contem-

porary descriptions of the city's growth. See for example John W. Francis, *Old New York*, 13–15. Hawthorne contemplated writing a story centered around what he described as "the devouring of the old country residences by the over-grown monster of a city," citing examples in his sketch book of streets running through what had once been ancestral homes. Homberger, *Scenes from the Life of a City*, 222.

20. M. Christine Boyer, *Manhattan Manners*, 9–15; Thomas Bender, *Toward an Urban Vision*, 173.

21. Quoted in Spann, *The New Metropolis*, 104.

22. New York *Mirror*, quoted in ibid., 158.

23. Quoted in Still, *Mirror for Gotham*, 99.

24. Cornelius Mathews, *A Pen-and-Ink Panorama of New-York City*, 178–9.

25. Lyon, *Recollections of an Old Cartman*, 8.

26. H. Arnold Barton, ed., *Letters from the Promised Land*, 37. For some other examples, see James Fenimore Cooper, *Home as Found*, 106–109; Mathews, *A Pen-and-Ink Panorama*, 92–101; Richard Gooch, *America and the Americans in 1833–34*, 20; Edward Dicey, *Spectator of America*, 15. Margaret Hall wrote of her 1827 visit, "One of the things that Basil has been most desirous of seeing at New York is a fire, and as one or two occur generally every week he would have been very unlucky had he not been gratified in this respect." See Una Pope-Hennessy, *The Aristocratic Journey*, 24; Spann, *The New Metropolis*, 154.

27. Asa Greene, *A Glance at New York*, 10; Bayard Tuckerman, ed., *The Diary of Philip Hone, 1828–1851*, 2:383. See also William Dodge's description of the collapse of his father-in-law's store in 1832. The brand-new building on the corner of Fulton and Cliff, which housed the mercantile firm of Phelps and Peck, "suddenly gave way from the foundation, and . . . fell in an instant, crushing to death seven persons." William E. Dodge, *Old New York*, 44.

28. Quoted in Gunther Barth, *City People*, 31.

29. Lyon, *Recollections of an Old Cartman*, 9.

30. Blackmar, *Manhattan for Rent*, 183–212, 276; Spann, *The New Metropolis*, 155.

31. Blackmar, *Manhattan for Rent*, 94–100; John Reps, *Town Planning in Frontier America*, 135–140; Hendrik Hartog, *Public Property and Private Power*, 158–175. For Mumford's general critique of gridiron plans as an agent of speculative capitalism that transformed the city into "a private commercial venture to be carved up in any fashion that might increase the turnover and further the rise in land values," see *The City in History*, 421–426. For Frederick Law Olmsted's famous criticism of the 1811 plan as resulting from "the chance occurrence of a mason's sieve near the map of the ground to be laid out," see Albert Fein, *Landscape Into Cityscape*, 352.

32. Philip Fisher, "Democratic Social Space: Whitman, Melville, and the Promise of American Transparency," in Fisher, ed., *The New American Studies*,

especially 72–77. See also Boyer, *Manhattan Manners*, 8. The slow and uneven trend toward land specialization north of Fourteenth Street had to overcome the powerful homogenizing impact of the city grid reinforced by a numbered street system that links different urban locations in terms of a continuous scale.

33. Ralph Bowen, ed. and trans., *A Frenchman in Lincoln's America* by Ernest Duvergier de Hauranne, 19–20.

34. Blackmar, *Manhattan for Rent*. In practice, other considerations (including development strategies, notions of social exclusivity, and of course speculation) would help determine land values in the antebellum city. See *Manhattan for Rent*, 98, and Spann, *The New Metropolis*, 106, 456. Still, the history of New York real estate largely confirmed the implications of the grid: that, in the words of Henry George, "The most valuable lands on the globe . . . are not lands of surpassing fertility, but lands to which a surpassing utility has been given by the increase of population." *Progress and Poverty*, 242.

35. Tuckerman, ed., *The Diary of Philip Hone*, 1:203; Blackmar, *Manhattan for Rent*, 273. Hone's experience was not simply the fortuitous result of speculative frenzies during the mid-1830s. Ten years after the Panic of 1837, William V. Brady (another ex-Mayor), invested in ten $300 lots on West Thirty-seventh and Thirty-eighth Streets, and then watched them appreciate almost 2000 percent over the next decade. Spann, *The New Metropolis*, 112.

36. Cooper, *Home as Found*, 102.

37. *Herald*, May 3, 1837. James L. Crouthamel, *Bennett's* New York Herald *and the Rise of the Popular Press*, 82.

38. Blackmar, *Manhattan for Rent*; Hartog, *Public Property and Private Power*.

39. Mumford, *The Culture of Cities*, 255.

40. "New York Daguerreotyped," *Putnam's Monthly*, I (February 1853). On the remarkable spread of photography in New York after its introduction in 1839, see Peter B. Hales, *Silver Cities*; Alan Trachtenberg, *Reading American Photographs*; Leo Braudy, *The Frenzy of Renown*, 493, Brand, *The Spectator and the City*, 165. While much of the early interest in daguerreotypes focused on personal portraiture, New York street scenes and building façades were also popular subjects in the antebellum era, especially in the work of Victor Prevost and in the stereoscopic pictures of Edward and Henry Anthony. For some of the best examples, see Mary Black, *Old New York in Early Photographs*, and Frederick Lightfoot, *Nineteenth-Century New York in Rare Photographic Views*. On bird's-eye views, see Kasson, *Rudeness and Civility*, 73, and chapter 3 of this study.

3. Commercial Impudence and the Dictatorship of the Perpendicular

1. Charles H. Haswell, *Reminiscences of an Octogenarian of the City of New York (1816–1860)*, 12–13.

2. Priscilla Parkhurst Ferguson, "Reading City Streets," 386.

3. I. N. Phelps Stokes, *The Iconography of Manhattan Island*, 856, 857.

4. One letter to Mayor DeWitt Clinton referred to street signs explicitly as "Direction Boards" (a term used for street signs by the Council as late as 1824), and a 1793 petition from the residents of Partition Street asked the Common Council "that a Board be put up at each end of every Street with the Name of the Street and an Index or hand pointed towards the Street painted thereon." Ibid., 1302–1303, 1417. See also the Common Council resolution of February 16, 1824 in *Minutes of the Common Council of the City of New York* 13:558. Though I have been unable to find any visual documentation of these pointing signs, there is a reference in the *Proceedings of the Board of Aldermen* 5:325 (November 2, 1833) to "sign or finger boards."

5. David Garrioch, *Neighborhood and Community in Paris, 1740–1790*, 29.

6. Stokes, *The Iconography of Manhattan Island*, 1310.

7. *Proceedings of the Board of Aldermen* 5:309–310 (October 14, 1833).

8. It is even stranger that resolutions to put signs on street corners managed to arouse discussion and in some cases controversy. An 1836 resolution to put signs on "any and all corners of streets, which are destitute of the name of the proper street" was tabled and followed two weeks later by the adoption of one calling for street names on "at least two corners of each intersection" and one on every designated street on Third Avenue. In 1837, the Street Committee of the Board of Aldermen refused to support a resolution of the Board of Assistant Aldermen to the same general effect, arguing that previous resolutions made it "not necessary to take any further action on the subject." Interestingly enough, the same committee had concurred with the resolution two months earlier, but had reconsidered it in light of some discussion. Ibid. 11:123, 213; 14:87.

9. Even a cursory perusal of the prints collected in the New York Public Library and the New-York Historical Society reveals numerous inconsistencies in how the city's verbal landscape is represented. To cite one example, an 1831 wood engraving of Holt's Hotel, in which the name of the hotel appears in huge letters on the front, shows the words "Water St." painted in black letters on a white sign attached to the corner building right above a black sign with white lettering that reads HOUSE OF. A contemporary engraving appearing in a pictorial reference work (as well as an 1835 woodcut) presents the same scene without any sign on the hotel, without the street sign, but with the HOUSE sign (though in this case the letters are black and the sign is white). Yet another engraving from the same period also depicts no hotel sign, also shows HOUSE OF in black letters, but has WATER STREET written out in full in black. The three engravings appear in the Eno (no. 144) and Stokes (no. 399.18) print collections of the New York Public Library. The 1835 woodcut appears in the print collections of the New-York Historical Society. Note that all reference numbers used here to designate prints in the Stokes collection refer to the catalogue of Gloria Gilda Deak, *Picturing America*.

10. See for example prints 392.1 and 399.18 in the Stokes Collection, prints 141 and 238 in the Eno Collection. For photographic evidence, see the Murray Street sign intersecting lower Broadway in the stereograph series *Anthony's Instantaneous Views* (no. 231). This particular image is housed at the New York Public Library, photography collection.

11. Edward March Blunt, *The Picture of New-York*, 141. See also Thomas A. Janvier, *In Old New York*, 57.

12. See Frederick Marryat, *A Diary in America*, 37. One mid-century engraving of a Broadway tobacco store shows the street name on the curb of the sidewalk. The image appears in Amy Gilman Srebnick, *The Mysterious Death of Mary Rogers*, 52.

13. Stokes, *The Iconography of Manhattan*, 1645. A decade later, English visitor J. S. Buckingham recommended placing house numbers on glass lamps "corresponding to the doors nearest to them, which could be seen by all in passing." James S. Buckingham, *America, Historical, Statistic and Descriptive* 1:222.

14. Anthony Trollope, *North America*, 1:193.

15. The words "Park Row" can be made out in *Anthony's Instantaneous View No. 290* (1860), a stereograph of Broadway as seen from Barnum's Museum. Prints of the image are housed in both the NYPL and the NYHS, though the more legible print is in the latter collection. See also numbers 181 and 188 in the same series.

16. The argument presented here is based on a review of images reproduced in dozens of printed collections and pictorial magazines listed in the bibliography, as well as those found in archives. For a sampling, see Kouwenhoven, *Columbia Historical Portrait*; Lightfoot, *Nineteenth-Century New York*; and Black, *Old New York in Early Photographs*.

17. For the early watercolors, see "Before Urban Renewal," *American Heritage* 24 (4) (June 1973): 23–28, and Kouwenhoven, *Columbia Historical Portrait*, 113.

18. *Proceedings of the Board of Aldermen* 7:140–141 (July 21, 1834). Similar rationales were used to approve name changes as well. See ibid., 4:148–149 (January 21, 1833), 4:394–395 (April 22, 1833), 5:412–413 (November 26, 1833), and 9:71 (June 22, 1835); 8:320–321 (March 23, 1838).

19. *Longworth's American Almanac*, 813.

20. See for example John F. Watson, *Annals and Occurrences of New York City and State in the Olden Time*, 350–354, and Dodge, *Old New York*.

21. As Walter Benjamin argues, the use of house numbers as opposed to names for structures in large cities (which he associates with Napoleonic standardization) marks an important moment in the history of modernization. *Charles Baudelaire*, 47. Like proprietary names, house numbers mark off private property, though by linking real estate in a shared field of reference they also mark that property as a commodity suitable for exchange.

22. New York *Evening Post*, July 19, 1839, quoted in Henry Hoffmann, "Changed House Numbers and Lost Street Names in New York of the Early Nineteenth Century and Later," *New-York Historical Society Quarterly* 21 (1937): 67.

23. *Proceedings of the Board of Aldermen* 38:363 (March 14, 1850).

24. A qualified exception would be the common signs inside omnibuses warning passengers to "beware of pickpockets." Buses were a form of public transit, of course, though the signs were not exactly outdoors, and were clearly identified with the authority of the privately owned (though publicly licensed) bus lines. As such, these signs functioned more as restrictions on liability than as public service announcements. It is also striking that few landmark signs or commemorative plaques appeared in New York before the Civil War, though of course a rich body of such signs emerges in later decades. See Albert Ulmann, *A Landmark History of New York*.

25. William Bobo, a visitor from South Carolina, records the advisory placard in his 1852 book on New York, excerpted in William S. Tryon, ed., *A Mirror for Americans*, 1:225.

26. Haswell, *Reminiscences of an Octogenarian*, 355–356.

27. Oliver Morhouse's recollections are printed in *Old New York*, 441; John Pintard, *Letters*, 1:83, 344; *Minutes of the Common Council* 18:654 (April 5, 1830). A picture of the 4-mile stone appears in James H. Callender, *Yesterdays in Little Old New York*, 298. See also Alvin F. Harlow, *Old Bowery Days*, 67–68.

28. Haswell, *Reminiscences of an Octogenarian*, 356.

29. For examples of this practice, see Kouwenhoven, *Columbia Historical Portrait*, 259, and print 150 in Eno Collection, NYPL.

30. Watson, *Annals and Occurrences of New York*, 355–356.

31. Aleksandr Borisovich Lakier, *A Russian Looks at America*, 63.

32. Marryat, *A Diary in America*, 37.

33. John Kouwenhoven argues that signs begin to appear in pictures of the city during the 1830s because of increased interest among artists and their customers in the business life of the city. But while lithographers (particularly those in the service of business directories) may have become increasingly attentive to sign details, it is certain that commercial signs were multiplying rapidly, if for no other reason than that businesses were spreading all over the city. At any rate, it would be perverse to attribute the steady rise in the concentration, size, and prominence of commercial signage (which continued well beyond the '30s) in the visual sources to iconographic developments governing the production of the pictures rather than iconographic (and commercial) developments governing the signs themselves. Moreover, as I argue later, concern for and sensitivity to the iconography of commerce in street pictures encouraged the proliferation of signs as well. Kouwenhoven, *Columbia Historical Portrait*, 146–147.

34. Joe Cowell, *Thirty Years Passed Among the Players in England and America*, 56;

Horace Greeley, *Recollections of a Busy Life*, 84; Susan Archer Weiss, *Home Life of Poe*, 109. On the other hand, signs could also send a visitor home, at least according to Richard Gooch, whose critical description of the United States in the 1830s included a story about a well-to-do English farmer who emigrated to New York but took the first ship back when, upon his arrival, he noticed a plethora of signs for "ready-made coffins." Gooch, *America and the Americans*, 91–92.

35. Dickens, *American Notes*, 82; Isabella Lucy Bird, *The Englishwoman in America*, 352. See also Evans, "Knickerbocker Hotels and Restaurants," 400.

36. Fanny Fern, *Ruth Hall and Other Writings*, 122. This scene anticipates, rather strikingly, the more famous description of Caroline Meeber's search for employment upon her arrival in Chicago in Theodore Dreiser's *Sister Carrie* (1900), a novel that develops the verbal landscape of the modern city in a fairly elaborate manner.

37. Jonathan Slick, *High Life in New York*, 14.

38. Thomas Hamilton, *Men and Manners in America*, 18.

39. Print 307 in the Eno Collection shows an 1853 view of Genin's store in which Jenny Lind Riding Hats are advertised. In print 287, drawn less than a year earlier, the same sign reads PREPARE FOR A RAINY DAY.

40. Quoted in Barbara J. Berg, *The Remembered Gate*, 97.

41. Watson, *Annals and Occurrences of New York*, 356.

42. Charles T. Harris, *Memories of Manhattan in the Sixties and Seventies*, 4.

43. Lakier, *A Russian Looks at America*, 64.

44. Pictures of the Five Points neighborhood frequently emphasized signage, as in fig. 6.4 of this study. See also the widely reproduced 1827 lithograph appearing in Paul A. Gilje, *The Road to Mobocracy*, 241.

45. See James D. McCabe Jr., *Lights and Shadows of New York Life*, 191–192, and Junius Henri Browne, *The Great Metropolis*, 140.

46. According to most reports, the signs on the houses read simply TO LET or, in Smith's story, THIS HOUSE TO LET, though James Boardman, an English visitor, noted that the rent amount was sometimes posted as well. Boardman's observations are excerpted in Still, *Mirror for Gotham*, 114.

47. Willis, *The Rag-Bag*, 101.

48. See "Old Taverns and Posting Inns," Haswell, *Reminiscences of an Octogenarian*, 169. Significantly, inn signs had already become a subject of antiquarian interest by the antebellum period. See for example William West, *Tavern Anecdotes, and Reminiscences of the Origin of Signs, Coffee-Houses, andc.* In Great Britain, where inn and tavern signs had an even more celebrated history, Jacob Larwood wrote in 1866: "In these modern days, the signboard is a very unimportant object: it was not always so. At a time when but few persons could read and write, house-signs were indispensable in city life." Larwood, *The History of*

Sign Boards from the Earliest Times to the Present Day, v. See also Clarence P. Hornung, *Treasury of American Design* 1:71–73.

49. John Berger, *Ways of Seeing*, 131.

50. Petrucci, *Public Lettering*, 73. For related developments in print advertising typography, see Clarence P. Hornung, *Handbook of Early Advertising Art*, xxiv–xxv.

51. Domingo Faustino Sarmiento, *Travels in the United States in 1847*, 129.

52. Stokes, *The Iconography of Manhattan*, plate 105. See also print 392.13 in Stokes Collection, NYPL. "Stationary" also appears in 392.14 of the same collection, and in 100a in the Eno Collection, NYPL. An 1820 painting of the building shown in the Stokes image also has the nonstandard spelling (though the stationery store has a different proprietor). The image is reprinted in Louis Auchincloss, ed., *The Hone and Strong Diaries of Old Manhattan*, 84.

53. Henry C. Southworth, a young New Yorker who worked as a clerk in a millinery store, was struck "with the peculiarity and manner of spelling different signs in New York," but his examples are "cigars" and "dyeing," both correct spellings. "Journal of Henry C. Southworth," New-York Historical Society ms., entry for June 8, 1850. The spelling "Segars" appears quite frequently in the pictorial sources. For another example of misspelling, see the nonstandard rendering of "restaurant" in Kouwenhoven, *Columbia Historical Portrait*, 226. English actor Joe Cowell, during his stay in New York in the 1840s, wrote of the word " 'restaurat' staring you in the face at every corner." Cowell, *Thirty Years Passed Among the Players*, 56. On dictionary wars, see Kenneth Cmiel, *Democratic Eloquence*, especially 82–90.

54. Pope-Hennessy, ed., *The Aristocratic Journey*, 17–18; Dicey, *Spectator of America*, 10.

55. See Still, *Mirror for Gotham*, 130; McCabe, *Lights and Shadows of New York Life*, 191–192; Dicey, *Spectator of America*, 10. On the role of signs in legitimating language groups and cultures in a different context, see Marc Shell's essay on Quebec in *Children of the Earth*, 41–57.

56. Willis quoted in Still, *Mirror for Gotham*, 88.

57. Abram C. Dayton, *Last Days of Knickerbocker Life in New York*, 134–135. Dayton wrote the book in 1871.

58. See Warner, *The Letters of the Republic*; Benedict Anderson, *Imagined Communities*.

59. Frazar Kirkland, *Cyclopaedia of Commercial and Business Anecdotes*, 320–321.

60. Reprinted in Fern, *Ruth Hall and Other Writings*, 262. The article "Have We Any Men Among Us?" appeared originally in *Musical World and Times*, September 24, 1853.

61. Dayton, *Last Days of Knickerbocker Life*, 133–134. The Canal St. Plan referred, in fact, to all-you-can-eat oysters for sixpence, a bargain reputedly undermined by the practice of slipping in a bad oyster to curb the appetites of

dangerously voracious customers. See Evans, "Knickerbocker Hotels and Restaurants," 400.

62. On graffiti, see Susan Stewart, "Ceci Tuera Cela: Graffiti as Crime and Art" in John Fekete, ed., *Life After Postmodernism*.

63. Quoted in Trachtenberg, *Reading American Photographs*, 15.

64. See Starn, "The Republican Regime of the 'Room of Peace'," 8.

65. On the importance of photography in the representation and self-presentation of American cities during the "information boom" of the 1850s, see Hales, *Silver Cities*, 42–47.

66. See Kasson, *Rudeness and Civility*, 73–74. For some examples of bird's-eye views of the city, including John Bachman's spectacular 1859 panorama, see Kouwenhoven, *Columbia Historical Portrait*, 188–195, 287. On the relationship between height and the sacred, see Amos Rapoport, *The Meaning of the Built Environment*, 116. On Belden's model of the city, which, according to the *Sun*, reproduced "every house, public and private, every tree, post andc.," see Ezekiel Porter Belden, *New-York As It Is*.

67. Robert Venturi, Denise Scott Brown, and Steven Izenour, *Learning From Las Vegas*.

68. Walter Benjamin, *Reflections*, 77–78. See also Michael Fried's intriguing discussion of the relationship between horizontal and vertical representation in the paintings of Thomas Eakins in *Realism, Writing, and Disfiguration*, especially 76–80. While associating writing with the horizontal plane, Fried notes that "there have been cultures and epochs that would have found that association positively unnatural," and considers the possibility that our own "technological society may be on the verge of doing so." In considering the traditional associations of perpendicular writing, it is worth recalling one of the earliest scenes of public script preserved in the Western literary tradition, namely the handwriting on the wall in Belshazzar's feast in the Book of Daniel. What frightens the Chaldean king in the biblical story may be more the appearance of the hand than the appearance of the script (the act of mural writing rather than its legible trace), but of course the severed hand itself provides a compelling metonym for the freestanding script, unattached to the visible presence of its author.

69. Warner, *The Letters of the Republic*.

70. See for example the mention of the 1834 petition of W. Pelby for permission to place a transparency in City Hall Park. *Proceedings of the Board of Aldermen* 7:277 (October 16, 1834).

71. Charles E. Beveridge and David Schuyler, eds., *Creating Central Park* 3:264–265, 279–280. See also Alan Trachtenberg, *The Incorporation of America*, 107–112.

72. *Minutes of the Proceedings of the Board of Commissioners of the Central Park for the*

Year Ending April 30, 1860 (September 23, 1859; reprint, New York, 1860), 138–141.

73. See Roy Rosenzweig and Elizabeth Blackmar, *The Park and the People*, especially 244–247.

74. Ibid., 246.

75. "List of Signs in use upon Central Park," ca. 1871, Frederick Law Olmsted Papers, Manuscript Division, Library of Congress. Central Park was also the site of a noteworthy advisory sign in the visual records. A popular Currier and Ives lithograph from the Civil War era shows ice skaters on the Central Park pond navigating around a small sign near the edge of the pond that reads DANGER. A Winslow Homer depiction of the same scene has the sign reading DANGEROUS. The sign is visible, though not legible, in other nonphotographic views of the park. See Harry T. Peters, *Currier and Ives*, plate 3; John A. Kouwenhoven, *Adventures of America, 1857—1900*, plate 23; Kouwenhoven, *Columbia Historical Portrait*, 290. For a photograph of the same scene a couple of years earlier, in which the sign does not appear, see ibid., 258.

76. Rosenzweig and Blackmar, *The Park and the People*. See also John Brinckerhoff Jackson, *American Space*, 217.

77. See Richard Sennett, *The Fall of Public Man*; Habermas, *The Structural Transformation of the Public Sphere*.

78. See for example the documents collected in David Brion Davis, *Antebellum American Culture*, 111–127.

4. Word on the Streets

1. Lakier, *A Russian Looks at America*, 66.

2. Robert Jay, *The Trade Card in Nineteenth-Century America*, especially 13–33; Bella Clara Landauer, *Early American Trade Cards from the Collection of Bella C. Landauer*; Thomas J. Schlereth, *Cultural History and Material Culture*, 125–126.

3. New York *Herald*, quoted in Stanley Nadel, *Little Germany*, 108–109.

4. Timothy J. Gilfoyle, *City of Eros*, 174.

5. As Elliott Gorn has pointed out, boxers' cards in mid-century New York drew on a tradition in dueling of using cards to express private grievances, but transformed the practice into a genre of advertisement. Gorn, *The Manly Art*, 86, 99–100.

6. Quoted in Tuckerman, ed., *The Diary of Philip Hone*, 2:159–60 (November 14, 1842).

7. Peter G. Buckley, "Culture, Class, and Place in Antebellum New York," 32.

8. Lyon, *Recollections of an Old Cartman*, 28–29.

9. "Journal of Henry C. Southworth," July 5, 1850.

10. Child, *Letters from New York*, 220.

11. Kirkland, *Cyclopaedia of Commercial and Business Anecdotes*, 309–310.

12. Lakier, *A Russian Looks at America*, 66. According to Clarence P. Hornung, sandwich boards first appeared in New York in the 1820s, followed shortly thereafter by wagons draped with banners. *Handbook of Early Advertising Art*, xxxi.

13. See Jay, *The Trade Card in Nineteenth-Century America*, 22.

14. *Minutes of the Common Council of the City of New York* 18:111 (June 1, 1829); 18:206 (July 27, 1829).

15. *People v. Moses Clements et al.*, Court of General Sessions, September, 13, 1830; the case is mentioned in Christine Stansell's study of antebellum New York, though she refers to the protagonists as the "Clements women." See *City of Women*, 60.

16. As Susan Stewart has argued in an essay on graffiti, "Writing and figuration in the wrong time and place fall into the category of obscenity" in a manner analogous to public displays of sexuality—even when the content of the graffiti is beyond reproach. "Ceci Tuera Cela: Graffiti as Crime and Art," 169.

17. Kirkland, *Cyclopaedia of Commercial and Business Anecdotes*, 323.

18. George G. Foster, *New York by Gas-Light and Other Urban Sketches*, 75.

19. Ibid., 152. The theme of overlapping or strikingly juxtaposed public notices is developed in Thomas La Clear's 1845 painting *Looking for Fun*. Melville adopts a related strategy and invokes a similarly urban trope for organizing information and events in the beginning of *Moby-Dick* (1851), when Ishmael imagines his whaling voyage as an item in the "grand programme of Providence," sandwiched between a contested presidential election and a battle in "Affghansitan." Herman Melville, *Moby-Dick*, 15.

20. Dicey, *Spectator of America*, 10; Bowen, ed., *A Frenchman in Lincoln's America*, I: 21–22; Bird, *The Englishwoman in America*, 386–287.

21. Foster, *New York by Gas-Light*, 152.

22. P. T. Barnum, *Struggles and Triumphs*; Barnum, *P. T. Barnum: The Greatest Showman on Earth*; Neil Harris, *Humbug: The Art of P. T. Barnum*; Bluford Adams, *E Pluribus Barnum*; Peter G. Buckley, "To the Opera House: Culture and Society in New York, 1820–1860," 469–540; Constance Mayfield Rourke, *Trumpets of Jubilee*, 369–426; Braudy, *The Frenzy of Renown*, 498–506; Jennifer Wicke, *Advertising Fictions*, 55–72; A. H. Saxon, *P. T. Barnum: The Legend and the Man*.

23. Wicke, *Advertising Fictions*, 63.

24. Barnum, *Struggles and Triumphs*, 119. Adams, *E Pluribus Barnum*, 96.

25. Barnum, *Struggles and Triumphs*, 108.

26. Quoted in Rourke, *Trumpets of Jubilee*, 369.

27. Barnum, *P. T. Barnum*, 51–52.

28. *Struggles and Triumphs*, 120. On the relationships and affinities between the American Museum and the pictorial press, see Adams, *E Pluribus Barnum*, 83–89, and Joshua Emmett Brown, "*Frank Leslie's Illustrated Newspaper*: Pictorial Journalism in Nineteenth-Century America," 67.

29. Barnum, *Struggles and Triumphs*, 129. Because of the constraints imposed by this advertising policy, Barnum had to buy a new blanket for all twelve performances of the Wedding Dance he staged with the help of some not-so-enthusiastic Native Americans (whose chief regarded the blankets as gifts rather than props) he had picked up in Iowa.

30. Ibid., 107.

31. Leo Hershkowitz, *Tweed's New York: Another Look*, 85.

32. Hamilton, *Men and Manners in America*, 18. See also J. S. Buckingham's description of political bills promoting "the whole ticket" in *America, Historical, Statistic and Descriptive* 1:70–71.

33. Joel Tyler Headley, *The Great Riots of New York: 1712–1863*, 102–110.

34. Dicey, *Spectator of America*, 283.

35. Poster appears in Lloyd Morris, *Incredible New York: High Life and Low Life of the Last Hundred Years*, 39.

36. *Tribune*, July 17, 1863.

37. Robert Moody, *The Astor Place Riot*, 130; Buckley, "To the Opera House," 315, 417; Headley, *The Great Riots of New York*, 111–128.

38. Moody, *The Astor Place Riot*, 178.

39. Ibid., 184.

40. Buckley, "To the Opera House," 518–519.

41. Nevins and Thomas, eds., *The Diary of George Templeton Strong* 3:574 (April 3, 1865). See also chapters 5 and 7 of this study.

42. *Herald*, November 6, 1841.

43. As Michael Warner argues, republican political discourse valorized an abnegation of the personal identity of individual authors. The kind of authority claimed by Benjamin Franklin's Mrs. Dogood or the framers of the Constitution was defined in opposition to and above individual identity and interest. Warner, *The Letters of the Republic*.

44. Headley, *The Great Riots of New York*, 82. The early date makes it unlikely that the poster was a sneaky abolitionist ploy to arouse antisouthern sympathy.

45. Wilentz, *Chants Democratic*, 291; Tuckerman, ed., *The Diary of Philip Hone*, 2:210–211 (June 6, 1836).

46. Edward Robb Ellis, *The Epic of New York City*, 251.

47. Headley, *The Great Riots of New York*, 82.

48. Ibid., 119.

49. Buckley, "To the Opera House," 72.

50. Tuckerman, ed., *The Diary of Philip Hone*, 2:234 (November 1, 1844).

51. Hershkowitz, *Tweed's New York*, 87.

52. Tuckerman, ed., *The Diary of Philip Hone*, 2:233 (October 30, 1844).

53. *Tribune*, July 14, 1863.

54. *Tribune*, July 17, 1863.

55. Ryan, "The American Parade," 133.

56. Susan G. Davis, *Parades and Power*, 4. The fact that parades were dramatic events that had a different (and no less powerful) impact from that of a political pamphlet is important, and the complaint about the underrepresentation of nonliterate media in modern historiography is fair to a point—it ignores, even as it epitomizes, a compensatory tendency to romanticize orality and dramaturgy as markers of more authentic, counterhegemonic traditions.

57. Cadwallader D. Colden, *Memoir, Prepared at the Request of a Committee of the City of New York . . . at the Celebration of the New York Canals*, 212–267.

58. Sean Wilentz, "Artisan Republican Festivals and the Rise of Class Conflict in New York City, 1788–1837," 37–77.

59. *Herald*, September 2, 1858.

60. Ibid., August 30, 1858.

61. *Herald*, September 2, 1858.

62. Quoted in Kouwenhoven, *Columbia Historical Portrait*, 309.

63. *Herald*, March 7, 1865

64. *Tribune*, October 15, 1842.

65. *Commercial Advertiser*, December 6, 1851.

66. *Herald*, September 2, 1858.

67. *Times*, April 20, 1865.

68. Ibid.

69. Ibid.

70. *Herald*, August 30, 1858.

5. Print in Public, Public in Print

1. Moritz Busch, *Travels Between the Hudson and the Mississippi, 1851–1852*, 33–34.

2. Terdiman, *Discourse/Counter-Discourse*, 117–146. Interestingly, Terdiman's critique of the modern newspaper, which links new market conditions and new technologies of communication as twin foes of holistic social understanding, resembles current attacks on television and digitial communication that mourn the decline of the typographic culture whose apotheosis Terdiman analyzes. See for example Birkerts, *The Gutenberg Elegies* and Postman, *Amusing Ourselves to Death*.

3. *National Police Gazette*, October 28, 1848, quoted in Dan Schiller, *Objectivity and the News*, 102.

4. Frank Luther Mott, *American Journalism*; Schudson, *Discovering the News*, 12–60; Schiller, *Objectivity and the News*; Barth, *City People*, 58–109; Alexander Saxton, *The Rise and Fall of the White Republic*, 95–108; David S. Reynolds, *Beneath the American Renaissance*, especially 170–175; Louis H. Fox, "New York City Newspapers, 1820–1850: A Bibliography."

5. Alexander Saxton, for example, sees the first two decades of the penny press as a unique window of political opportunity in the history of print technology, when low production costs coexisted with low consumption costs. Michael Schudson attributes the technological changes to the rise of the very political culture whose emergence Saxton is trying to explain. And while Schudson emphasizes the affinities between the new press and the ideology of the urban middle classes, Dan Schiller connects the success of those papers to their appeal to the artisan population. Perhaps not inconsistent with Schudson, Gunther Barth's version of the story has the press projecting an image of common humanity, in which urban residents of all classes and ideologies are implicitly linked by their shared pursuit of material success. Stuart Blumin makes similar claims for the causal role of print technology in his introduction to George G. Foster's *New York by Gas-Light*, 11–19. See also Mott, *American Journalism*, 215, where he proclaims "Behind it all was the machine"; Saxton, *The Rise and Fall of the White Republic*, 95–108; Schudson, *Discovering the News*; Schiller, *Objectivity and the News*; Barth, *City People*, 58–59. Significantly, both Schudson and Schiller link the ideology of the mass-circulation press to that of Jacksonian democracy, though Schudson is mostly interested in the decline of deferential politics while Schiller, following Sean Wilentz, stresses the roots of Jacksonian-era egalitarianism in urban craft traditions and in emerging class consciousness. In his recent survey of the period, Charles Sellers (drawing on Saxton and Schiller) portrays the penny press as straying from its mechanic roots and its antibourgeois origins, becoming more apolitical with the infusion of large-scale capital (sometime in the '40s, it seems, though his choice of villains suggests a decline as early as 1835!). See Sellers, *The Market Revolution: Jacksonian America*, 386. For an alternative interpretation that stresses the role of evangelism and tract societies in the emergence of mass journalism in the first third of the century, see David Paul Nord, "The Evangelical Origins of Mass Media in America, 1815–1835," 88.

All of these studies draw heavily (some almost exclusively) on New York sources and examples. Another recent work, Gerald Baldasty's *The Commercialization of News in the Nineteenth Century*, uses newspapers from smaller cities and comes up with a strikingly different story. Baldasty's thesis that the nineteenth century saw a gradual shift from a press driven by partisan politics (which "produced political debate of potential value for the broad public," 143) to a press driven by advertising (which did not) would not account for the emergence of the penny press in New York (and in other large eastern cities), whose development, as I argue here, blurred and complicated the very distinction (invidious or neutral) between political and commercial journalism that he underscores and simplifies. Schiller, *Objectivity and the News*, 15.

6. Habermas, *The Structural Transformation of the Public Sphere*, 14–18. An excessively rigid separation between the penny papers and the sixpennies also glosses

over significant differences among the former themselves. While some, like the *Sun*, the *Herald*, and the early *New Era*, flaunted their nonpartisan status, the *Tribune* proudly identified itself with the Whigs from the very first issue. George Henry Evans's *Man* (1834–35), another penny daily, had an even more explicit (radical) political agenda, and conformed to none of the general patterns of sensationalism and heavy advertising.

7. Schudson, *Discovering the News*, 31–35; Blumin, *New York by Gas-Light*, 11–19; Barth, *City People*, 90–92. Mott, *American Journalism*, 203–204; Frank Presbrey, *The History and Development of Advertising*, 186.

8. Ibid., 186–194; Fox, "New York City Newspapers, 1820–1850," 6.

9. Quoted in Crouthamel, *Bennett's* New York Herald, 11.

10. Isaac Pray, *Memoirs of James Gordon Bennett and His Times*, 197.

11. *Herald*, May 6, 1835.

12. *Age*, May 12, 1838.

13. *New Era*, October 3, 1836; *Herald*, May 11, 1835.

14. Pray, *Memoirs of James Gordon Bennett*, 198.

15. Tuckerman, ed., *The Diary of Philip Hone*, 1:271 (September 23, 1837).

16. Philadelphia *Public Ledger*, March 25, 1836, quoted in Mott, *American Journalism*, 241.

17. Fanny Fern, *Fern Leaves from Fanny's Port-Folio*, 178–179. Interestingly, Fern combines these references to public reading with a number of domestic scenarios ("Where did . . . papas find solace when the coffee was muddy? What screen did husbands dodge behind, when their wives asked them for money?"), and her litany includes female as well as male readers ("What did love-sick damsels do for 'sweet bits of poetry' and 'touching continued stories?' ").

18. Augustus Maverick, *Henry J. Raymond and the New York Press*, 52; Bird, *The Englishwoman in America*, 342.

19. Pray, *Memoirs of James Gordon Bennett*, 397. Pray also describes public reading of the *Herald* on Nassau Street during the first year of its publication, pages 218–219.

20. Foster, *New York by Gas-Light*, 113. Newsboys made similarly poignant characters in the urban reform literature of the period. Lydia Maria Child describes her 1842 encounter with a four-year-old "little ragged urchin," whom she imagines sleeping on dirty straw, being beaten for failing to "bring home pence enough for his parents grog," and being tempted into the life of vice from which "one tone like a mother's voice might have wholly changed his earthly destiny." See *Letters from New York*, 95. To Charles Loring Brace, another reformer, the newsboys were model citizens of the urban underworld who were lighthearted, honorable, and rarely drank. "Their kindness to one another, when are all in the utmost destitution," Brace observed, "is a credit to human nature." *The Dangerous Classes of New York, and Twenty Years' Work Among Them*, 97–99. Several aspects of the mythology of the antebellum newsboy are captured in

John Morrow's 1860 memoir, the foreword to which presents the book as a description of a much broader slice of urban experience, since " 'Newsboy' . . . properly embraces all those of either sex who at a tender age are compelled to rely upon their own wits and exertions for support." *A Voice From the Newsboys*, xii. For examples of the romance of the newsboy in popular fiction, see Adrienne Siegel, *The Image of the City in Popular Literature, 1820–1870*, 82.

21. Frances S. Osgood, *The Cries of New-York*; Luc Sante, *Low Life: Lures and Snares of Old New York*, 61–62. Sante traces the decline of the street crier to the aural competition from transportation conveyances and other sources, though this explanation would not seem to account for the survival of the newsboy.

22. *Sunday Times and Noah's Weekly Messenger*, February 11, 1849.

23. The crying of an extra became a standard moment of public discovery, as suggested in Caroline Woolsey's letter to a relative after Lincoln's assassination. "What can one do? We are all dumb with grief. The extra has just been cried giving the awful moment of his death. What a moment for America!" Georgeanna Woolsey Bacon and Eliza Woolsey Howland, *Letters of a Family During the War for the Union, 1861–1865*, 659–660.

24. Lyon, *Recollections of an Old Cartman*, 57–58.

25. Whitman quoted in Ellis, *The Epic of New York City*, 262.

26. Bacon and Howland, *Letters of a Family During the War for the Union*, 110.

27. Browne, *The Great Metropolis*, 93–95. In an unpublished dissertation, Joshua Emmett Brown has demonstrated how physiognomic illustrations in the pictorial press ordered the promiscuous world of urban strangers by segmenting the city into exclusive social types. Arrayed side by side in the streets of the city, however, newspapers and magazines could reinforce images of abrupt collisions that the pictorial press sought to smooth over. See Brown, *"Frank Leslie's Illustrated Newspaper,"* especially 144–146.

28. *Tribune*, May 3, 1841; New York *Transcript*, May 25, 1836, quoted in Fox, "New York City Newspapers, 1820–1850," 5.

29. *Morning Courier and New-York Enquirer*, April 14, 1845.

30. Terdiman, *Discourse/Counter-Discourse*, 124.

31. Pray, *Memoirs of James Gordon Bennett*, 350.

32. Reynolds, *Beneath the American Renaissance*, 174; Pray, *Memoirs of James Gordon Bennett*, 214–215.

33. *Tribune*, May, 3, 1841.

34. See for example Henry Bright's use of daily newspaper advertisements in his 1852 travel diary. Anne Henry Ehrenpreis, ed., *Happy Country This America: The Travel Diary of Henry Arthur Bright*, 82–91.

35. See Presbrey, *The History and Development of Advertising*, 210.

36. Pray, *Memoirs of James Gordon Bennett*, 397.

37. A handful of advertisements extended for two columns during the sec-

ond half of the 1830s, but these were striking exceptions. See Presbrey, *The History and Development of Advertising*, 208.

38. See for example the *Courier and Enquirer* for the year 1861.

39. *Herald*, June 25, 1845. See Brown, *"Frank Leslie's Illustrated Newspaper,"* 22. The *Herald* did periodically include illustrations, especially maps (an early example of which appears on the front page of the November 2, 1841 issue), which were all the more striking for their singularity. See Crouthamel, *Bennett's New York Herald*, 34.

40. Presbrey, *The History and Development of Advertising*, 176.

41. For an example of an especially delirious exploitation of these possibilities, see Hornung, *Handbook of Early Advertising Art*, xxxvii.

42. See Presbrey, *The History and Development of Advertising*, 233–239; Crouthamel, *Bennett's* New York Herald, 52.

43. Jay Fliegelman, *Declaring Independence*, 26.

44. Anderson, *Imagined Communities*, 35.

45. *Herald*, November 21, 1837.

46. Willis, *The Rag-Bag*, 13

47. Warner, *The Letters of the Republic*.

48. Frederic Trautmann, ed. and trans., "New York Through German Eyes: The Travels of Ludwig Gall, 1819," 452–455.

49. Anderson, *Imagined Communities*, 35–36.

50. Presbrey, *The History and Development of Advertising*, 208.

51. George P. Rowell, *The Men Who Advertise*, 4.

52. See other examples in chapter 7.

53. *Times*, December 21, 1861; McCabe, *Lights and Shadows of New York Life*, 611–614. Interestingly, earlier forms of the personal ad sought unknown partners for marital connections, much in the spirit of a help wanted announcement. It was not until the end of the antebellum era, however, after public spaces and public papers had grown in a mutually clarifying fashion into sites of promiscuous circulation, that this particular kind of notice began to appear with some frequency. See Gilfoyle, *City of Eros*, 114.

54. *Report of the Special Committee Appointed by the Common Council . . . for the Reception of Gov. Louis Kossuth*, 93, 237.

55. *Times*, December 8, 1851.

56. Pray, *Memoirs of James Gordon Bennett*, 417.

57. Ibid., 353. By the end of the war, the Tribune was spending more than $100,000 per year on "intellectual labor" and another $100,000 on telegraphing and correspondence. Greeley, *Recollections of a Busy Life*, 142.

58. On the immigrant press, see Robert Ernst, *Immigrant Life in New York City, 1825–1863*, 150–161.

59. Edward Neufville Tailer Jr., "Journal of Some of the Events Which Have

Occurred in My Life." The journal fills 57 volumes and spans the years 1848 to 1917. For more information on Tailer, see Allan Stanley Horlick, *Country Boys and Merchant Princes*, 121–143.

60. Tailer, "Journal," September 29, 1857; November 28, 1857.

61. Ibid., January 22, 1858.

62. See for example ibid., March 29, 1863.

63. When Tailer leaves New York for a ten-month trip to Europe, the clippings practically disappear, and the journey is bracketed neatly by two passenger listings in the press, marking his departure and his return. See ibid., December 11, 1858–October 30, 1859.

64. Ibid., July 2, 1858.

65. Ibid., March 11, 1861.

66. Most antebellum diaries, despite the aura of intimacy and introversion that frequently surrounds the genre, reflect a certain consciousness of wider readerships, anticipated or imagined, but Tailer goes further. An 1860 entry, for example, introducing an uncited clipping, observes that "the following acct. of the improvements about to be made on Broadway may not prove uninteresting when a few years shall have rolled away." Ibid., April 19, 1860.

67. Ibid., December 31, 1862.

68. Compare to the case cited by Augustus Maverick, in his biography of *Times* founder Henry J. Raymond, of a New England man who reputedly composed a hand-printed mini-weekly for his own consumption, providing "the only instance on record of a man being his own editor, printer, publisher, and reader." Maverick, *Henry J. Raymond and the New York Press*, 51.

69. Lakier, *A Russian Looks at America*, 77.

70. Tuckerman, ed., *The Diary of Philip Hone*, 2:11 (February 25, 1840); C. Astor Bristed, *The Upper Ten Thousand*, 211.

71. Edgar Allan Poe, "Marginal Notes," in Poe, *Essays and Reviews*, 1370.

72. Tuckerman, ed., *The Diary of Philip Hone*, 2:11 (February 25, 1840).

73. James Fenimore Cooper, *The American Democrat*, 182. Others offered different explanations why writing is less trustworthy than speech. Poe thought that "we place on paper without hesitation a tissue of flatteries, to which in society we could not give utterance, for our lives, without either blushing or laughing outright," and observed elsewhere that "the greater amount of truth is impulsively uttered; thus the greater amount is spoken, not written." Edgar Allan Poe, "The Literati of New York City," in Poe, *Essays and Reviews*, 1119; Poe, "Marginalia," in ibid., 1322.

74. See Halttunen, *Confidence Men and Painted Women*. For a broader history of the association between writing and fraudulence, to be discussed at greater length in the next chapter, see Ziff, *Writing in the New Nation*.

75. Pray, *Memoirs of James Gordon Bennett*, 473.

76. *Herald,* May 6, 1835. On Matthias, see Paul E. Johnson and Sean Wilentz, *The Kingdom of Matthias: A Story of Sex and Salvation in Nineteenth-Century America.*

77. On Locke and Poe, see Reynolds, *Beneath the American Renaissance,* 241; Poe, "The Literati of New York City," in *Essays and Reviews,* 1214–1222; Poe, "The Balloon Hoax," in *Complete Tales and Poems of Edgar Allan Poe,* 71–81. Newspaper hoaxes were recurring affairs in the antebellum era, describing apocryphal battles, fictitious discoveries, and even bogus presidential pronouncements.

6. Promiscuous Circulation

1. *Evening Post,* August 6, 1834, reprinted in William Leggett, *Democratick Editorials,* 73.

2. Lynn Glaser, *Counterfeiting in America,* 82.

3. See examples in John A. Muscalus, *Odd Bank Note and Scrip Denominations in American Monetary History.*

4. Sociologist Viviana A. Zelizer has offered a compelling critique of the classical understanding of money as a uniform system of quantification, rationalizing human interactions and liquidating all social values. Through elaborate rituals of earmarking, Zelizer argues, we differentiate a wide range of monies and monetary uses in everyday life, inscribing various social formations and preserving noncommensurate and unfungible differences. Zelizer reminds us that money is multiple even when it appears to be uniform. When money appears in so many different guises and denominations, subject to varying rates of discount and degrees of suspicion, its social meanings are probably even more complex. Of course, in that case we may be more interested in the way so many different kinds of paper become a single thing recognized as money, rather than in how differences are imposed onto that single thing. The point of this chapter is not to probe the ways in which everyday people differentiated their money (an important question that lies beyond the scope of this project), but rather to consider how everyday New Yorkers, negotiating a city saturated with writing, experienced their money as a set of print claims that were *already* differentiated, but that could often be substituted and exchanged. See Zelizer, *The Social Meaning of Money.*

5. Dodge, *Old New York,* 43.

6. Eric P. Newman, *The Early Paper Money of America,* 11. John Kenneth Galbraith has written: "If the history of commercial banking belongs to the Italians and of central banking to the British, that of paper money issued by a government belongs indubitably to the Americans." *Money: Whence It Came, Where It Went,* 45.

7. Newman, *The Early Paper Money of America,* 26–29. See also Glaser, *Counterfeiting in America,* 11–52.

8. Clinton Rossiter, ed., *The Federalist Papers*, 281 (Federalist 44).

9. Marc Shell, *Money, Language, and Thought*, 1.

10. Michel Chevalier, *Society, Manners, and Politics in the United States*, 31–32; William H. Dillistin, *Bank Note Reporters and Counterfeit Detectors, 1826–1866*, 80.

11. A. Barton Hepburn, *A History of Currency in the United States*. See also Henry Wysham Lanier, *A Century of Banking in New York, 1822–1922*; Bray Hammond, *Banks and Politics in America from the Revolution to the Civil War*, 105–106.

12. Dodge, *Old New York*, 43. Other observers describe a similar situation around the time of the Panic of 1819. See Lanier, *A Century of Banking in New York*, 24, 52.

13. Galbraith, *Money*, 88–89. See also Viviana Zelizer, "Making Multiple Monies," 197. According to one estimate, 12,000 different banknote issues were in circulation in 1863, on the eve of the establishment of a national currency. Ernest A. McKay, *The Civil War and New York City*, 255.

14. David R. Johnson, *Illegal Tender*.

15. Marvin Meyers, *The Jacksonian Persuasion*, especially 16–32; Hammond, *Banks and Politics in America*, 328–329; Sellers, *The Market Revolution*, especially 325–326; Walter Hugins, *Jacksonian Democracy and the Working Class*, especially 32–35, 179–186. For an example of the depth of antipaper sentiment within more radical labor sentiment, see George Henry Evans's short-lived daily paper *The Man*, February 20, 1834. For the purposes of this chapter, it makes little difference whether Jackson's anti-Bank rhetoric expressed the fundamental hostility of an agrarian majority toward the market economy or masked the self-aggrandizing ambitions of a particular entrepreneurial class seeking to wrest control over that economy from the hands of older elites. The plausibility and effectiveness of the rhetoric depended, to some degree, on links among paper, cities, and the marketplace explored here for particular purposes. Interestingly, the historiographical tide has shifted somewhat in the last decade or two, away from Counterprogressive critiques of Jacksonian democracy, and recent surveys of the period tend to take the republican and agrarian rhetoric rather seriously. See Harry L. Watson, *Liberty and Power*; Sellers, *The Market Revolution*; Richard B. Latner, "Preserving 'the natural equality of rank and influence': Liberalism, Republicanism, and Equality of Condition in Jacksonian Politics," in Haskell and Teichegraeber, eds., *The Culture of the Market*, 189–230. For an account of some of the historiographical debates surrounding Jacksonian politics, see Sean Wilentz, "On Class and Politics in Jacksonian America."

16. Nevins and Thomas, eds., *The Diary of George Templeton Strong* 1:57 (April 12, 1837). Tuckerman, ed., *The Diary of Philip Hone*, 1:252 (April 28, 1837).

17. The story appears in Hill, *Their Sisters' Keepers*, 123.

18. Lyon, *Recollections of an Old Cartman*, 92–101.

19. Michael O'Malley, "Specie and Species: Race and the Money Question in Nineteenth-Century America," 374.

20. Hepburn, *A History of Currency in the United States*, 165; the second study is quoted in Glaser, *Counterfeiting in America*, 86.

21. Quoted in *Day's New-York Bank Note List, Counterfeit Detector and Price Current*, November 28, 1837.

22. Quoted in ibid., December 4, 1840.

23. *Bankers Magazine* quoted in W. L. Ormsby, *A Description of the Present System of Bank Note Engraving, Showing Its Tendency to Facilitate Counterfeiting*, 15.

24. Johnson, *Illegal Tender*, 37. *Times*, July 30, 1862.

25. Leggett, *Democratick Editorials*, 83–84. James Gordon Bennett offered a variant of this charge, in his claim that a rival publisher pawned off bad notes on "hard-driven" employers who pass them on to their workers. *Herald*, December 4, 1841.

26. McKay, *The Civil War and New York City*, 139–140; John Jay Knox, *United States Notes*, 100–105; Marryat, *A Diary in America*, 27.

27. Horatio Alger Jr., *Ragged Dick and Struggling Upward*, 11–14; Supplement to *New-York Bank Note List*, March 21, 1842. In Isaac Lyon's story about the deadbeat clergyman, the butcher identifies what's wrong with the Canadian bill with "a hasty glance." Lyon, *Recollections of an Old Cartman*, 101.

28. Cowell, *Thirty Years Passed Among the Players*, 56.

29. *The Banker's Method of Detecting Bad Money*, 4.

30. Kirkland, *Cyclopaedia of Commercial and Business Anecdotes* 1:96–97.

31. The history of counterfeit detectors presented in this chapter relies heavily on William Dillistin's excellent monograph, *Bank Note Reporters and Counterfeit Detectors*.

32. *The New Monthly Messenger, General Bank Note List and New-York Prices Current*, August 5, 1842.

33. Harris, *Memories of Manhattan in the Sixties and Seventies*, 22.

34. Melville, *The Confidence-Man*, 331.

35. The question of confidence in *The Confidence Man* can be read as a reflection on the process by which print and writing are used to negotiate relations among strangers in public. As if to drive the point home, the novel opens with three separate public displays of writing—a placard announcing the reward for the capture of an impostor, a beggar's slate preaching the virtues of charity, and a barber's sign bearing the ominous inscription NO TRUST. Confidence on the *Fidèle* is acquired and regulated as much with the flash of a text as with the wink of an eye.

36. Halttunen, *Confidence Men and Painted Women*; Johannes Dietrich Bergmann, "The Original Confidence Man"; Reynolds, *Beneath the American Renaissance*, 187,

300–304; William E. Lenz, *Fast Talk and Flush Times*. The analogy between the paradoxical function of antebellum counterfeit detectors and that of Halttunen's etiquette books also appears in O'Malley, "Specie and Species," 375.

37. *Day's New-York Bank Note List, Counterfeit Detector and Price Current*, June 28, 1832.

38. The case is summarized in *Niles Weekly Register*, April 16, 1836, 124–125.

39. *The Banker's Method of Detecting Bad Money*, 4; See also A. S. Gear, *The United States Bank Note Detector*, 26.

40. Ormsby, *A Description of the Present System of Bank Note Engraving*, 63.

41. *Sylvester's Reporter, Counterfeit Detector, New-York Price Current, and General Advertiser*, September 18, 1834.

42. *Day's New-York Bank Note List*, November 28, 1837.

43. *The Banker's Method of Detecting Bad Money*, 5.

44. On brothel guides, see Gilfoyle, *City of Eros*, 131–132; Hill, *Their Sisters' Keepers*, 214–215.

45. *The Bank Note and Commercial Reporter*, January 23, 1851.

46. *The Banker's Method of Detecting Bad Money*, 13. The particular copy of the book was sent from Edw. L. Murray to Henry F. Vail Esq. a year before the publication date, with a letter attached asking Vail for his opinion of the work. The penciled suggestion could thus be Murray's own.

47. Weekly *Herald*, November 6, 1841.

48. See for example *The New-York Bank Note List*, March 21, 1842. On Thompson, see Dillistin, *Bank Note Reporters and Counterfeit Detectors*, 78–93. Interestingly, after the introduction of national banknotes, Thompson established the first national bank in New York City.

49. *Sylvester's Reporter*, September 24, 1830.

50. Mahlon Day, to take a significant example, also printed pamphlets, handbills, circulars, and trade cards. See advertisement in *Day's New-York Bank Note List, Counterfeit Detector and Price Current*, June 28, 1832.

51. *Evening Post, Man*. Bennett's fickle position on Jackson and the Bank Veto and his subtle fluctuations in editorial party preferences should not obscure his enduring antipathy to banks, paper money (which he consistently referred to as "shinplaster"), and credit. See Crouthamel, *Bennett's* New York Herald, 80–85.

52. Weekly *Herald*, November 6, 1841. Interestingly enough, *Tribune* editor and publisher Horace Greeley's first major printing job was S. J. Sylvester's *Bank-Note Reporter*. Greeley, *Recollections of a Busy Life*, 91.

53. Weekly *Herald*, November 27, 1841; Dillistin, *Bank Note Reporters and Counterfeit Detectors*, 48–51.

54. Weekly *Herald*, November 27, 1841.

55. *Sylvester's Reporter, Counterfeit Detector, New-York Price Current, and General Advertiser.*, September 13, 1838.

56. Weekly *Herald*, November 6, 1841.

57. Newman, *The Early Paper Money of America*, 27

58. *Day's New-York Bank Note List and Counterfeit Detector*, November 2, 1841.

59. See for example *Herald*, January 10, 1842. Significantly, it was by observing discrepancies in handwriting that the *Times* managed to avoid falling for the notorious draft hoax of May 1864, in which a local journalist forged an Associated Press bulletin bearing a proclamation from the president calling for the conscription of 400,000 additional troops. See McKay, *The Civil War and New York City*, 248–249.

60. Melville, *The Confidence-Man*, 108.

61. *A New Security for Protecting Bank Notes From Alterations and Photographic Counterfeits*, 17–18.

62. *Second Annual Report of the Board of Managers of the Association of Banks for the Suppression of Counterfeiting*, 10.

63. Quoted in Dillistin, *Bank Note Reporters and Counterfeit Detectors*, 36–38.

64. *The Banker's Method of Detecting Bad Money*, 15–16.

65. Ormsby, *A Description of the Present System of Bank Note Engraving*, 80–81. Many of New York's finest engravers were involved in the production of banknotes, as was the painter Asher Durand. See Kouwenhoven, *Columbia Historical Portrait*, 235.

66. A. S. Gear, *The United States Bank Note Detector, at Sight*, 25. Gear also cites the examples of Winfield Scott, John Fremont, and Franklin Pierce to dispute the notion that a faithful rendering of a human subject in the vignette would include an attractive head of hair.

67. Johnson, *Illegal Tender*, 44.

68. Gear, *The United States Bank Note Detector*, 8, 25.

69. *The Banker's Method of Detecting Bad Money*, 11.

70. *A New Security for Protecting Bank Notes*, 7.

71. *The Banker's Method of Detecting Bad Money*, 10.

72. Kirkland, *Cyclopaedia of Commercial and Business Anecdotes* 1:97. A New York bank teller worried that "when even bank officers, themselves, receive false issues with false signatures of their own bank without detection . . . there would seem to be a danger that the whole system of bank paper for currency may yet have to be abandoned." Quoted in Glaser, *Counterfeiting in America*.

73. Alger, *Ragged Dick*, 34–36.

74. Ormsby, *A Description of the Present System of Bank Note Engraving*, 19.

75. Uniform currency further extended these central features of antebellum currency, features we are now in a position to appreciate as paper money begins to pass from view. Cash transactions, especially large ones, are becoming obsolete, preserved in fetishized form in the bill wads and stuffed suitcases of our cinematic imagination. While credit cards, ATMs, and new forms of electronic

cash would seem to make money even lighter and more portable, our new forms of doing business presuppose fixed personal identity and are attended and burdened by an astonishing amount of personal history. Thus while our money is becoming less and less immanent, in other ways we are returning to a state before the advent of a cash economy, before widepsread urbanization, when personal acquaintance served as security for exchange.

7. *Epilogue: Words of War*

1. *Frank Leslie's Illustrated Newspaper*, March 25, 1865.

2. Greeley, *Recollections of a Busy Life*, 296. See also George Lippard's 1864 novel set in and around New York, *The Empire City*, in which two characters—"Number Ninety-one" and "Nameless"—meet en route to the city.

3. Benjamin, *Charles Baudelaire*, 47.

4. Bowen, ed., *A Frenchman in Lincoln's America*, 1:21–22.

5. *Times*, April 15, 1861.

6. *Herald*, July 4, 1862.

7. Bacon and Howland, *Letters of a Family During the War for the Union*, 659–660. On time lags in the circulation of news in antebellum America, see Pred, *Urban Growth and City-Systems*, 146–148; Richard D. Brown, *Knowledge Is Power*, 245–267.

8. McKay, *The Civil War and New York City*, 304–305.

9. See for example Jane Woolsey's 1861 letter to her daughters after the Confederate rout at Manassas, which had been misreported in the New York papers: "We have had an exciting night and morning. Just as we were going to bed last night, we heard the distant sound of an 'Extra;' it was very late; everybody in bed. . . . We were all undressed, but waited with anxiety till the sound approached nearer and nearer; but made up our minds not to rush down and buy one, as it might be a hoax—till at last a tremendous howl of three boys gave us the news of a 'great battle at Bull's Run.' 'Rebels defeated! Batteries all taken!' We thanked God for this much, and went to our beds to try and sleep patiently till morning. We have now had the newspaper accounts as far as they go, but long for further and later." Bacon and Howland, *Letters of a Family During the War for the Union*, 123.

10. *Herald*, April 15, 1861.

11. See for example *Herald*, April 20, 1861; Herman Melville, *Billy Budd, Sailor and Other Stories*, 99.

12. Frederick Van Wyck, *Recollections of an Old New Yorker*, 30.

13. Shortly after the outbreak of the fighting, ads linking patriotism to the purchase of particular products began appearing in the newspapers. See for examples the large notices for Dr. Underhill's Pure Union Wine, *Times*, April 16, 1861 and for Radway's Ready Relief, *Times*, April 18, 1861.

14. Edward Dicey was struck by the scarce evidence of public response to Union successes at Roanoke Island, Bowling Green, and Fort Donaldson in 1862, but remarked on "a notice that Barnum's Museum would be illuminated in honor of the Union victories, by that patriotic proprietor." *Spectator of America,* 17.

15. *Times,* July 13, 1862.

16. Knox, *United States Notes,* 100–105. See also McKay, *The Civil War and New York City,* 139–140; *Times,* July 13, 1862.

17. *Times,* July 6, 1862.

18. It is worth observing that a far greater portion of the information necessary for a stranger to negotiate daily life—with the significant exception of legal information—was visible in the outdoor spaces of antebellum New York than in many late twentieth-century cities, where much information has migrated indoors to telephones, televisions, and computer monitors. It is also important to keep in mind that gender norms, class distinctions, criminal intimidation, and the rise of a centralized police force, to take a few examples, placed limits on the free and equal street access that Manhattan's urban texts appeared to presuppose. Still, New York streets were sites of significant heterogeneous intermingling. See Mary P. Ryan, *Civic Wars,* 43–57.

19. The quoted advertisements appear in the *Herald,* January 1 and July 2, 3, and 4, 1862.

Bibliography

MANUSCRIPTS AND PRINT COLLECTIONS

New-York Historical Society
*Edward Neufville Tailer Jr., "Journal of Some of the Events Which Have Occurred in My
    Life Time"*
"Journal of Henry C. Southworth"
Print Collections

New York Public Library, Astor, Lenox, and Tilden Foundations
Eno Collection, Division of Prints and Photographs
I. N. Phelps Stokes Collection, Division of Prints and Photographs

Other
"List of Signs in Use Upon Central Park," ca. 1871, Frederick Law Olmsted
    Papers. Manuscript Division, Library of Congress, Washington, D.C.
Nineteenth-Century Currency Collection (New York State). American Anti-
    quarian Society, Worcester, Massachusetts.
Court of General Sessions, Indictment Papers, 1830. Municipal Archives, City
    of New York.

NEW YORK NEWSPAPERS, MAGAZINES, AND OTHER PERIODICALS

Age
American Magazine of Useful and Entertaining Knowledge
Commercial Advertiser
Morning Courier and Enquirer
Day's New-York Bank Note List and Counterfeit Detector
Evening Post
Frank Leslie's Illustrated Newspaper
Gleason's Pictorial Drawing-Room Companion
Harper's Magazine

Herald
Humorist, or, Real Life in New York
Journal of Commerce
Illustrated London News
Ledger
The Man
New Era
Owl
National Police Gazette
New Monthly Messenger, General Bank Note List and New-York Prices Current
New-York Bank Note List
Niles Weekly Register
Penny Daily Gazette
Putnam's Magazine
Spirit of the Times
Sylvester's Reporter
Sun
Sunday Times and Noah's Weekly Messenger
Thompson's Bank Note and Commercial Reporter
Times
Tribune

PUBLISHED PRIMARY SOURCES

Literature

Alger, Horatio Jr. *Ragged Dick and Struggling Upward*. New York: Penguin, 1985.

Auchincloss, Louis, ed. *The Hone and Strong Diaries of Old Manhattan*. New York: Abbeville, 1989.

Bacon, Georgeanna Woolsey and Eliza Woolsey Howland, eds. *Letters of a Family During the War for the Union, 1861–1865*. 2 vols. New York: privately printed, 1899.

The Banker's Method of Detecting Bad Money, Showing How Bank Notes Are Made, and How to Detect Counterfeits on Scientific Principles. New York: J. Craft, 1863.

Barnum, P. T. *P. T. Barnum: The Greatest Showman on Earth*. Ed. Andrew E. Norman. 1855; reprint, New York: Chelsea House, 1983.

———. *Struggles and Triumphs*. Ed. Carl Bode. 1855; reprint, New York: Penguin, 1981.

Barton, H. Arnold, ed. *Letters from the Promised Land: Swedes in America, 1840–1914*. Minneapolis: University of Minnesota Press, 1975.

Belden, Ezekiel Porter. *New-York as It Is; Being the Counterpart of the Metropolis of America*. New York: J. P. Prall, 1849.

Beveridge, Charles E. and David Schuyler, eds. *Creating Central Park, 1857–1861*. Volume 3 of the Frederick Law Olmsted Papers. Baltimore: Johns Hopkins University Press, 1983.

Bird, Isabella Lucy. *The Englishwoman in America*. 1856; reprint, Madison: University of Wisconsin Press, 1966.

Blunt, Edward March. *The Picture of New-York, and Stranger's Guide to the Commercial Metropolis of the United States*. New York: A. T. Goodrich, 1828.

Bowen, Ralph, ed. and trans. *A Frenchman in Lincoln's America: Huit Mois en Amerique: Lettres et Notes de Voyage, 1864–1865, Ernest Duvergier de Hauranne*. Chicago: R. R. Donnelley, 1974.

Brace, Charles Loring. *The Dangerous Classes of New York and Twenty Years' Work Among Them*. New York: Wynkoop and Hallenbeck, 1872.

Bristed, C. Astor. *The Upper Ten Thousand: Sketches of American Society*. New York: Stringer and Townsend, 1852.

Browne, Junius Henri. *The Great Metropolis: A Mirror of New York*. Hartford: American Publishing Company, 1869.

Buckingham, James S. *America, Historical, Statistic and Descriptive*. Vol. 1. London: Fisher, 1841.

Busch, Moritz. *Travels Between the Hudson and the Mississippi, 1851–1852*. Ed. and trans. Norman Binger. Lexington: University of Kentucky Press, 1971.

Callender, James H. *Yesterdays in Little Old New York*. New York: Dorland Press, 1929.

Caruthers, William Alexander. *The Kentuckian in New-York*. New York: Harper and Bros., 1834.

Chevalier, Michel. *Society, Manners, and Politics in the United States*. Ed. John William Ward. Trans. after the T. G. Bradford edition (1839). Ithaca: Cornell University Press, 1961.

Child, Lydia Maria. *Letters from New York*. 11th ed. New York: C. S. Francis, 1850.

Colden, Cadwallader D. *Memoir, Prepared at the Request of a Committee of the City of New York . . . at the Celebration of the New York Canals*. New York: W. A. Davis, 1825.

Conway, Alan, ed. *The Welsh in America: Letters From the Immigrants*. Minneapolis: University of Minnesota Press, 1961.

Cooper, James Fenimore. *The American Democrat*. New York: Penguin, 1969.

——. *Home as Found: A Novel of Social Criticism and Observation*. New York: Capricorn, 1961.

Cowell, Joe. *Thirty Years Passed Among the Players in England and America*. New York: Harper and Bros., 1844.

Dayton, Abram C. *Last Days of Knickerbocker Life in New York*. New York: G. P. Putnam's Sons, 1897.

Diamond, Sigmund, ed. *A Casual View of America: The Home Letters of Salomon de Rothschild, 1859–1861*. Stanford: Stanford University Press, 1961.

Dicey, Edward. *Spectator in America*. 1863; reprint, Chicago: Quadrangle, 1971.

Dickens, Charles. *American Notes: A Journey*. 1842; reprint, New York: Fromm International, 1985.

Dodge, William E. *Old New York: A Lecture*. New York: Dodd, Mead, 1880.

Ehrenpreis, Anne Henry, ed. *Happy Country This America: The Travel Diary of Henry Arthur Bright*. Columbus: Ohio State University Press, 1978.

Fay, Theodore S. *Views of the City of New York and Its Environs*. New York: Peabody, 1831.

Fein, Albert, ed. *Landscape Into Cityscape: Frederick Law Olmsted's Plans for a Greater New York City*. New York: Van Nostrand, 1967.

Fern, Fanny. *Fern Leaves from Fanny's Port-Folio*. Second series. Auburn, N.Y.: Miller, Orton and Mulligan, 1854.

———. *Ruth Hall and Other Writings*. Ed. Joyce W. Warren. New Brunswick: Rutgers University Press, 1986.

Foster, George G. *New York by Gas-Light and Other Urban Sketches*. Ed. Stuart Blumin. Berkeley: University of California Press, 1990.

Francis, John W. *Old New York: Or, Reminiscences of the Past Sixty Years*. New York: W. J. Widdleton, 1865.

Gear, A. S. *The United States Bank Note Detector, at Sight. The Only Infallible System of Detecting Counterfeit and Altered Bank Notes*. Nashua, N.H.: A. S. Gear and G. B. Fiske, 1859.

George, Henry. *Progress and Poverty*. 1879; reprint, New York: Robert Schalkenbach Foundation, 1990.

Gooch, Richard. *America and the Americans—in 1833–4*. Ed. Richard Toby Widdicombe. New York: Fordham University Press, 1994.

Greeley, Horace. *Recollections of a Busy Life*. New York: J. B. Ford, 1869.

Greene, Asa. *A Glance at New York*. New York: A. Greene, 1837.

Hamilton, Thomas. *Men and Manners in America*. 1833; reprint, New York: Augustus M. Kelley, 1964.

Hardie, James. *The Description of the City of New-York*. New York: Samuel Marks, 1827.

Harris, Charles T. *Memories of Manhattan in the Sixties and Seventies*. New York: Derrydale Press, 1928.

Haswell, Charles H. *Reminiscences of an Octogenarian of the City of New York (1816–1860)*. New York: Harper and Bros., 1896.

Havens, Catherine Elizabeth. *Diary of a Little Girl in Old New York*. New York: Henry Collins Brown, 1920.

Headley, Joel Tyler. *The Great Riots of New York: 1712–1873*. 1873; reprint, Indianapolis: Bobbs Merrill, 1970.

Kimball, Richard B. *Undercurrents of Wall Street: A Romance of Business*. New York: G. P. Putnam's Sons, 1862.

Kirkland, Frazar. *Cyclopaedia of Commercial and Business Anecdotes*. 2 vols. New York: D. Appleton, 1864.

Ladies of the Mission. *The Old Brewery and the New Mission House at the Five Points*. New York: Stringer and Townsend, 1854.

Lakier, Aleksandr Borisovich. *A Russian Looks at America: The Journey of Aleksandr Borisovich Lakier in 1857*. Ed. Arnold Schrier. Trans. Joyce Story. Chicago: University of Chicago Press, 1979.

Larwood, Jacob. *The History of Sign Boards from the Earliest Times to the Present Day*. London: Chatto and Windus, 1866.

Leggett, William. *Democratick Editorials: Essays in Jacksonian Political Economy by William Leggett*. Ed. Lawrence H. White. Indianapolis: Liberty Press, 1984.

Levasseur, A. *Lafayette in America in 1824 and 1825; Or, a Journal of a Voyage to the United States*. 1829; reprint, Philadelphia: Carey and Lea, 1970.

Lippard, George. *The Empire City, or New York by Night and Day*. Philadelphia: T.B. Peterson, 1864.

Longworth, Thomas. *Longworth's American Almanac, New-York Register, and City Directory*. New York: Longworth, 1841.

Lyon, Isaac. *Recollections of an Old Cartman*. 1872; reprint, New York: New York Bound, 1984.

McCabe, James D. Jr. *Lights and Shadows of New York Life; or, the Sights and Sensations of the Great City*. Philadelphia: National Publishing Company, 1872.

Marryat, Frederick. *A Diary in America: With Remarks on Its Institutions*. 1839; reprint, New York: Knopf, 1962.

Mathews, Cornelius. *A Pen-and-Ink Panorama of New-York City*. New York: J. S. Taylor, 1853.

Maverick, Augustus. *Henry J. Raymond and the New York Press*. Hartford: A. S. Hale, 1870.

Melville, Herman. *Billy Budd, Sailor and Other Stories*. New York: Penguin, 1967.

———. *The Confidence-Man: His Masquerade*. New York: Oxford University Press, 1989.

———. *Moby-Dick*. New York: Bantam, 1967.

———. *Pierre: Or, The Ambiguities*. New York: New American Library, 1964.

Minutes of the Common Council of the City of New York. New York: Common Council, 1917.

Morhouse, Oliver. "A Boy's Reminiscences." Part 2. *Old New York* (January 1890): 440–447.

Morrow, John. *A Voice From the Newsboys*. [New York]: John Morrow, 1860.

Myers, J. C. *Sketches on a Tour Through the Northern and Eastern States, the Canadas, and Nova Scotia.* Harrisonburg: J. H. Wartmann, 1849.

Nevins, Allan and Milton Halsey Thomas. *The Diary of George Templeton Strong.* 4 vols. New York: Macmillan, 1952.

A New Security for Protecting Bank Notes From Alterations and Photographic Counterfeits, by the Use of the Patent Green Tint Conjointly with Black Carbon Ink. As printed by Rawdon, Wright, Hatch, and Edson, Bank Note Engravers, New-York. New York: W. H. Arthur, 1858.

New York City Board of Aldermen. *Proceedings of the Board of Aldermen.* New York: 1828–1860.

New York City Board of Commissioners of the Central Park. *Minutes of the Proceedings of the Board of Commissioners of the Central Park.* New York: 1859–1863.

Ormsby, W. L. *A Description of the Present System of Bank Note Engraving, Showing Its Tendency to Facilitate Counterfeiting: to Which Is Added a New Method of Constructing Bank Notes to Prevent Forgery.* New York: W. L. Ormsby, 1852.

Osgood, Frances S. *The Cries of New-York.* New York: J. Doggett Jr., 1846.

Pachter, Marc, ed. *Abroad in America: Visitors to the New Nation, 1776–1914.* Reading, Mass.: Addison-Wesley, 1976.

Pintard, John. *Letters from John Pintard to His Daughter Eliza Noel Pintard Davidson, 1816–1833.* 4 vols. New York: New-York Historical Society, 1940–1941.

Poe, Edgar Allan. *Complete Tales and Poems of Edgar Allan Poe.* New York: Vintage, 1975.

———. *Essays and Reviews.* New York: Library of America, 1984.

Pope-Hennessy, Una. *The Aristocratic Journey, Being the Outspoken Letters of Mrs. Basil Hall, Written During a Fourteen Months' Sojourn in America 1827—1828.* 1827; reprint, New York: G. P. Putnam, 1931.

Pray, Isaac. *Memoirs of James Gordon Bennett and His Times.* New York: Stringer and Townsend, 1855.

Report of the Special Committee Appointed by the Common Council of the City of New York, to Make Arrangements for the Reception of Gov. Louis Kossuth, the Distinguished Hungarian Patriot. New York: Common Council, 1852.

Robinson, Solon. *Hot Corn: Life Scenes in New York Illustrated.* New York: De Witt and Davenport, 1853.

Rossiter, Clinton, ed. *The Federalist Papers.* New York: New American Library, 1961.

Rowell, George P. *The Men Who Advertise: An Account of Successful Advertisers, Together With Hints on the Method of Advertising.* New York: Geo. P. Rowell, 1870.

Sarmiento, Diego Faustino. *Travels in the United States in 1847.* Trans. Michael Aaron Rockland. Princeton: Princeton University Press, 1970.

Second Annual Report of the Board of Managers of the Association of Banks for the Suppression of Counterfeiting. Boston: William A. Hall, 1855.

Slick, Jonathan. *High Life in New York.* New York: Bunce and Brother, 1854.

Smith, Seba. *May Day in New York: Or House Hunting and Moving.* New York: Burgess, Stringer, 1845.

Squints Through an Opera Glass, by a Young Gent. Who Hadn't Any Thing Else to Do. New York: Merchants' Day-Book, 1850.

Thompson, John. *The Autographical Counterfeit Detector, Companion to the Bank Note Reporter.* New York: Wm. W. Lee, [several years].

de Tocqueville, Alexis. *Democracy in America.* Trans. George Lawrence. Garden City, N.Y.: Doubleday, 1969.

Trautmann, Frederic, ed. and trans. "New York Through German Eyes: The Travels of Ludwig Gall, 1819." *New York History* 62 (4) (October 1981).

Trollope, Anthony, *North America.* 2 vols. 1862; reprint, New York: St. Martin's, 1986.

———. *The Struggles of Brown, Jones, and Robinson.* New York: Oxford University Press, 1992.

Trollope, Frances. *Domestic Manners of the Americans.* 1832; reprint, New York: Vintage, 1960.

Tryon, William S, ed. *A Mirror for Americans: Life and Manners in the United States, 1790–1870, as Recorded by American Travelers.* 3 vols. Chicago: University of Chicago Press, 1952.

Tuckerman, Bayard, ed. *The Diary of Philip Hone, 1828–1851.* 2 vols. New York: Dodd, Mead, 1889.

Van Wyck, Frederick. *Recollections of an Old New Yorker.* New York: Liveright, 1932.

Watson, John F. *Annals and Occurrences of New York City and State in the Olden Time.* Philadelphia: H. F. Anners, 1846.

West, William. *Tavern Anecdotes, and Reminiscences of the Origin of Signs, Coffee-Houses, andc.* London: W. Cole, 1825.

Whitman, Walt. *New York Dissected.* New York: Rufus Rockwell Wilson, 1936.

Willis, Nathaniel Parker. *The Rag-Bag, A Collection of Ephemera.* New York: Charles Scribner, 1855.

Pictorial Collections

Black, Mary. *Old New York in Early Photographs: 196 Prints, 1853–1901, From the Collections of the New-York Historical Society.* New York: Dover, 1973.

Deák, Gloria-Gilda. *American Views: Prospects and Vistas.* New York: Viking, 1976.

———. *Picturing America: 1497–1899.* Princeton: Princeton University Press, 1988.

Grafton, John. *New York in the Nineteenth Century: 317 Engravings from* Harper's Weekly *and Other Contemporary Sources.* New York: Dover, 1977.

Johnson, Henry and Frederick S. Lightfoot. *Maritime New York in Nineteenth-Century Photographs*. New York: Dover, 1980.

Kouwenhoven, John A. *Adventures in America, 1857–1900*. New York: Harper, 1938.

———. *The Columbia Historical Portrait of New York: An Essay in Graphic History*. New York: Harper and Row, 1972.

Lightfoot, Frederick S. *Nineteenth-Century New York in Rare Photographic Views*. New York: Dover, 1981.

Peters, Harry T. *Currier and Ives: Printmakers to the American People*. Garden City, N.Y.: Doubleday, 1942.

Stokes, I. N. Phelps. *The Iconography of Manhattan Island, 1498–1909*. 6 vols. New York: R. H. Dodd, 1915–1928.

Watson, Edward B. *New York Then and Now: 83 Manhattan Sites Photographed in the Past and Present*. New York: Dover, 1976.

SECONDARY SOURCES

Adams, Bluford. *E Pluribus Barnum: The Great Showman and the Making of U.S. Popular Culture*. Minneapolis: University of Minnesota Press, 1997.

Agnew, Jean-Christophe. *Worlds Apart: The Market and the Theater in Anglo-American Thought, 1550–1750*. Cambridge: Cambridge University Press, 1986.

Albion, Robert Greenhalgh. *The Rise of New York Port*. 1939; reprint, New York: Scribner, 1970.

Allen, Irving Lewis. *The City in Slang: New York Life and Popular Speech*. New York: Oxford University Press, 1993.

Anderson, Benedict. *Imagined Communities: Reflections on the Origin and Spread of Nationalism*. London: Verso, 1983.

Baldasty, Gerald. *The Commercialization of News in the Nineteenth Century*. Madison: University of Wisconsin Press, 1992.

Barth, Gunther. *City People: The Rise of Modern City Culture in Nineteenth-Century America*. New York: Oxford University Press, 1980.

Baym, Nina. *Novels, Readers, and Reviewers: Responses to Fiction in Antebellum America*. Ithaca: Cornell University Press, 1984.

"Before Urban Renewal." *American Heritage* 24 (4) (June 1973): 28–35.

Bender, Thomas, ed. *The Antislavery Debate: Capitalism and Abolitionism as a Problem in Historical Interpretation*. Berkeley: University of California Press, 1992.

Bender, Thomas. *New York Intellect: A History of Intellectual Life in New York City, From 1750 to the Beginnings of Our Own Time*. New York: Knopf, 1987.

———. *Toward an Urban Vision: Ideas and Institutions in Nineteenth-Century America*. Lexington: University Press of Kentucky, 1975.

———. "Wholes and Parts: The Need for Synthesis in American History." *Journal of American History* (June 1986).

Benjamin, Walter. *Charles Baudelaire: Lyric Poet in the Age of High Capitalism.* Trans. Harry Zohn. London: NLB, 1973.

———. *Reflections: Essays, Aphorisms, Autobiographical Writings.* Ed. Peter Demetz. Trans. Edmund Jephcott. New York: Schocken, 1978.

Berg, Barbara J. *The Remembered Gate: Origins of American Feminism: The Woman and the City, 1800–1860.* New York: Oxford University Press, 1978.

Berger, John. *Ways of Seeing.* London: Penguin, 1972.

Bergmann, Johannes Dietrich. "The Original Confidence Man." *American Quarterly* 21 (Fall 1969): 560–577.

Bernstein, Iver. *New York City Draft Riots: Their Significance for American Society and Politics in the Age of the Civil War.* New York: Oxford University Press, 1990.

Birkerts, Sven. *The Gutenberg Elegies: The Fate of Reading in an Electronic Age.* New York: Fawcett Columbine, 1994.

Blackmar, Elizabeth. *Manhattan for Rent, 1785–1850.* Ithaca: Cornell University Press, 1989.

Blau, Joseph L., ed. *Social Theories of Jacksonian Democracy.* New York: Liberal Arts Press, 1954.

Blumin, Stuart M. "George G. Foster and the Emerging Metropolis." Introduction to George G. Foster, *New York by Gas-Light and Other Urban Sketches.* Berkeley: University of California Press, 1990.

Boyer, M. Christine. *The City of Collective Memory.* Cambridge: MIT Press, 1994.

———. *Manhattan Manners: Architecture and Style, 1850–1900.* New York: Rizzoli, 1985.

Brand, Dana. *The Spectator and the City in Nineteenth-Century American Literature.* Cambridge: Cambridge University Press, 1991.

Braudy, Leo. *The Frenzy of Renown: Fame and Its History.* New York: Oxford University Press, 1986.

Bridges, Amy. *A City in the Republic: Antebellum New York and the Origins of Machine Politics.* Cambridge: Cambridge University Press, 1984.

Brodhead, Richard H. *Cultures of Letters: Scenes of Reading and Writing in Nineteenth-Century America.* Chicago: University of Chicago Press, 1993.

Brown, Henry Collins. *Fifth Avenue Old and New, 1824–1924.* New York: The Fifth Avenue Association, 1924.

———. *Glimpses of Old New-York.* New York: Anderson Galleries Building, 1917.

Brown, Joshua Emmett. *"Frank Leslie's Illustrated Newspaper: The Pictorial Press and the Representations of America, 1855–1889."* Ph.D. diss. Columbia University, 1993.

Brown, Richard D. *Power and Knowledge: The Diffusion of Information in Early America, 1700–1865*. New York: Oxford University Press, 1989.

Buckley, Peter G. "Culture, Class, and Place in Antebellum New York." In John Hull Mollenkopf, ed., *Power, Culture, and Place: Essays on New York City*. New York: Russell Sage Foundation, 1988, 25–52.

——. "To the Opera House: Culture and Society in New York, 1820–1860." Ph.D. diss., SUNY Stony Brook, 1984.

Bushman, Richard L. *The Refinement of America: Persons, Houses, Cities*. New York: Knopf, 1992.

Calhoun, Craig, ed. *Habermas and the Public Sphere*. Cambridge: MIT Press, 1992.

Carby, Hazel V. *Reconstructing Womanhood: The Emergence of the Afro-American Woman Novelist*. New York: Oxford University Press, 1987.

de Certeau, Michel. *The Practice of Everyday Life*. Trans. Steven Rendall. Berkeley: University of California Press, 1984.

Chartier, Roger. *The Cultural Uses of Print in Early Modern France*. Ithaca: Cornell University Press, 1987.

Charvat, William. *The Profession of Authorship in America, 1800–1870*. 1968; reprint, New York: Columbia University Press, 1992.

Cmiel, Kenneth. *Democratic Eloquence: The Fight Over Popular Speech in Nineteenth-Century America*. Berkeley: University of California Press, 1990.

Cohen, Patricia Cline. *A Calculating People: The Spread of Numeracy in Early America*. Chicago: University of Chicago Press, 1982.

Cooper, George. *Lost Love: A True Story of Passion, Murder, and Justice in Old New York*. New York: Pantheon, 1994.

Cornelius, Janet Duitsman. *"When I Can Read My Title Clear": Literacy, Slavery, and Religion in the Antebellum South*. Columbia: University of South Carolina Press, 1991.

Crouthamel, James L. *Bennett's* New York Herald *and the Rise of the Popular Press*. Syracuse: Syracuse University Press, 1989.

——. *James Watson Webb: A Biography*. Middletown: Wesleyan University Press, 1969.

Darnton, Robert. *The Kiss of Lamourette: Reflections in Cultural History*. New York: Norton, 1990.

Davidson, Cathy N. *Revolution and the Word: The Rise of the Novel in America*. New York: Oxford University Press, 1986.

–-, ed., *Reading in America: Literature and Social History*. Baltimore: Johns Hopkins University Press, 1989.

Davis, David Brion, ed. *Antebellum American Culture: An Interpretive Anthology*. Lexington, Mass: D. C. Heath, 1979.

Davis, Susan G. *Parades and Power: Street Theatre in Nineteenth-Century Philadelphia*. Berkeley: University of California Press, 1986.

Dillistin, William H. *Bank Note Reporters and Counterfeit Detectors, 1826–1866.* Numismatic Notes and Monographs No. 114. New York: American Numismatic Society, 1949.

Domosh, Mona. *Invented Cities: The Creation of Landscape in Nineteenth-Century New York and Boston.* New Haven: Yale University Press, 1996.

Dunshee, Kenneth Holcomb. *As You Pass By.* New York: Hastings House, 1952.

Eisenstein, Elizabeth L. *The Printing Press as an Agent of Change: Communications and Cultural Transformations in Early-Modern Europe.* 2 vols. Cambridge: Cambridge University Press, 1979.

———. *The Printing Revolution in Early Modern Europe.* Cambridge: Cambridge University Press, 1983.

Ellis, Edward Robb. *The Epic of New York City.* New York: Coward-McCann, 1966.

Ernst, Robert. *Immigrant Life in New York City, 1825–1863.* New York: King's Crown Press, 1949.

Ethington, Philip J. *The Public City: The Political Construction of Urban Life in San Francisco, 1850–1900.* Cambridge: Cambridge University Press, 1994.

Evans, Meryle R. "Knickerbocker Hotels and Restaurants, 1800–1850," *The New-York Historical Society Quarterly* 36 (October 1952): 377–409.

Febvre, Lucien and Henri-Jean Martin. *The Coming of the Book: The Impact of Printing, 1450–1800.* Trans. David Gerard. London: Verso, 1984.

Ferguson, Priscilla Parkhurst. "Reading City Streets." *The French Review* 61 (February 1988): 386–397.

Fisher, Philip. "Democratic Social Space: Whitman, Melville, and the Promise of American Transparency." In Philip Fisher, ed., *The New American Studies: Essays from Representations.* Berkeley: University of California Press, 1991, 70–111.

Fliegelman, Jay. *Declaring Independence: Jefferson, Natural Language, and the Culture of Performance.* Stanford: Stanford University Press, 1993.

Foucault, Michel. *The Archaeology of Knowledge and the Discourse on Language.* Trans. A. M. Sheridan Smith. New York: Pantheon, 1972.

———. *The Order of Things: An Archaeology of the Human Sciences.* New York: Vintage, 1970.

Fox, Louis H. "New York City Newspapers, 1820–1850: A Bibliography." *Papers of the Bibliographical Society of America* 21 (1927): 1–131.

Fried, Michael. *Realism, Writing, and Disfiguration: On Thomas Eakins and Stephen Crane.* Chicago: University of Chicago Press, 1987.

Fritzsche, Peter. *Reading Berlin, 1900.* Cambridge: Harvard University Press, 1996.

Galbraith, John Kenneth. *Money: Whence It Came, Where It Went.* Boston: Houghton Mifflin, 1975.

Garrioch, David. *Neighborhood and Community in Paris, 1740–1790.* Cambridge: Cambridge University Press, 1986.

Gates, Henry Louis Jr. *Figures in Black: Words, Signs, and the Racial Self.* New York: Oxford, 1987.

Genovese, Eugene D. *Roll, Jordan, Roll: The World the Slaves Made.* New York: Vintage, 1972.

Gilfoyle, Timothy J. *City of Eros: New York City, Prostitution, and the Commercialization of Sex, 1790–1920.* New York: Norton, 1992.

Gilje, Paul A. *The Road to Mobocracy: Popular Disorder in New York City, 1763–1834.* Chapel Hill: University of North Carolina Press, 1987.

Glaser, Lynn. *Counterfeiting in America: The History of an American Way to Wealth.* New York: Clarkson N. Potter, 1968.

Goffman, Erving. *The Presentation of Self in Everyday Life.* Garden City, N.Y.: Doubleday Anchor Books, 1959.

Goodwin, Maud Wilder, Alice Carrington Royce, Ruth Putnam, and Eva Palmer Brownell, eds. *Historic New York.* Vol. 2. New York: G. P. Putnam's Sons, 1899.

Goody, Jack and Ian Watt. "The Consequences of Literacy." In Jack Goody, ed., *Literacy in Traditional Societies.* Cambridge: Cambridge University Press, 1968.

Gorn, Elliott J. *The Manly Art: Bare-Knuckle Prize Fighting in America.* Ithaca: Cornell University Press, 1986.

Graff, Harvey J. *The Legacies of Literacy: Continuities and Contradictions in Western Culture and Society.* Bloomington: Indiana University Press, 1987.

———. *The Literacy Myth: Literacy and Social Structure in the Nineteenth-Century City.* New York: Academic Press, 1979.

Habermas, Jürgen. *The Structural Transformation of the Public Sphere: An Inquiry Into a Category of Bourgeois Society.* Trans. Thomas Burger. Cambridge: MIT Press, 1989.

Hales, Peter B. *Silver Cities: The Photography of American Urbanization, 1839–1915.* Philadelphia: Temple University Press, 1984.

Hall, David D. *Cultures of Print: Essays in the History of the Book.* Amherst: University of Massachussetts Press, 1996.

Halttunen, Karen. *Confidence Men and Painted Women: A Study of Middle-Class Culture in America, 1830–1870.* New Haven: Yale University Press, 1982.

Hammond, Bray. *Banks and Politics in America from the Revolution to the Civil War.* Princeton: Princeton University Press, 1957.

Harlow, Alvin F. *Old Bowery Days: The Chronicles of a Famous Street.* New York: D. Appleton, 1931.

Harris, Neil. *Humbug: The Art of P. T. Barnum.* Boston: Little, Brown, 1973.

Hartog, Hendrik. *Public Property and Private Power: The Corporation of the City of New*

York in American Law, 1730–1870. Chapel Hill: University of North Carolina Press, 1983.

Haskell, Thomas L. and Richard F. Teichgraeber III, eds. *The Culture of the Market: Historical Essays*. Cambridge: Cambridge University Press, 1993.

Henkin, David M. "City Reading: The Written Word and the Urban Public in New York City, 1825–1865." Ph.D. diss., University of California, Berkeley, 1995.

Hepburn, A. Barton. *A History of Currency in the United States*. 1924; rev. ed., New York: A. M. Kelley, 1967.

Hershkowitz, Leo. *Tweed's New York: Another Look*. Garden City, N.Y.: Anchor Books, 1978.

Hill, Marilynn Wood. *Their Sisters' Keepers: Prostitution in New York City, 1830–1870*. Berkeley: University of California Press, 1993.

Hodges, Graham Russell. *New York City Cartmen, 1667–1850*. New York: New York University Press, 1986.

Hoffmann, Henry B. "Changed House Numbers and Lost Street Names in New York of the Early Nineteenth Century and Later." *New-York Historical Society Quarterly* 21 (1937): 67–92.

Homberger, Eric. *The Historical Atlas of New York City: A Visual Celebration of Nearly 400 Years of New York City's History*. New York: Henry Holt, 1994.

———. *Scenes From the Life of a City: Corruption and Conscience in Old New York*. New Haven: Yale University Press, 1994.

Horlick, Allan Stanley. *Country Boys and Merchant Princes: The Social Control of Young Men in New York*. London: Associated University Presses, 1975.

Hornung, Clarence P., ed. *Handbook of Early Advertising Art: Mainly From American Sources*. 2 vols. New York: Dover, 1956.

———. *Treasury of American Design*. New York: Harry N. Abrams, 1972.

Hugins, Walter. *Jacksonian Democracy and the Working Class: A Study of the New York Workingmen's Movement, 1829–1837*. Stanford: Stanford University Press, 1960.

Hutton, Frankie. *The Early Black Press in America, 1827 to 1860*. Westport: Greenwood Press, 1993.

Jackson, John Brinckerhoff. *American Space: The Centennial Years, 1865–1876*. New York: Norton, 1972.

Janvier, Thomas A. *In Old New York*. New York: Harper and Bros., 1894.

Jay, Robert. *The Trade Card in Nineteenth-Century America*. Columbia: University of Missouri Press, 1987.

Johnson, David R. *Illegal Tender: Counterfeiting and the Secret Service in Nineteenth-Century America*. Washington, D.C.: Smithsonian Institution Press, 1995.

Johnson, Paul E. and Sean Wilentz. *The Kingdom of Matthias: A Story of Sex and Salvation in Nineteenth-Century America*. New York: Oxford University Press, 1994.

Joyce, William, David Hall, Richard Brown, and John Hench, eds. *Printing and Society in America*. Worcester: American Antiquarian Society, 1983.

Kaestle, Carl F. *The Evolution of an Urban School System: New York City, 1750–1850*. Cambridge: Harvard University Press, 1973.

———. *Pillars of the Republic: Common Schools and American Society*. New York: Hill and Wang, 1983.

Kaestle, Carl F., Helen Damon-Moore, Lawrence C. Stedman, Katherine Tinsley, and William Vance Trollinger Jr. *Literacy in the United States: Readers and Reading Since 1880*. New Haven: Yale University Press, 1991.

Kasson, John F. *Rudeness and Civility: Manners in Nineteenth-Century Urban America*. New York: Hill and Wang, 1990.

Knox, John Jay. *United States Notes: A History of the Various Issues of Paper Money by the Government of the United States*. New York: Charles Scribner's Sons, 1899.

Landauer, Bella Clara. *Early American Trade Cards from the Collection of Bella C. Landauer*. Critical notes by Adele Jenny. New York: W. E. Rudge, 1927.

Landes, Joan B. *Women and the Public Sphere in the Age of the French Revolution*. Ithaca: Cornell University Press, 1988.

Langdon, William Chauncey. *Everyday Things in American Life, 1776–1876*. New York: Charles Scribner's Sons, 1941.

Lanier, Henry Wysham. *A Century of Banking in New York, 1822–1922*. New York: George H. Doran, 1922.

Lears, Jackson. *Fables of Abundance: A Cultural History of Advertising in America*. New York: Basic Books, 1994.

Lenz, William E. *Fast Talk and Flush Times: The Confidence Man as a Literary Convention*. Columbia: University of Missouri Press, 1985.

Levine, Lawrence W. *Black Culture and Black Consciousness: Afro-American Folk Thought from Slavery to Freedom*. New York: Oxford University Press, 1977.

Lindstrom, Diane. "Economic Structure, Demographic Change, and Income Inequality in Antebellum New York." In John Hull Mollenkopf, ed., *Power, Culture, and Place: Essays on New York City*. New York: Russell Sage Foundation, 1988, 3–23.

Lofland, Lyn. *A World of Strangers: Order and Action in Urban Public Space*. New York: Basic Books, 1973.

Long, Elizabeth. "Textual Interpretation as Collective Action." In Jonathan Boyarin, ed., *The Ethnography of Reading*. Berkeley: University of California Press, 1993, 180–211.

Lynch, Kevin. *The Image of the City*. Cambridge, MIT Press, 1960.

Machor, James L., ed. *Readers in History: Nineteenth-Century American Literature and the Contexts of Response*. Baltimore: Johns Hopkins University Press, 1993.

McKay, Ernest A. *The Civil War and New York City*. Syracuse: Syracuse University Press, 1990.

McKay, Richard C. *South Street: A Maritime History of New York*. Riverside, Conn.: 7 C's Press, 1934.

McLuhan, Marshall. *The Gutenberg Galaxy: The Making of Typographic Man*. Toronto: University of Toronto Press, 1962.

Mandelbaum, Seymour J. *Boss Tweed's New York*. New York: Wiley, 1965.

Martin, Henri-Jean. *The History and Power of Writing*. Trans. Lydia Cochrane. Chicago: University of Chicago Press, 1994.

Meyers, Marvin. *The Jacksonian Persuasion: Politics and Belief*. 1957; reprint, New York: Vintage, 1960.

Michaels, Walter Benn. *The Gold Standard and the Logic of Naturalism*. Berkeley: University of California, 1987.

Minnigerode, Meade. *The Fabulous Forties, 1840–1850: A Presentation of Private Life*. New York: G. P. Putnam's Sons, 1924.

Mitchell, W.J.T. *Iconology: Image, Text, Ideology*. Chicago: University of Chicago Press, 1986.

Monaghan, Frank and Marvin Lowenthal. *This Was New York: The Nation's Capital in 1789*. Garden City, N.Y.: Doubleday, 1943.

Monkkonen, Eric. *America Becomes Urban: The Development of U.S. Cities and Towns, 1780–1980*. Berkeley: University of California Press, 1988.

Moody, Richard. *The Astor Place Riot*. Bloomington: Indiana University Press, 1958.

Morris, Lloyd. *Incredible New York: High Life and Low Life of the Last Hundred Years*. New York: Random House, 1951.

Mott, Frank Luther. *American Journalism: A History of Newspapers in the United States Through 250 Years, 1690 to 1940*. New York: MacMillan, 1941.

——. *A History of American Magazines, Volume II: 1850–1865*. Cambridge: Harvard University Press, 1938.

Mumford, Lewis. *The City in History: Its Origins, Its Transformations, Its Prospects*. New York: Harcourt, Brace, and World, 1961.

Muscalus, John A. *Odd Bank Note and Scrip Denominations in American Monetary History*. Bridgeport, Penn.: Historical Paper Money Research Institute, 1967.

Nadel, Stanley. *Little Germany: Ethnicity, Religion, and Class in New York City, 1845–80*. Urbana: University of Illinois Press, 1990.

Newhall, Beaumont. *The Daguerreotype in America*. New York: Dover, 1961.

Newman, Eric P. *The Early Paper Money of America*. 3rd ed. Iola, Wisc.: Krause Publications, 1990.

Nord, David Paul. "The Evangelical Origins of Mass Media in America, 1815–1835." *Journalism Monographs* 88 (1984).

Nunberg, Geoffrey, ed. *The Future of the Book*. Berkeley: University of California Press, 1996.

————. "The Place of Books in the Age of Electronic Reproduction." *Representations* 42 (Spring 1993): 13–37.

O'Malley, Michael. "Specie and Species: Race and the Money Question in Nineteenth-Century America." *American Historical Review* (April 1994): 369–395.

Ong, Walter J. *Orality and Literacy: The Technologizing of the Word.* London: Methuen, 1982.

Pessen, Edward. *Riches, Class, and Power Before the Civil War.* Lexington, Mass.: D. C. Heath, 1973.

Petrucci, Armando. *Public Lettering: Script, Power, and Culture.* Trans. Linda Lappin. Chicago: University of Chicago Press, 1993.

Postman, Neil. *Amusing Ourselves to Death: Public Discourse in the Age of Show Business.* New York: Penguin, 1985.

Pred, Allan R. *Urban Growth and the Circulation of Information: The United States System of Cities, 1790–1840.* Cambridge: Harvard University Press, 1973.

————. *Urban Growth and City-Systems in the United States, 1840–1860.* Cambridge: Harvard University Press, 1980.

Presbrey, Frank. *The History and Development of Advertising.* Garden City, N.Y.: Doubleday, 1929.

Rapoport, Amos. *The Meaning of the Built Environment: A Nonverbal Communication Approach.* Tucson: University of Arizona Press, 1982.

Reps, John. *Town Planning in Frontier America.* 1965; reprint, Columbia: University of Missouri Press, 1980.

Reynolds, David S. *Beneath the American Renaissance: The Subversive Imagination in the Age of Emerson and Melville.* Cambridge: Harvard University Press, 1988.

Rosenberg, Charles. *The Cholera Years: The United States in 1832, 1849, and 1866.* Chicago: University of Chicago Press, 1971.

Rosenwaike, Ira. *Population History of New York City.* Syracuse: Syracuse University Press, 1972.

Rosenzweig, Roy and Elizabeth Blackmar. *The Park and the People: A History of Central Park.* Ithaca: Cornell University Press, 1992.

Rourke, Constance Mayfield. *Trumpets of Jubilee.* London: Jonathan Cape, 1927.

Ryan, Mary P. "The American Parade: Representations of the Nineteenth-Century Social Order." In Lynn Hunt, ed., *The New Cultural History.* Berkeley: University of California Press, 1989, 131–153.

————. *Civic Wars: Democracy and Public Life in the American City During the Nineteenth Century.* Berkeley: University of California Press, 1997.

————. *Women in Public: Between Banners and Ballots, 1825–1880.* Baltimore: Johns Hopkins University Press, 1990.

Sante, Luc. *Low Life: Lures and Snares of Old New York.* New York: Vintage, 1991.

Saxon, A. H. *P. T. Barnum: The Legend and the Man*. New York: Columbia University Press, 1989.

Saxton, Alexander. *The Rise and Fall of the White Republic: Class Politics and Mass Culture in Nineteenth-Century America*. London: Verso, 1990.

Scherzer, Kenneth. *Unbounded Community: Neighborhood Life and Social Structure in New York City, 1830–1875*. Durham: Duke University Press, 1992.

Schiller, Dan. *Objectivity and the News: The Public and the Rise of Commercial Journalism*. Philadelphia: University of Pennsylvania Press, 1981.

Schlereth, Thomas J. *Cultural History and Material Culture: Everyday Life, Landscapes, Museums*. Charlottesville: University of Virginia Press, 1990.

Schudson, Michael. *Discovering the News: A Social History of American Newspapers*. New York: Basic Books, 1978.

Sellers, Charles. *The Market Revolution: Jacksonian America, 1815–1846*. New York: Oxford University Press, 1991.

Sennett, Richard. *The Conscience of the Eye: The Design and Social Life of Cities*. New York: Norton, 1990.

——. *The Fall of Public Man: On the Social Psychology of Capitalism*. New York: Vintage, 1978.

Shell, Marc. *Children of the Earth: Literature, Politics, and Nationhood*. New York: Oxford University Press, 1993.

——. *Money, Language, and Thought: Literary and Philosophic Economies from the Medieval to the Modern Era*. Berkeley: University of California Press, 1982.

Siegel, Adrienne. *The Image of the American City in Popular Literature, 1820–1870*. Port Washington, N.Y.: Kennikat Press, 1981.

Simmel, Georg. *The Sociology of Georg Simmel*. Ed. and trans. Kurt Wolff. New York: Free Press, 1950.

Soltow, Lee and Edward Stevens. *The Rise of Literacy and the Common School in the United States: A Socioeconomic Analysis to 1870*. Chicago: University of Chicago Press, 1981.

Spann, Edward K. *The New Metropolis: New York City, 1840–1857*. New York: Columbia University Press, 1981.

Spufford, Margaret. "First Steps in Literacy: The Reading and Writing Experiences of the Humblest Seventeenth-Century Spiritual Autobiographers." *Social History* 4 (1979): 407–435.

Srebnick, Amy Gilman. *The Mysterious Death of Mary Rogers: Sex and Culture in Nineteenth-Century New York*. New York: Oxford University Press, 1995.

Stansell, Christine. *City of Women: Sex and Class in New York, 1789–1860*. Urbana: University of Illinois Press, 1986.

Starn, Randolph. "The Republican Regime of the 'Room of Peace' in Siena, 1338–1340." *Representations* 18 (Spring 1987): 1–34.

Stewart, Susan. "Ceci Tuera Cela: Graffiti as Crime and Art." In John Fekete, ed., *Life After Postmodernism: Essays on Value and Culture*. New York: St. Martin's Press, 1987.

Still, Bayrd. *Mirror for Gotham: New York as Seen by Contemporaries from Dutch Days to the Present*. New York: New York University Press, 1956.

Stott, Richard B. *Workers in the Metropolis: Class, Ethnicity, and Youth in Antebellum New York City*. Ithaca: Cornell University Press, 1990.

Terdiman, Richard. *Discourse/Counter-Discourse: The Theory and Practice of Symbolic Resistance in Nineteenth-Century France*. Ithaca: Cornell University Press, 1985.

Trachtenberg, Alan. *The Incorporation of America: Culture and Society in the Gilded Age*. New York: Hill and Wang, 1982.

———. *Reading American Photographs: Images as History: From Matthew Brady to Walker Evans*. New York: Hill and Wang, 1989.

Ulmann, Albert. *A Landmark History of New York*. New York: D. Appleton-Century, 1939.

Venturi, Robert, Denise Scott Brown, and Steven Izenour. *Learning from Las Vegas: The Forgotten Symbolism of Architectural Form*. Rev. ed. Cambridge: MIT Press, 1977.

Warner, Michael. *The Letters of the Republic: Publication and the Public Sphere in Eighteenth-Century America*. Cambridge: Harvard University Press, 1990.

Warner, Sam Bass Jr. *The Private City: Philadelphia in Three Periods of Its Growth*. Philadelphia: University of Pennsylvania Press, 1968.

Watson, Harry L. *Liberty and Power: The Politics of Jacksonian America*. New York: Farrar, Straus & Giroux, 1990.

Weber, Adna Ferrin. *The Growth of Cities in the Nineteenth Century: A Study in Statistics*. 1899; reprint, Ithaca: Cornell University Press, 1963.

Weiss, Susan Archer. *The Home Life of Poe*. New York: Broadway, 1907.

White, Shane. *Somewhat More Independent: The End of Slavery in New York City, 1770–1810*. Athens: University of Georgia Press, 1991.

Wicke, Jennifer A. *Advertising Fictions: Literature, Advertising, and Social Reading*. New York: Columbia University Press, 1988.

Wilentz, Sean. "Artisan Republican Festivals and the Rise of Class Conflict in New York City, 1788–1837." In Michael H. Frisch and Daniel J. Walkowitz, eds., *Working-Class America*. Urbana: University of Illinois Press, 1983.

———. *Chants Democratic: New York City and the Rise of the American Working Class, 1788–1850*. New York: Oxford University Press, 1984.

———. "On Class and Politics in Jacksonian America." *Reviews in American History* 10 (1982): 43–63.

Wright, Richardson. *Hawkers and Walkers in Early America*. Philadelphia: Lippincott, 1927.

Zboray, Ronald J. *A Fictive People: Antebellum Economic Development and the American Reading Public.* New York: Oxford University Press, 1993.

Zelizer, Viviana A. "Making Multiple Monies." In Richard Swedberg, ed., *Explorations in Economic Sociology.* New York: Russell Sage Foundation, 1993.

——. *The Social Meaning of Money: Pin Money, Paychecks, Poor Relief, and Other Currencies.* Princeton: Princeton University Press, 1994.

Ziff, Larzer. *Writing in the New Nation: Prose, Print, and Politics in the Early United States.* New Haven: Yale University Press, 1991.

Illustration Credits

3.1 Lightfoot Collection/Archive Photos.

3.2 Eno Collection, Prints Division, The New York Public Library.

3.3 © Collection of The New-York Historical Society.

3.4 Lightfoot Collection/Archive Photos.

3.5 Lightfoot Collection/Archive Photos.

3.6 Collection of Edward W. C. Arnold; photograph courtesy of Museum of the City of New York.

3.7 Courtesy Main Library, University of California–Berkeley.

3.8 The Museum of the City of New York, The J. Clarence Davies Collection, 29.100.2481.

3.9 Lightfoot Collection/Archive Photos.

4.1 Eno Collection, Miriam and Ira D. Wallach Division of Art, Prints and Photographs, The New York Public Library, Astor, Lenox, and Tilden Foundation.

4.2 © Collection of The New-York Historical Society.

4.3 The Museum of the City of New York, Gift of Miss Sarah F. deLuze, 39.253.7.

4.4 Lightfoot Collection/Archive Photos.

4.5 The New-York Historical Society.

4.6 Library of Congress.

4.7 © Collection of The New-York Historical Society.

4.8 © Collection of The New-York Historical Society.

5.1 The Lucille and Walter Rubin Collection.

5.2 The New-York Historical Society.

5.3 The New-York Historical Society.

5.4 The New-York Historical Society.

5.5 The New-York Historical Society.

6.1 Courtesy American Antiquarian Society.

6.2 Courtesy American Antiquarian Society.

6.3 Courtesy Main Library, University of California–Berkeley.

6.4 The Museum of the City of New York, The J. Clarence Davies Collection, 29.100.2355.
6.5 Courtesy American Antiquarian Society.
6.6 Courtesy American Antiquarian Society.

Index